Mississippi:
The Real State of Our State

A True Story

Rick Ward

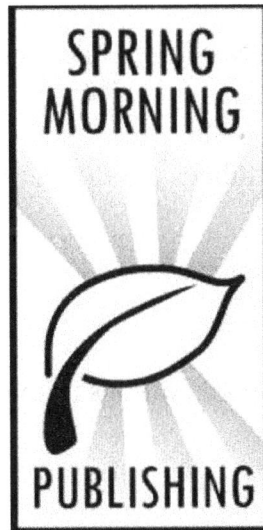

SPRING
MORNING

PUBLISHING

Mississippi: The Real State of Our State

Copyright © 2011 by Rick Ward

Spring Morning Publishing, Inc.

For more information, please contact: info@springmorningpublishing.org

Cover photograph by: Christopher Meredith, Jackson, Mississippi, (chmeredith@gmail.com)   "Storm Brewing over the Capitol"

Printed in the United States of America

The Real State of Our State

Rick Ward

1. Title   2. Author   3. Nonfiction/ Politics, Crime, Corruption

Library of Congress Control Number - 2011914525

ISBN 13 978-0-9828099-3-8 (Paperback)

ISBN 10 0-9828099-3-X

ISBN 13 978-0-9828099-4-5 (E-book, various formats)

ISBN 10 0982809948

TABLE OF CONTENTS

EPIGRAPH

"Commercial gambling is technically a swindle. The payoffs on bets must be less than fair, and the overwhelming majority of the investors must eventually lose their money, if the gambling enterprise is to survive and prosper. The case for legalized gambling is simply an argument in favor of the government raising revenues by swindling its citizens rather than by taxing them."

Professor Irving Kristol

Professor Kristol (1920-2009) was described by <u>The Daily Telegraph</u> as "perhaps the most consequential public intellectual of the latter half of the 20th century."

I

Preface

This book is written for the average Mississippi registered voter, absent fancy words, phrases, or political buzzwords. It is not intended to be a collegiate or a scholarly publication, but rather a simple manuscript with facts, comparisons, and proof of its claims. The original version is written in a digital format so readers can click on the references for additional information without having to refer to footnotes, endnotes, or bibliographies. Hard copy readers can still reap the same benefit by typing the URL addresses into a search engine on the internet.

It relies heavily on the use of each state of the state address given by Governor Haley Barbour during his two terms in office. The information sometimes conflicts with his statements, highlights his pet peeves, and enlightens you on subjects that have not been discussed. It will show you how crimes committed by certain state agencies have been pointed out by other state agencies, and will show crimes committed in industry that go unpunished.

This book is predicated on the fact that our state's soul has been sold to the gaming industry. Although we chose to legalize gambling, we treat it as a "speak easy." Like the serpent in the Garden of Eden that convinced Eve it was okay to partake of the forbidden fruit, so did our devilish leaders convince us. You will read herein more about politicians, and their actions, or lack of action, than you will read about gaming itself. Gaming has provided jobs, entertainment, tourism dollars, and tax revenues. Some good has come from it. The spacious, smooth, well-lit highways, enlarged police agencies, fire departments, and state agencies are only a fraction of material cost's gaming has been to us, aside from crime, addiction, and disappointed dreams. I fear the governors in the future will cut other essential services to replace those light bulbs or re-pave those roads leading to the casinos. I have no doubt where their priorities are.

Having said all that, I am not necessarily an opponent of casinos, or bingo, but rather a proponent of law enforcement. Our politicians have become so paranoid that this big cash cow is going to find greener pastures that they are willing to forgive any crimes the industry commits, and tie the hands of law enforcement officers we pay to enforce the laws. Gaming officials hide behind the truth and claim discretion, but develop policies in direct violation of the law.

We know that politicians often do not tell us the whole truth, and sometimes omit or twist issues of great importance to us. Mississippians who live outside the Jackson area rarely know what's really going on in the governor's office, or in the legislature.

We see our politicians every four years in our hometown coffee shops, dressed like us, in denim clothes, wearing a ball cap and high-top working boots, telling us what we want to hear. They go back to Jackson, dress in their suits, and become as inaccessible as the president -- until the next election.

We rely on the governor each year to tell us in his state of the state address where we have been, where we are going, our accomplishments, and our downfalls. He is the cheerleader, patting himself on the back, while giving credit to the legislature -- with extra high praise for the more powerful members who give him what he wants. Some of the more constant topics include jobs, new business, family income, state revenue, education, roads, catastrophes, crime, criminals, children, healthcare, and taxes. You can usually discern the governor's pet projects and organizations by listening to or reading the state of the state addresses.

Neither of our governors since Ray Mabus' last speech has uttered one word about gaming, casinos, or bingo in the state of the state addresses. Each of them has talked all around the subject bragging about scores of industries that have given us increased revenue, jobs, tourism, and economic growth. Governor Ronnie Musgrove introduced all the state executive directors in his first speech, but never mentioned the Mississippi Gaming Executive Director.

The tragedies of Katrina, floods along the river, loss of revenue, layoffs, and damage, have failed to muster up one word in a speech to our legislature or our citizens about gaming. That industry is protected at all costs, coddled like a child, its vices overlooked, crimes never considered for enforcement action. It's like a cancer spreading silently, and most of us never know it's there. Is there any hope for our future? Back rooms, greed, deals made over a bourbon glass, suspicious activity, fear of prosecution, and shame has made our leaders hide behind the fig leaf, unworthy of an animal's skin, unwilling to "fess up," take responsibility, and tell us what they have done.

III

Chapter One

THE GOVERNOR'S VERSION

"Mothers may still want their favorite sons to grow up to be President, but . . . they do not want them to become politicians in the process"

John F. Kennedy

Why would anybody spend $11 million dollars to land a job that pays $122,160 per year? We have at least one small bingo-funded charity in Mississippi with only five people employed, and the director makes more money than the head of our state. Two of the remaining four employees also make over a $100 thousand dollars annually.

Businessmen use a term called Return on Investment or "ROI." It is a simple process. You just divide the total dollars you intend to spend by the total dollars you would earn in a year, and you determine when your investment is recovered and when you start turning a profit. You find out whether or not it would make business sense to embark on that venture. In this case, the answer to that is over 90 years. A man in his mid to late 50's could easily see that wouldn't be a good investment or business proposition if he wanted to live to see the fruits of his labors. It wouldn't be a good investment for anybody since our expected life spans are under 80 years. But then again, that wasn't the governor's money that he spent. It was people who count on him, not you and me, the average Joe. It would take too many contributions from us to make that much, and, there aren't that many people who vote. That much money took big businesses, lawyers, lobbyists, and gold diggers. You and I know, politicians don't care about somebody else's money, and are quick to throw it around. But the people that gave it, are looking for something in return -- most likely big business ventures.

There is no question Governor Barbour has brought big business, and as a result more jobs to the state. In Ronnie Musgrove's 2001 state of the state address, he bragged of the first Nissan vehicle which would roll off the assembly line in the summer of 2003. Why didn't any governor talk about the first customer that entered the Hard Rock Café or the first night spent in one of the casino hotels?

Governor Barbour came to our state Capitol with a storm cloud already hanging over his head the first day he took office. It would hang over our Capitol for eight years. Most of us didn't know it at that time, but he did. *Bloomberg* reported during his run for reelection in 2007 that back in 2004, Barbour had an interest and stock ownership in his lobbying firm at reporting time. His name still appeared in the company of Barbour, Griffith and Rogers. *Bloomberg* reported that his attorney said he complied with Mississippi law and the Mississippi Ethics Commission agreed that he had complied with the law. *Bloomberg* also said he was able to hide it because of the Mississippi law but it would have been required reporting based on federal laws in the executive branch of government. Maybe that's the reason he decided not to run for president. Then again, it may be because he has a number of skeletons in his closet during his eight years in office as governor. *USA Today* on Politics had their own thoughts about his motives, linked below if you care to read.

http://www.usatoday.com/news/politics/2011-04-12-haley-barbour-2012-lobbying.htm

For more on this story and additional information, please read the entire article at: http://www.bloomberg.com/apps/news?pid=newsarchive&sid=a3O8w8_QJ6KU

For a related story on "mum Barbour" about his friends benefitting from Katrina click here:

http://www.bloomberg.com/apps/news?pid=washingtonstory&sid=aG1fHyzJA56A

As a follow-up to that story, the *Washington Note* suggested impeachment. They say that Barbour's family, and friends, including his "old lobbying firm" benefited by the work done on the Gulf Coast following Hurricane Katrina. They said there were at least four companies doing work that permitted the casinos to re-open.

To read more click here:

http://www.thewashingtonnote.com/archives/002303.php

This book is based on research and information already available that the readers may or may not have seen before in the various forms of media or through public record research. However we forget the bad too quickly as the politicians preach on their way out what a great job they did while in office. We remember them as saints. That's nothing new in our history. Later I will address an interesting account involving events from the 1800's which happened right here in Mississippi where Barbour claims close ties to Greenwood Leflore. But I think it is important for us to look back on the Mississippi State of the State addresses each of the eight years of Barbour's reign before he leaves.

You can read about the same old stuff like no money, lots of money, bad times, and good times, as they fluctuate. Don't forget about the great job the legislature is doing either. I will give you the links to those sites year by year as I provide small summaries and quotes with emphasis on certain words or phrases which I will bring to the readers' attention by underlining. I will analyze those topics at the end of each year's address.

We are already going to give Barbour an A+ for his work in business, which includes jobs. These statements are all quotes from his speeches. The URL link at the end of each set of quotes will take you directly to that particular speech.

2004 – Governor Barbour's State of the State address
First and foremost, my budget will state very clearly that <u>we do not need to raise anybody's taxes -- period</u>.

An essential element of such a business climate is to <u>keep taxes down</u>. That's why <u>I consider not raising taxes</u> the first point of our economic development plan.

Beyond that, <u>raising taxes is the enemy</u> of controlling spending, and controlling spending is the way to get our budget back in line over the next two years, which is my goal.

I want to let you know that <u>the largest increase in my budget will be to restore some of what has been cut from our universities and community colleges.</u>

In the area of corrections, <u>we incarcerate criminals to protect the public's safety</u>. My goal is to house prisoners at the least cost. My administration <u>will make increased use of county-owned regional jails and private prisons</u> to save money.

People around the country underestimate Mississippi. They underestimate our people and our potential. What's worse, we too often underestimate ourselves. I ask you to join me in putting that kind of thinking behind us. We don't have to be last.

In addition, I ask this legislature to grant me the authority to house state prisoners and different classifications of prisoners at the private Tutwiler facility. If the State of

Alabama can house prisoners twelve miles from Parchman at 36% less cost than we can house them ourselves, common sense says we need to capture those savings for Mississippi and with your help we will. We will be reopening the Delta Regional Correctional Facility at Greenwood.

We are blessed to be a tourist destination in a fabulous location, here in the center of the fastest growing region of the country, flanked by two great waterways, with outstanding ports on the Gulf.

Click on the URL link below to read the actual speech or verify anything quoted herein.

http://www.stateline.org/live/details/speech?contentId=16208

      I think we can reasonably conclude from the statements highlighted, that the governor believes in:

- No Tax Increase
- Obedience of the Law
- Law Enforcement
- Prison Expansion
- More Funding for Higher Education
- Not being last (our state)
- Tourism

2005 – Governor Barbour's State of the State address

This legislature enacted a merger of the Bureau of Narcotics into the Department of Public Safety. Drug arrests are up 73% over 2003, and because of the reforms you *allowed us to make in <u>our prison system</u>, we're <u>housing these criminals</u> at the lowest possible cost to taxpayers. <u>Safer communities</u> create more jobs.*

<u>You've seen my budget</u>, so I won't go through it in detail. <u>It gives the highest priority to K-12 education, law enforcement and homeland security and Medicaid.</u>

To help in this effort, my budget level funds the <u>Mississippi Bureau of Narcotics</u> and the <u>Department of Public Safety</u>, while <u>adding funds for a long overdue trooper school</u>, which will add <u>50 new, trained and equipped officers</u> to the Highway Patrol. Our <u>law enforcement</u> people are doing a great job. Let's strengthen them.

Too often <u>law enforcement</u> finds crystal meth labs in homes where <u>children are present</u>. Those <u>kids</u> are exposed to both the risk of a meth lab explosion and to long-term chemical contamination. We should <u>toughen the punishment for drug criminals</u> who manufacture drugs in the <u>presence of a child</u>, and we should have additional penalties for buying or selling drugs in a <u>child's presence</u>.

While my education reforms seek to educate <u>our children</u>, I have another set of proposals designed to better protect <u>our children</u>. We're attacking drug <u>crime</u> in Mississippi because drug crime can destroy our communities and <u>our children</u>.

http://www.stateline.org/live/details/speech?contentId=16584

The theme that stands out most to me for 2005 seems to be a focus on law enforcement, with emphasis on drug enforcement, and protecting children.

- Drug Enforcement
- State Troopers
- Law Enforcement
- Prison
- Our children's welfare and safety

2006 – Governor Barbour's State of the State address

<u>We will also assist the Tupelo Furniture Market</u> in its national and international promotion in the amount of $200,000 a year, based again on a 50-50 cost share.

We've underline{eliminated this $700 million budget hole without raising anybody's taxes!}

http://www.stateline.org/live/details/speech?contentId=79585

The 2006 state of the state address was a lot of the same old stuff, but emphasis was placed on helping a failing furniture business -- and of course, Katrina.

2007 – Governor Barbour's State of the State address

Another priority we have focused on is law enforcement. Our Highway Patrol and other state law enforcement have received the biggest pay raises in history to get them on a level with our neighboring states. Two trooper schools in one year. . . one paid for with federal funds after Katrina . . . have added ninety-two new highway patrolmen to the force. We plan a third trooper school in the next fiscal year to get us back closer to the authorized number of troopers.

The Bureau of Narcotics continues to excel, and legislation you passed two years ago has greatly reduced the number of crystal methamphetamine labs in the state. Drugs continue to be a major problem, and most crime is drug-related, but you are doing things to combat it.

This year I ask you to do three more things: To pass laws that lengthen the mandatory prison sentence for committing a felony with a gun, and to lengthen the prison sentence for a felon possessing a gun. These changes will give prosecutors better tools to punish criminals who use guns to commit crimes, and they will not violate the constitutional rights of law-abiding citizens to keep and bear arms.

I also ask you to increase the number of narcotics agents by fifty or nearly half.

While most policing is done at the local level by police and sheriffs' departments, we need to give them all the support we can to protect our citizens and families.

State Revenue is up a third or more since I became governor. Part of that is because our economic picture has improved so much…with more people working and making higher incomes. More tax revenue without raising anybody's taxes.

"The <u>most important things</u> for our State's financial well-being <u>are for us to abide by</u> <u>the law</u> that says only 98% of General Fund revenue can be appropriated and that the 2% set aside goes into the Rainy Day Fund until built up to the <u>amount set by law</u>."

http://www.stateline.org/live/details/speech?contentId=171376

- Drug Enforcement
- State Troopers
- Prison
- Abide by law
- Katrina

Barbour said in 2007 that law enforcement is a priority. He deviated from his initial request to have a trooper school, and actually had two, increasing their numbers by 92. Still he wanted a third school. It is clear his focus is on his Mississippi Department of Public Safety (DPS) which includes Mississippi Bureau of Narcotics (MBN), and Mississippi Highway Patrol (MHP).

2008 – Governor Barbour's State of the State address

But again, how can you not do whatever it takes for those people…our people…the people who sent us here to get results…to <u>spend their tax dollars wisely</u>…to <u>take as few of their dollars in taxes as possible.</u>

I think the governor was out of steam in 2008 from the reelection campaign. It looks like he pulled in language from his campaign speeches. He just regurgitated a lot of the same old stuff – as always including pats on the backs for key people. He did mention Medicaid 13 times though.

http://www.stateline.org/live/details/speech?contentId=273885

2009 – Governor Barbour's State of the State address

In the last five years I have joined you in more than speeches. <u>At the beginning we</u> <u>addressed a $720 million dollar budget hole;</u> we ended lawsuit abuse with comprehensive tort reform; we overhauled and greatly improved workforce development and job training; we used Momentum Mississippi to accelerate economic development and job creation; we upgraded education and increased state spending *on all three levels – K-12, community colleges and universities – by record amounts; and <u>we did it all without raising anybody's taxes.</u>*

Most of our viewers are probably aware that Mississippi's Constitution and our statutes require the State to have a balanced budget. They probably don't know how <u>our laws mandate we meet that requirement.</u>

That <u>law requires</u> state and local governments to pay a twenty-five percent match.

<u>There is a law</u> . . . a statute . . . <u>Section 27 104 13 of the Mississippi Code</u> that <u>orders the governor</u> to make enough cuts in appropriated state spending to eliminate any deficit spending, if State revenue comes in lower than the estimate on which the appropriations were made by the legislature. <u>As required by law</u> I submitted my Executive Budget Recommendation last November.

The choices haven't changed: <u>We can give the hospitals a ninety million dollar tax break and raise somebody else's taxes to allow the hospitals not to pay their fair share; or, we can give the hospitals a ninety million dollar tax break and cut Medicaid spending accordingly, which amounts to two hundred seventy-five million a year,</u> including the federal share; or, <u>the hospitals can pay their fair share, ninety million and not cut the program.</u>

To me, it is a clear choice. <u>We should reinstate the hospital tax,</u> and the hospitals, who asked for this provider fee because it pays them back six dollars for every one they pay in taxes, should pay their fair share as they did all those years.

<u>The law gives me very little latitude</u> about how I can distribute these cuts. <u>The law says I can</u> cut any department or agency by five percent of its appropriation; however, <u>I cannot cut any department or agency by more than five percent</u> until every department and agency has been cut five percent.

http://www.stateline.org/live/details/speech?contentId=368942

- State laws apply to governor (can't violate)
- Law Enforcement
- Budget issues

- Hospital Tax

This is the first time in six years the governor has conceded that he is held accountable by law. They are the laws that he and the legislators make. They become state statutes codified in the Mississippi Code. He says things like, "*our law requires it, as required by law, the law gives me little latitude, the Mississippi code orders me, and laws mandate.*"

Please remember those comments because they will come back to haunt him.

2010 – Governor Barbour's State of the State address

That law says the governor can cut any department, agency or line by up to 5 percent, but can't cut any account by more than 5 percent, until every department and agency had been cut by 5 percent, except debt service. Then the law goes on to say, any cuts above 5 percent must be the same for every department and agency with no exemption but debt service. I have asked you to change that law to allow the governor the flexibility to cut departments and agencies up to 10 percent.

As an example of why the 10 percent bill with flexibility is critically needed, let me refer you to the Corrections budget, for our prison system. An 8.1 percent cut would equal nearly $26 million. To make such a cut for the rest of this fiscal year would require 3,400 to 4,000 convicts to be let out of prison: 3,400 to 4,000 convicts, who are not approved for parole, have not gone through pre-release preparation or training and for whom there are very, very few jobs.

We know we must have a balanced budget, and it appears to me there is no appetite for tax increases. I agree. In a recession, when our businesses and families are hard pressed and their incomes are down, the last thing we should do is further reduce their incomes by raising taxes.

I cannot believe anyone watching this speech on TV or hearing it on the radio would vote to turn 3,400 to 4,000 convicts loose onto civil society, on to the public.

By state law the governor is required to make cuts to appropriated spending sufficient to align spending with actual revenue. You may recall that I cut about $226 million in state spending last Fall. Another $211 million must be cut, based on an 8.1 percent revenue shortfall.

http://www.stateline.org/live/details/speech?contentId=452651

I am so glad to see that the governor is so concerned about not releasing prisoners and that he realizes he cannot ignore the laws.

- Corrections
- Against releasing prisoners
- Taxes
- Governor can't ignore the state laws

2011 – Governor Barbour's State of the State address

While it took two plus years, we got our budget back to where the state spent no more than it received in annual revenue, and we quit raiding balances in special funds. <u>We replenished the Rainy Day Fund to its statutory limit of $375 million</u> and created other reserves to cover potential federal liability. <u>And we did it without raising anybody's taxes</u>.

Not only do <u>I urge you not to consider tax increases this year</u>, I implore you to <u>keep spending</u> at a level this year that protects more of our reserves for next year. <u>That is the way to stop any tax increases in 2012</u>.

In <u>law enforcement</u>, we have fought the scourge of illegal narcotics with a vengeance. In 2005 you passed laws to reduce the production and use of crystal methamphetamine. When the <u>criminals</u> learned how to get around those laws, you made the necessary changes, and they are working.

<u>Congratulations to the Bureau of Narcotics, the Department of Public Safety</u>, and to you for making the needed legislative changes To <u>keep law enforcement where we want it</u>, I'm announcing tonight that <u>I will dedicate $7.3 million of the governor's discretionary funds to hold</u>

<u>a troopers' school this calendar year</u>. If you will join me in <u>moving motor carrier enforcement from MDOT to the Department of Public Safety</u>, freeing up 40 current highway patrolmen, that would mean nearly <u>100 more state troopers</u> on the road.

http://www.stateline.org/live/details/speech?contentId=540495

I wonder if the governor puts as much emphasis on other laws as he does drug enforcement and traffic enforcement.

- Money Pots overflowing
- Back Patting for MBN and DPS
- No Increase in Taxes
- Almost a hundred new troopers added to enforce traffic laws
- Desire to add enforcement officers from the Department of Transportation (DOT) to Department of Public Safety (DPS)

It sounds like the governor is catering to the Mississippi Commissioner of Public Safety and is building an empire for himself. The Department of Homeland Security is on his radar too. Looks like a man with power wanting more power -- complete control of these agencies.

I also smell a rat in the governor offering up $7.3 million dollars from his discretionary fund to pay for trooper schools, etc. during his January 11, 2011 state of the state address, when his buddy State Senator and candidate for Lieutenant Governor Billy Hewes was asking for the same amount of money ($7,284,121.00) for the same purpose a week before the governor's speech in a bill he introduced on January 4, 2011, in what appears to be an attempt to back-fill the governor's coffer. It wasn't very likely they could have known whether or not the legislature would have approved the funding after only submitting the request seven days before and having another month and a half before it was to be reported out of the committee. See the following link for Hewes' actions:

http://billstatus.ls.state.ms.us/documents/2011/pdf/SB/2100-2199/SB2161IN.pdf

History of the bill, when it was introduced, rejected, etc. The bill didn't die in committee until February 23, 2011, so why would the governor have offered up the money from his own discretionary funds a week after Hewes proposed the bill? Something looks very suspicious about that.

http://billstatus.ls.state.ms.us/2011/pdf/history/SB/SB2161.xml

Throughout the Governor's state of the state addresses, he continually talked about businesses in Mississippi --how much money they brought in, how much they will bring in, how many jobs they will create, how much revenue they added to the state's coffers, and how we were going to help them. I don't know how many of these businesses he was responsible for bringing in to the state. Other sources I have read only list a handful. The list below is not an all-inclusive list of names that he throws around in his speeches, but I think you will get the picture.

Toyota, GE Aviation, PACCAR, Stion, EADS, Twin Creek Technologies, Schulz, Nissan, Semi-South, FNC Oxford, Warm Kraft, General Electric, Raspet Flight Center, Polymer Institute, Mississippi Power, Chevron, Gulf LNG, Bluefire, Denbury, Ergon and Bunge, Enerkem, Soladigm, Kior, Rentech, Severstal, Cooper Tire, ACT Electronics with Ayreshire Electronics, PSL- North America, Cisco and Bell South, SeverCorr, Strategic Petroleum Reserve, Franklin Center for Furniture Manufacturing

Governor Barbour made a comment in one of his addresses that I liked, **"Don't take my word for it."** I didn't, and I urge you not to either. Trust, but verify. That includes everything you read in this book.

Chapter Two

OMISSIONS, REVIEW AND ANALYSIS

"Three groups spend other people's money, children, thieves and politicians. All three need supervision."

Dick Armey

Let's consider issues that were not addressed. Some of these areas intermingle with others and many people may not be aware of the need for addressing them:

- Term Limits
- Holding Government Accountable (especially the Executive Branch)
- Ethics (Real ethics laws that provide adequate punishment -- not what we have now)
- Taxing Industry to bring in more revenue (not cutting state budgets across the board)
- Campaign Finance Reform (not the mealy-mouth junk we have presently)
- Constitutional Amendment that would allow voters to put anything on the ballot
- Downsizing the legislature
- Release of Violent Prisoner
- Integrity and Honesty in Office
- Clear and concise, unhindered Public Records Disclosure Laws (without threats)
- Performance Based Budgets (set a benchmark, reward those above, fire those below)
- Redistricting (it is sad that we have to run to the feds because we can't agree on a plan)
- Lobbying Reform (Think the lobbyists will persuade the politicians on this one?)

- Legislative Performance (or lack thereof) – much more on this subject later
- Eminent Domain (Take our property and give it to another person or corporation?)

Issues like Medicaid, K-12 school funding, required spending and discretionary spending, are issues that Barbour addressed over and over. Those are very important issues, but they became so convoluted, I don't even want to address them. Robbing from Peter to pay Paul in those areas made it a topic that would only confuse the reader.

These are the issues that stand out in my mind that he raised in one or more of his state of the state addresses:

- More Drug Agents
- More State Troopers
- Putting DOT officers under the DPS
- Prisoners/Prisons
- Longer sentencing for violent offenders
- Child Safety
- Health Care
- Katrina recovery
- No Tax Increase for Citizens
- Need for Additional Revenue

I will break those topics down into four broader categories and address them as we go along:

- Prisoners
- Health Care as related to Taxes/Revenues
- Legislation
- Law Enforcement

Prisons, prisoners (especially felons), and retention of violent offenders seemed to be a common theme.

The governor made it clear that he was concerned about the safety of the public with emphasis on our children. Let's take a look at what he really thinks about our safety. He claims the budget cut required of the Corrections Department would result in the mandatory release of 3,000 to 4,000 prisoners. He says, "I cannot believe anyone watching this speech on TV or hearing it on the radio would vote to turn 3,400 to 4,000 convicts loose onto civil society, onto the public."

First of all, any time a large amount of prisoners are released from prison, they are of the lowest threat prisoners we have. That includes people convicted of nonviolent crimes such as larceny, drug possession, car theft, embezzlement, false pretense, and so on. I don't feel threatened by those people. I drive past many of them every day while stopping at red lights in Rankin County with them (many of them women) watering, or cutting grass in the median a few feet away from me. These are minimum security prisoners; the first to go in a mass release. Recognizing that requirement and the propensity for having to release prisoners, Senator Terry Burton introduced Senate Bill 2987 in 2011 to review the definition of nonviolent offenders eligible for parole. So at least somebody in the state realized these would be nonviolent prisoners.

http://billstatus.ls.state.ms.us/documents/2011/pdf/SB/2900-2999/SB2987IN.pdf

Additionally the governor wanted to contract prisoner housing out for lower threat prisoners near Parchman Prison. That was early in first administration, and I don't recall reading much, if anything, about that again in the state of the state addresses.

He talked in several of the addresses about going after criminals, with emphasis on felons, drug manufacturers, and convicted felons in possession of weapons. Those are dangerous felons that could have been a threat to our public safety and most of all our children. However, there is another class of dangerous felons that he didn't mention -- violent criminals. At any rate, either class would be dangerous to release on society around our families. These would only be released as an absolute last resort.

Governor Barbour has his own hand-picked police force of state troopers around him to protect him every day, so he isn't worried about violent criminals, not even killers. He even permits them to work around his mansion. In fact he has given killers a "get-out-of-jail-free" card many times (Senator Watson introduced

Senate Bill 2587 in 2011, if passed it would have prohibited prisoners convicted of murder from working at the governor's mansion). Click here:

http://billstatus.ls.state.ms.us/documents/2011/pdf/SB/2500-2599/SB2587IN.pdf

The Biloxi Sun Herald reported on March 25, 2011 that convicted killer Joseph Goff was released by Barbour in Executive Order 956 months before his sentence was to be commuted by the Mississippi Department of Corrections (MDOC). He had served only eight years of a 20 year sentence. Goff had done work in the community after major storms. Goff's victim, a 19 year old, was shot next to his Gautier family's Christmas tree – killed by a bullet that came through the window – fired by a coward hiding outside. There was no joyous occasion for that family that year. Kyle Todd died in his mother's arms.

http://www.mcclatchydc.com/2011/03/25/111074/mississippi-gov-barbour-had-hand.html

In July 2008, Barbour signed an order to release and suspend the sentence of Michael David Graham who had stalked his ex-wife, and shot her in the head with premeditation using a 12 gauge shotgun as she sat in her car at a red light in Pascagoula. Graham had done work around the governor's mansion. Friends/family of victim outraged.

http://www.cbsnews.com/stories/2008/08/02/national/main4316708.shtml

The governor also pardoned Willie James Kimble for the robbery and murder of a Leake County man who was lured out of his house by Kimble with a story of car trouble, then shot in the back of the head, and robbed by two of Kimble's accomplices. Kimble received life behind bars in 1992. Barbour pardoned him in July 2008, giving him a clean record.

Bobby Clark of Batesville murdered his "occasional girlfriend" with a .25 caliber gunshot to her carotid artery. He committed aggravated assault by beating her "new boyfriend" in her house with a mop handle. He was already a convicted felon in possession of a firearm, which was another felony in itself. He had already been convicted of aggravated assault once before. Charged with murder, in 1996,

Clark was allowed to plead to a lesser charge of manslaughter, and received an 18 year sentence. Barbour pardoned him in 2008.

In 1992 Clarence Jones of Vicksburg confessed to hiding out in his ex-girlfriend's home, and attacking her with a knife when she arrived home, stabbing her more than 20 times. He was sentenced to life imprisonment, eligible for parole in 2002. But release was not good enough for Barbour. He pardoned him. The man no longer even has a felony conviction.

In 1989 Paul "Jody" Warnock, also of Vicksburg, shot his girlfriend in the back of the head while she slept. She suffered all night and died the next day. Warnock was convicted, and sentenced to life in prison in 1993, but was released in 2006. Barbour also pardoned him. He too, has no felony conviction for that crime. For a detailed report of facts about all these cases, please refer to an excellent story by the Jackson Free Press on July 28, 2008 (link below).

http://www.jacksonfreepress.com/index.php/comments/barbour_helps_domestic_killers_073008

On January 3, 2009, the Jackson Free Press reported that Leslie Bowlin, who was convicted of rape, kidnapping, aggravated assault, and burglary of an occupied dwelling, had been released. The victim was a Mississippi State student who was taken out into the woods to be tied up, but was miraculously saved by a passing-by hunter. Bowlin was sentenced to life plus 25 years. It was clear that the judge and jury wanted him to remain behind bars for a very long time. However, on December 20, 2008, Governor Barbour released him to go home to Louisiana for 90 days during Christmas. Louisiana Attorney General Buddy Caldwell was furious, having received no prior notice. He sent a letter to Mississippi's Attorney General Jim Hood asking for his assistance in dealing with Governor Barbour. He even threatened to sue for Barbour's action calling it "unbelievable and insane".

www.jacksonfreepress.com/index.php/site/comments/barbour_furloughs_rapist_then_retracts/

The order called for Mississippi probation officers to supervise Bowlin during the absence although no interstate agreement had been negotiated with Louisiana and Mississippi probation officers had no jurisdiction in Louisiana The monitoring device that was supposed to be on Bowlin was not there, according to the sheriff in the Parish where Bowlin resided.

Bowlin (supposedly released for a psychological exam), would not have needed a 90 day release for that purpose. That could have been done in one day at the prison. After the media disclosed the real information concerning the details of his release, Barbour must have known at that point he had been caught with his pants down. He ordered the return of Bowlin. Read here:

http://www.wlbt.com/story/9582433/barbour-revokes-order-sex-offender-will-be-returned-to-prison?redirected=true

Notice that every single one of these actions by Barbour took place in his second term. He would have had serious backlash in his bid for reelection had he made these decisions in his first term, likely causing his loss of the reelection. He knew what he was doing, and he had it timed perfectly. All of the permanent releases and/or pardons took place within seven months after he took office for the second time. He knew he was serving his last term because of term limits of two terms for governors. He had nothing to lose. But why did he do it? Did he have something to gain that we don't know about?

What we have is a governor who has ignored the fact that some people who have made the mistakes of committing far less serious crimes, have a record that will follow them to their graves. But he released murderous felons, and pardoned most of them, giving them a clean slate. Felons that were responsible for putting innocent people in their graves – people that deserved to live.

The next issues we will look at have to do with the governor's honesty regarding his concerns for health care, children and taxes. He included in three of his state of the state addresses that he and the legislature had pulled us out of a $720 million deficit, and, best of all, it happened in only two years, "without raising anybody's taxes." He was able to say that around his "buddy rubs" in the legislature, and he had one over on most of us, who viewed his addresses on television. However, one day while in Chicago, speaking to the chamber of commerce, he blurted that out again. But this time an alert and determined reporter named Andy Kroll from Motherjones.com (an online watchdog site) decided to take him to task and check his "facts."

Kroll said Barbour had raised taxes a half dozen times, and had cut budgets that prevented Mississippians from having essential services, not to mention education. Here is an excerpt from MotherJones.com dated March 16, 2011.

In 2003, before Barbour took office, the state's tax on hospitals was $1.50 a bed per night. The tax for nursing homes with mentally disabled patients was $4.00 per night. In 2004, he raised the tax from $4.00 to $6.00 for <u>nursing homes, children's psychiatric facilities,</u> and care <u>centers for the mentally disabled</u>. In 2005, he signed a bill that more than doubled the daily bed rate for hospitals. He approved legislation that taxed approximately 110 hospitals between $60 and $90 million dollars a year according to Michael Bailey, senior vice-president of the Mississippi Hospital Association.

In Barbour's "Equity and Solvency" bill, according to Kroll, was a buried tax that was supposed to increase the unemployment insurance trust fund. It would also lower the burden on new business while doubling the taxes on existing businesses, only businesses that were having to lay people off.

One member of the legislature would speak out about the reality of Barbour's claims. "He's raised taxes, made budget cuts, laid off people, used up reserve funds, and he wants to say he's got this budget magic," says State Representative Cecil Brown. "Well, there's nothing magic about that."

Kroll also said Barbour raised cigarette taxes twice in only three months. The first raise almost quadrupled the tax from 18 to 61 cents per pack A couple of months later, there was a tax increase of another 25 cents a pack on cheaper cigarettes. Barbour claimed it was for health reasons instead of budgetary issues. A spokesman from his office defended Barbour's actions by giving reasons for each of the tax increases. He wasn't asked for reasons, or excuses, but rather was confronted about claiming they did this great job of filling a $720 million budget deficit without raising anyone's taxes. That simply was not true, and Barbour knew it. He made that claim in several of his addresses.

http://motherjones.com/politics/2011/03/haley-barbour-budget-fact-check

Let's move on for a moment from these misrepresentations themselves, and look at other tax issues. In the 2010 address, Barbour said his PEER Committee called for budget cuts. This was to be done "across the board with no sacred cows". However, further on down on that same page, he raised the issue of not granting a tax amnesty to people, or to small companies that weren't able to pay their taxes. He also said the tax amnesty in 2004 produced about $9 million dollars in revenue. However, he said his budget proposal would not allow for such an amnesty. Instead, he was going to give an <u>increase</u> to the Mississippi Bureau of Revenue (now MDR, formerly Mississippi State Tax Commission) budget to allow for more tax collection efforts. He increased the size of the MHP and MBN.

Barbour took money from other state agencies offering essential services and stuffed more money into the "Rainy Day Fund". I could save money too if I neglected paying my bills. He took the MGC out from under legislative budget control to let them earn their own keep.

What happened to those "sacred cows"? It sounds to me like he had a herd of sacred cows. They are grazing in Kentucky bluegrass now, thanks to him. He could not have bolstered those agencies by cutting their budgets.

So we know he has taxed the sick and mental patients, as well as children, and now he wants to go after people who, because of the poor economy, have had trouble paying all their taxes. Follow the 2010 address link below.

http://www.stateline.org/live/details/speech?contentId=452651

Chapter Three

TRUST BUT VERIFY

"For everything you have missed, you have gained something else, and for everything you gain, you lose something else."

Ralph Waldo Emerson

There is one issue I didn't cover in the chapter two rebuttals that was hot on the governor's mind, especially during the latter years of each term. That topic is law enforcement. The governor made use of that phrase quite often as I will point out to you.

2007 Speech

Another <u>priority</u> we have focused on is <u>law enforcement</u>. Our <u>Highway Patrol</u> and other <u>state law enforcement</u> have received the biggest pay raises in history to get them on a level with our neighboring states. <u>Two trooper schools in one year</u>. . . one paid for with federal funds after Katrina . . . have added <u>ninety-two new highway patrolmen</u> to the force. We <u>plan a third trooper school</u> in the next fiscal year to get us back closer to the authorized <u>number of troopers</u>.

<u>The Bureau of Narcotics</u> continues to excel, and legislation you passed two years ago has greatly reduced the number of crystal methamphetamine labs in the state. <u>Drugs</u> continue to be a major problem, and <u>most crime</u> is drug-related, but you are doing things to combat it.

This year I ask you to do three more things: To pass laws that <u>lengthen the mandatory prison sentence</u> for <u>committing a felony with a gun</u>, and to <u>lengthen the prison sentence for a felon possessing a gun</u>. These changes will give prosecutors better tools to <u>punish criminals</u> who use guns to <u>commit crimes</u>, and they will not violate the constitutional rights of law-abiding citizens to keep and bear arms.

I also ask you to increase the <u>number of narcotics agents by fifty or nearly half</u>.

While most <u>policing</u> is done at the local level by <u>police and sheriffs' departments</u>, we <u>need to give them all the support we can to protect our citizens and families.</u>

2011 Speech

In <u>law enforcement</u>, we have fought the scourge of illegal narcotics with a vengeance. In 2005 you passed laws to reduce the production and use of crystal methamphetamine. When the <u>criminals</u> learned how to get around those laws, you made the necessary changes, and they are working.

<u>Congratulations to the Bureau of Narcotics, the Department of Public Safety</u>, and to you for making the needed legislative changes To <u>keep law enforcement where we want it</u>, I'm announcing tonight that <u>I will dedicate $7.3 million of the governor's discretionary funds to hold a troopers' school this calendar year</u>. If you will join me in <u>moving motor carrier enforcement</u>.

This is not what it appears. The average person looking at these priorities would think he is a very pro law enforcement person. The fact is the MHP has long been the right hand of the governor and the "class pet."

http://motherjones.com/mojo/2011/03/haley-barbours-bodyguard-boondoggle

Most people will agree we have some of the worst roads in the country (except those leading to gaming establishments). But, Barbour uses state-funded troopers as bodyguards on his trips around the US and the world. Other governors use state troopers as bodyguards. However, the real issue here is his frequent jet-setting. Click the Clarion Ledger link below for more:

http://blogs.clarionledger.com/ecrisp/2010/12/28/gov-barbour-under-scrutiny/

Troopers are either protecting him, writing tickets/accident reports, or looking for little stickers on the windshields of politicos. These stickers are outlines of the state, in various colors depending on your position, i.e. judge, legislator, etc. The other thing is the license plates indicating the driver is a member of the legislature. They make a political statement, *"Write me a ticket, and forget the legislation the governor is proposing, or your pay raises, and your wish-list for equipment, and additional manpower."* I encourage you to submit a public records request, and ask for the number of legislators who have received citations in the last ten years. Ask them what the purpose of the windshield stickers is and how they determine who gets them. They have exempted themselves from the traffic laws they enforce and I would surmise are the biggest breakers of those laws. I have had several friends over the years that have been patrolmen and at one time worked extensively with their criminal investigative division (CID). I have ridden with them plenty of times. It didn't matter which patrolman, or where we were going --if the trip was of any significant distance, they had the pedal to the metal. These officers are good people, but there is nobody to police them.

When the cat's away, the mice will play. Children left unsupervised will get into just about anything. Adults left without some policing efforts will do the same. Even the police, without some authority over them, will run amuck. I'll give you a good example. Drive up or down Interstate 55 during any day from Jackson to Southaven, and you will most likely pass at least three MHP vehicles. You will also notice that unless they are out trolling for speeders, they are the biggest violators of the speed laws themselves. That doesn't mean they are bad guys, any more than you and I are when we speed, or our kids when they misbehave. But when you are doing the maximum speed limit of 70 miles per hour and they pass you like you are sitting still --unless they are using their lights and sirens --they have no right to break the laws themselves. If they have an accident under those conditions, they will most likely be at fault. Even if they have their lights and sirens on, if they fail to use caution and good judgment while approaching intersections, they may take a life, and be held at fault. When you are heading north, and they are heading south (or vice versa), and you see that tall low-band antenna on the back of their cars bent so far backwards it is pointing towards the road behind it, they are far exceeding the speed limit. So again, who will police them? The answer is, "nobody".

I don't think people realize how dangerous it is for a trooper headed in one direction who passes a speeder going 85 miles per hour in the other direction. If there are no emergency crossovers to the other side of the interstate, the trooper is forced to either go to the next exit or cross the median. If that median is wet, that could cause him to slide into oncoming traffic. Assuming he gets to the other side safely, how fast will he have to drive to catch that person? Speeds in excess of 100 miles per hour are not uncommon at all. When the trooper cars run up behind a casual driver, they could look in their rearview mirror, panic, and slam on their brakes. Is it worth it?

Troopers are highly unlikely to ticket the drivers of those cars that have a "get out of jail free" yellow, red, or other color sticker in the shape of the state on their windshield. That means that high speed pursuit to stop one of those vehicles, while endangering the rest of the public, is done in vain. So they are above the law, and there is nobody higher on the food chain to police the would-be enforcers. The same is true with our legislature and other top state government officials. Who will police them in their day-to-day activities that might be against the law?

When Mike Moore was in office it happened frequently. State, county and city officials were charged with crimes and removed from office through the Public Integrity Division.

The Alcohol and Beverage Control (ABC) laws are interesting. Their statute, Section 67-1-91 of the Mississippi Code, requires them and other officers to strictly enforce the alcohol laws and makes it a crime if they fail to do so. (After you go to this link you will have to click on the folder in the upper left corner that says MS Code of 1972, enter the statute number (67-1-91) in the search box on the top left. It will take you to a list of statutes on the center right. Look for that one (67-1-91) and read it.) This link can be used to research any of our state laws.

http://www.michie.com/mississippi/lpext.dll?f=templates&fn=main-h.htm&cp=mscode

At any rate, you and I are a part of the problem if we are not part of the solution. We have a voice, a phone, a pen and paper, a word processor, a car, access to media, and a free mind to vote for anybody we want and to report unlawful conduct. We have to be the police for those agencies with no higher authority, or a higher authority that turns a blind eye.

As far as the increase in State Narcotics Agents is concerned, I strongly support it, having worked for them myself in the late 1970's. We never got that kind of support back then. They are getting support now because they are under the wing of the Mississippi Department of Public Safety (DPS), and have a program that allows troopers, and agents to swap back and forth between the MHP to the MBN and back if approved. I think the more people they can get, the better off our state will be. However, the way they do it now is political, because of whom they belong to.

The DPS also owns the crime lab, and the sex offender program on the internet, in addition to the MBN. As you can see, they are now trying to get the enforcement officers from the DOT. There won't be much time left before we become a police state. They will be running law enforcement agencies through their political appointees, and really, the governor will be calling day-to-day operational shots.

Speaking of the governor, in addition to his insistence on having to abide by the law himself, his determination that we do too, and his desire to populate his own "pet" agencies with everything they need, I would like to bring another one to your attention. This is where the governor will cringe, and his blood will boil.

The MGC (MGC) has law enforcement officers in most of their divisions, including investigations, intelligence, enforcement, and charitable gaming (bingo). The only arrests they make on the casino side of the house are persons who commit crimes against the casinos – employees caught stealing or patrons caught cheating. There are never any charges when the casino management is caught violating the law. They occasionally impose administrative fines, but the casinos have already factored that in as a cost of doing business.

A couple of years ago, I requested information from the MGC about certain bingo hall charities and the commission's arrest records since I left their employment on August 1, 2000. I got a complete runaround from the attorney general lawyers embedded in MGC. They wanted me to hire a part-time temp employee to conduct the research. That was just a ploy to get me to back off. If you don't think our own agencies will do anything like that, look at this site where a reporter requested access to Governor Barbour's e-mails. He was told it would take 832 hours over a 20 week period, and he would have to pay the cost of research, man hours and paper:

Motherjones.com reporter David Corn reported that a nationally recognized expert in IT matters, David Gerwitz said, "The idea that it will take 832 hours over a span of 20 weeks is ludicrous, unless literally they're trying to get it off the bottom of the ocean." He added that if that were the case, Mississippi would have to be using antiquated systems with materials stored elsewhere in an "Indiana Jones" type warehouse. The cost would be in upwards of $200 thousand dollars. E-mails are not likely stored that way, rather downloaded from a server.

http://motherjones.com/politics/2011/03/haley-barbour-emails-mississippi

I have seen these things myself, and I am confident that part of it is due to incompetence, and the other part is due to arrogance, sometimes even corruption. Neither should be tolerated. The techniques these state offices are using are the way they are, by design, and simply circumvent the Mississippi Public Records Act. They try to discourage you with this run around scheme, or they send you material you didn't request, as if they can't read or understand English. The attorney general provides these lawyers to several of the state agencies. We have computers these days and most of them are run by low level clerks. Records should be immediately accessible (and are) for a reasonable cost. In most cases, a database program, or Excel spreadsheet can be produced using the proper queries with very little effort, or time consumed.

I was invited to go to work for MGC, and began my employment on August 1, 1998 with marching orders to "clean up bingo." I was chosen because of my prior work with the Attorney General's Office under Mike Moore -- because of my reputation of not backing down from politicians, and being what Mike described as "a bulldog" -- which he liked at the time. I don't think MGC knew about the hornet's nest they were about to disturb.

In 1992, the public agreed to allow bingo operations, with the understanding that they would be operated for a charitable purpose, and only if certain actions by the charity, or the bingo operators were made illegal. Legislators passed criminal statutes. In order to make sure they were enforced, the law gave the MGC authority to enforce those laws.

http://www.mgc.state.ms.us/pdf/cgd/cgd_charbingolaw.pdf

Knowing that sometimes there are special circumstances or minor issues that could be addressed by a group of three commissioners, designated by the governor, we agreed to a set of regulations. Those regulations gave the commissioners some leeway in interpreting the law (with the assistance of lawyers provided by the attorney general), passing judgment, and imposing, or not imposing, some form of punishment or administrative action less severe – regulatory or non-criminal. The regulations were not meant to be a regurgitation of the laws.

http://www.mgc.state.ms.us/pdf/cgd/cgd_charitable_gaming_regs.pdf

When we agreed through our legislators to accept the bingo laws under those circumstances, what we expected was that the MGC would "regulate" the halls and charities by monitoring their activities. However, we approved, and funded, trained law enforcement agents. These agents were required to spend many weeks at the law enforcement academy so that they would be trained to enforce the laws and make arrests, if, during their regulatory duties, they discovered a crime being committed.

Having lenient laws or not enforcing them eventually made the industry look bad. What we have now is history repeating itself. Please read this excerpt from a California library that is all too similar to what is going on right now in our state and I urge you (when you have time) to go to this link and read the entire historical article from the 1850's.

Public Opinion Quickly Turns Against Gambling. <u>Gamblers were affiliated with municipal corruption</u> and were blamed for the depression that was occurring at the time. Lynching of professional gamblers occurred in San Francisco in 1856, in <u>part a result of the fight for political control of the city.</u> The <u>gamblers were strong backers of one political faction.</u>

Initially, <u>the state laws were weak</u> and <u>had little real effect on gambling.</u> The statutes outlawed specific games, making the <u>laws difficult to enforce</u> as new and unnamed variants were used and <u>only light penalties were provided.</u>

http://www.library.ca.gov/crb/97/03/Chapt2.html

In 1998, the MGC's former director in charge of bingo agents passed away. He was a very gentle man but had no law enforcement background. No one really knows for sure if the lack of enforcement in the bingo division then was driven by the legislature, or based on his personality, or his lack of law enforcement experience. Since the position is an appointed higher-level position within the agency, and the fact that the appointee normally has political connections, legislative intervention would rate a close look. I am sure he was a fine man. However, during his tenure of several years, nobody was arrested except one person. That case was lost.

Also in 1998, the MGC came under new leadership. They were of the opinion that bingo was an ugly duckling, operating in smoke-filled, formerly abandoned, strip malls that were taking money away from the plush casinos. The games being played in bingo halls looked and operated very much like the games in casinos. At any rate, my "rudder orders" from the new leadership was verbatim to "kick ass, and take names" in the bingo industry. I knew absolutely nothing about bingo. However, I read the law, saw the problem, and implemented a strategy to correct the problem. The senior staff and commissioners were elated -- initially.

One problem was the charity laws that let anybody and everybody form a charity. It was obvious just from the titles of some of them that they were as bogus as a three dollar bill. I pointed out to the director and his assistant that arrests and convictions would lead to disqualification for further operation. I began making arrests through my agents who were finally very happy that they were allowed to do the job they were hired for. Morale was very high at this time.

The bingo laws that we used to go after these people were very weak. However, even with those weaknesses, 45 of the 46 that we arrested entered guilty pleas. These individuals were advised before entering pleas what affect that plea would have on their future in the gaming industry. They would not have pled guilty -- knowing they would be barred from bingo operations -- had they not been guilty. There were two classes of offenses. I will call the first "less serious" and the second "more serious." However, in either case, the punishment only amounts to a misdemeanor, which is a crime punishable by less than one year imprisonment, and/or a fine of less than $1 thousand. In this case, both classes were misdemeanors, hence my claim of weakness in the law.

I asked for clarification from the attorney general's office of the definition of a misdemeanor and a felony, with emphasis on a felony, and got three different answers. According to an assistant attorney general, in order for a law to be a felony, it must have one (but not necessarily all) of the following statements spelled out within the statute:

1. The punishment must be for "more" than one year imprisonment.
2. It must say in the statute that this offense is a "felony"
3. It must provide that the offender is sentenced to more than one year in the "state penitentiary". Whether or not he serves that full sentence is immaterial.

I wanted to push for stronger laws with a more robust bite. I felt that people in this all-cash business would be less likely to commit an offense if they faced prison time. I sought assistance to change the law, but failed. But that gives fodder for future issues to be ignored by our legislators who can simply say, "We need to change the laws." If you EVER hear that phrase, you are most likely being patronized, and taken for a fool, or considered a "chump" especially as it pertains to the bingo laws. Unless your legislator gets numerous, strong colleagues to join him on a bill, he doesn't care about getting it passed.

Why can't the attorney general's lawyers embedded in the MGC draft a law to fix the wording of the current law? They won't for two reasons. One is the "industry-friendly" MGC doesn't want it, and the other is because it will never get passed. There are too many people in the legislature, and people influenced by the legislature, who have other reasons not to pass the law. It would be simple. If you wanted to rewrite the punishment, and ensure that certain violations were felonies, all you would have to do is say:

"This crime is a felony and any person convicted of this crime will be punished by imprisonment in the state penitentiary for more than one year, but less than five years."

How hard would that be? It would sew up the hole in the law that currently exists. The problem is neither the bingo hall operators, nor the legislators, want to subject the law to scrutiny, for fear of what may happen, nor for fear that it could be detrimental to either of them. Therefore, it is what it is, and even the Chairman of the Gaming Committee in the Mississippi Legislature can rarely get a change passed. I saw that when he attempted to change the law that would prohibit gaming agents from being what we wanted them to be when the first law was written -- which is "Peace Officers." Having that status basically allowed them to have powers of arrests over any crime. I turned the table upside down during my tenure because of that.

Since the bingo laws had no teeth and only misdemeanor charges, I went outside the bingo laws, and used other criminal statutes to go after criminals. I charged them with felonies like, embezzlement and false pretense. It infuriated the bingo industry and its associates.

All the chairman's proposal would have done is prevented them from making an arrest. You and I, and anybody else, can conduct an investigation just like the national television media does. You can gather evidence (video, audio, documents, etc.), and turn it in to a prosecutorial authority who may use you and your evidence to prosecute, or may use your evidence for a basis to conduct his own investigation and have the sheriff's department or police department make the arrest. Who cares, as long as the crook goes to jail? This video of the Today Show is the result of an NBC investigative team targeting vehicle warranty fraud.

http://www.msnbc.msn.com/id/21134540/vp/43560209#43560209

After reviewing the video, authorities chose to pursue the offenders already exposed by the media. That investigation led to a 40 state Attorneys General investigation, started by the Missouri Attorney General, arrests of the owners of US Fidelis, closing of the company, and millions of dollars in fines. After you review the video, you will agree that this is a classic example of oversight agencies ignoring the backgrounds of people entrusted with millions of dollars and how that led to massive criminal activity. I am confident that the MSNBC reporters were not the ones who arrested these clowns, but who cares who made the arrest?

You and I can make these type investigations if nobody else will. The Missouri Attorney General took this action only because he saw the investigation on television.

After the "Cold War" ended, spy equipment companies almost went broke. They had to downsize their agencies and started selling cheaper equipment to the public in order to survive. You can now get micro-cameras in just about anything your mind can imagine -- from buttons to ball caps, sunglasses to wall receptacles, televisions to radios, and smoke alarms to Teddy Bears. They have been made so easy to use that an average fifth grader could put a recorder under your car seat, run a wire under your carpet and up to a sun visor. Better yet, get a wireless system. You can then drive down to your local State Inspection Station and video the mechanic putting the sticker on your car without inspecting it. The same goes for cameras under the hood to catch a mechanic dusting out your air filter, but charging you for a new one.

You can turn the videos over to prosecutors, and if they laugh you off, go to the television stations with it -- the pressure from local citizens will likely change their mind. Remember, you are not enforcing the law and should never represent yourself as such. You are merely collecting information that may become evidence of a crime that should be turned over to prosecutors, or you are collecting evidence that something newsworthy occurred just like anybody. Everybody is doing the same thing with cell phone video these days.

If this information is read in states other than Mississippi, I recommend you talk to a lawyer to find out the laws in that state. Even in Mississippi you can never audio tape anybody unless you or some other consenting party is in the room, car, etc. You may have to capture video without a microphone. In other words, you can't go into your bosses' office and leave a device that captures audio and walk out, only to tape him and a phone call he is making. On the other hand, if you are in his office, you are that consenting party and you can. Just don't let the boss know or you will probably get fired.

Never, ever tap anybody's phone line. You may think, *I am not that stupid.* While that may be true, one of our own Professors of Criminal Justice at a major Mississippi University did that one time and got caught. He had to negotiate a misdemeanor plea deal with the feds to stay out of jail. Too bad we don't have a law called "felony stupidity."

Don't ever put an audio or video by itself in any place where a person has "a reasonable expectation of privacy." If a person gets inside their car and closes the door, they would most likely have a reasonable expectation of privacy while talking on their cell phone. However, if they are sitting out on the hood in public, they don't. I am not a lawyer and don't profess to be and I am not giving you legal advice. I am telling you the rules as I know them from many years of experience. If you question your own activities, go see a lawyer. Don't take my word at face value.

I am telling you all this because there is corruption in our midst and you just may be that trusted soul that can talk to somebody seeking a payoff or whatever. Let them approach you though, so you will know they are dirty and that have intent. Don't entrap anybody by enticing them to commit a crime they would not normally commit for the purpose of prosecuting them.

http://www.dinodirect.com/spy-cameras/?affid=422&kwid=85ef7a22185e2294&gclid=CNfdgbTH66kCFQ8r7Aod
ECRhWg

I didn't mean to get so far off my subject, but people need to know there are things they can do to help bring crooks to justice. That is especially true when you know the law enforcement agencies responsible are not going to do anything to enforce the law.

Please keep in your mind from previous chapters how committed the governor was to obeying the law. Keep in mind how much he wanted our law enforcement officers to enforce the law. Compare that mentality with what you are about to see.

Chapter Four

DIRECT IMPACT OF LOST CASINO REVENUE

"Sometimes it is better to lose and do the right thing than to win and do the wrong thing."

Tony Blair

Our politicians' constantly complain about budget deficits -- usually due to casinos not producing the expected revenue because of floods, hurricanes, the economy or something else.

(23 March 2010) Mississippi Announces More Budget Cuts in March 2010
Governor Haley Barbour ordered another $40.6 million in budget cuts for 2010 bringing the total this year to $499.1 million dollars.

http://econpost.com/mississippieconomy/mississippi-announces-more-budget-cuts-march-2010

(27 December 2010) Mississippi Casino Revenue Down in November to $170.6m
Over the same month in previous year which was $185.4 million.

http://www.onlinepoker.net/poker-news/casino-news/mississippi-casino-revenue-november-1796m/8889

(20 September 2010) Casinos' revenues down slightly from last year
Mississippi's 30 casinos almost matched the take from gamblers

http://msbusiness.com/2010/09/casinos-revenues-down-slightly-from-last-year/

(3 September) 2009 Falling State Revenues Demand Reductions in FY 2010 Budget
"Although we struggled very hard last year to spare education from the budget axe, and were successful to a large extent, Mississippi cannot control spending without addressing the largest line item of our budget: education," Governor Barbour said.

http://www.gulfcoastnews.com/gcnarchive/2009/gcnnewsmorestatebudgetcuts090309.htm

You can go back in the media as early as three or four years after casinos started, and you will find articles that show the "woe is me," and the gloom, and doom stories by the casinos. However, if you want the real story, read these charts from the Mississippi Department of Revenue (DOR) that show gross by district, month and year. Look at the bottom lines on the far right.

MONTH	YEAR	GULF COAST COUNTIES	MISSISSIPPI RIVER COUNTIES	TOTALS
JANUARY	2010 $	90,495,763.50	$ 102,350,756.93	$ 192,846,520.43
FEBRUARY		95,769,139.68	125,088,774.33	220,857,914.01
MARCH		95,599,468.15	116,853,041.10	212,452,509.25
APRIL		92,505,892.33	105,664,788.13	198,170,680.46
MAY		95,250,993.44	107,836,991.64	203,087,985.08
JUNE		87,073,953.34	102,385,249.77	189,459,203.11
JULY		97,663,468.44	126,454,531.53	224,117,999.97
AUGUST		101,208,922.50	100,535,258.90	201,744,181.40
SEPTEMBER		90,643,486.11	100,609,256.25	191,252,742.36
OCTOBER		88,068,481.61	103,529,254.04	191,597,735.65
NOVEMBER		85,640,980.74	93,938,807.12	179,579,787.86
DECEMBER		86,591,448.00	97,238,605.67	183,830,053.67
TOTALS 2010	$	1,106,511,997.84	$ 1,282,485,315.41	$ 2,388,997,313.25

MONTH	YEAR	GULF COAST COUNTIES	MISSISSIPPI RIVER COUNTIES	TOTALS
JANUARY	2009 $	96,331,446.76	$ 121,570,538.26	$ 217,901,985.02
FEBRUARY		99,620,106.22	116,883,977.40	216,504,083.62
MARCH		101,865,555.73	130,886,115.74	232,751,671.47
APRIL		92,599,924.09	112,518,907.60	205,118,831.69
MAY		97,694,523.00	124,981,734.05	222,676,257.05
JUNE		84,179,574.29	105,022,078.86	189,201,653.15
JULY		104,182,136.91	120,650,399.89	224,832,536.80
AUGUST		95,918,380.35	109,265,385.92	205,183,766.27
SEPTEMBER		85,272,881.08	101,192,983.60	186,465,864.68
OCTOBER		86,306,891.64	107,228,643.59	193,535,535.23
NOVEMBER		87,213,101.72	98,278,807.11	185,491,908.83
DECEMBER		83,594,292.87	101,413,762.72	185,008,055.59
TOTALS 2009	$	1,114,778,814.66	$ 1,349,883,334.74	$ 2,464,662,149.40

MONTH	YEAR	GULF COAST COUNTIES	MISSISSIPPI RIVER COUNTIES	TOTALS
JANUARY	2008	$106,700,195.50	$117,954,542.99	$224,654,738.49
FEBRUARY		110,487,423.99	143,283,033.48	253,770,457.47
MARCH		120,793,839.02	139,756,702.86	260,550,541.88
APRIL		96,138,319.43	112,719,549.87	208,857,869.30
MAY		107,475,155.36	128,247,298.48	235,722,453.84
JUNE		116,421,705.77	120,855,557.79	237,277,263.56
JULY		115,598,626.68	133,569,637.32	249,168,264.00
AUGUST		111,502,155.05	126,788,529.60	238,290,684.65
SEPTEMBER		84,714,439.42	107,507,666.70	192,222,096.12
OCTOBER		96,762,293.35	114,184,273.19	210,976,566.54
NOVEMBER		96,248,681.29	109,099,419.96	205,348,100.25
DECEMBER		95,481,676.12	108,818,505.12	204,300,181.24
TOTALS 2008		$1,258,354,510.98	$1,462,784,705.36	$2,721,139,216.34

MONTH	YEAR	GULF COAST COUNTIES	MISSISSIPPI RIVER COUNTIES	TOTALS
JANUARY	2007	$106,885,866.56	$139,795,804.09	$246,681,670.65
FEBRUARY		109,743,756.00	138,169,366.29	247,913,124.29
MARCH		117,574,933.38	146,459,283.83	264,034,217.21
APRIL		107,209,635.51	134,101,129.22	241,310,764.73
MAY		104,265,352.50	135,594,570.58	239,859,923.08
JUNE		107,728,460.99	128,208,252.03	235,936,713.02
JULY		124,686,197.82	143,002,204.92	267,688,402.74
AUGUST		108,591,631.34	130,680,256.30	239,271,889.64
SEPTEMBER		111,367,810.67	127,011,905.32	238,379,715.99
OCTOBER		96,897,914.39	120,287,028.33	217,184,942.72
NOVEMBER		103,946,733.95	120,942,210.00	224,888,943.95
DECEMBER		103,204,074.19	125,192,044.73	228,396,118.92
TOTALS 2007		$1,302,102,369.30	$1,589,444,057.84	$2,891,546,426.94

MONTH	YEAR	GULF COAST COUNTIES	MISSISSIPPI RIVER COUNTIES	TOTALS
JANUARY	2006	$64,217,676.26	$159,636,516.62	$223,854,192.88
FEBRUARY		58,863,432.29	139,078,908.83	197,942,341.12
MARCH		63,504,018.93	159,310,451.21	222,814,470.14
APRIL		59,562,681.07	134,997,938.00	194,560,619.07
MAY		62,586,313.13	135,369,700.37	197,956,013.50
JUNE		64,813,749.75	134,294,444.58	199,108,194.33
JULY		74,639,807.67	148,231,022.58	222,870,830.25
AUGUST		66,532,312.26	135,195,444.54	201,727,756.80
SEPTEMBER		109,505,693.69	131,126,780.34	240,732,474.03
OCTOBER		92,201,035.56	129,234,298.73	221,435,334.29
NOVEMBER		95,454,027.01	124,606,551.34	220,060,578.35
DECEMBER		98,725,594.80	129,105,186.17	227,830,780.97
TOTALS 2006		$910,606,342.42	$1,660,187,243.31	$2,570,883,585.73

MONTH	YEAR	GULF COAST COUNTIES	MISSISSIPPI RIVER COUNTIES	TOTALS
JANUARY	2005	$118,790,205.28	$144,898,946.31	$263,689,151.59
FEBRUARY		109,052,869.58	135,923,544.00	244,976,413.58
MARCH		117,781,093.90	141,673,922.24	259,455,016.14
APRIL		100,918,858.30	120,947,066.14	221,865,923.44
MAY		113,062,691.54	130,995,661.18	244,058,352.72
JUNE		107,484,265.94	125,595,628.56	233,079,894.50
JULY		101,673,142.63	135,907,651.48	237,580,794.11
AUGUST		105,900,778.98	126,553,826.80	232,454,605.78
SEPTEMBER		0.00	118,549,040.08	118,549,040.08
OCTOBER		0.00	137,501,346.58	137,501,346.58
NOVEMBER		0.00	129,515,696.61	129,515,696.61
DECEMBER		11,494,128.88	134,156,504.88	145,650,633.76
TOTALS 2005		$886,158,035.03	$1,582,318,835.86	$2,468,476,870.89

Pay close attention to 2005 (the year of Katrina). You would think there had been a huge drop even in the years to follow.

So even if the casinos have their woes just like all other businesses do, how does the governor or the legislature determine how to deal with it? You either have to cut services, or charge more taxes to bring in more revenue. No politician wants to increase taxes, so you can see from the news stories I have already shown, that in most cases the choice has been to cut services, by cutting the state agency budgets.

The politicians will tell you that casino revenue is not our biggest source of income. However, watch the news, and almost any time you see casinos poor-mouthing, you will see politicians talking about cutting state budgets. That's not to say that the governor hasn't increased taxes, which I have already shown, but taxes haven't increased to burden the casinos. They are not to be offended. Notice in the next chart that you can count down to see the gaming industry ranks seventh, of thirty-six in terms of dollars provided to the state, although no ranking is assigned to this chart from the MS DOR and they aren't worth talking about at state of the state addresses.

I would also urge you to read this article from my friend Sid Salter. It will prepare you for the remaining information.

http://nems360.com/bookmark/12525406-SID-SALTER-Gaming-tax-discussion-expected-after-%E2%80%9911-state-elections

CASH REPORT
APRIL 2011

TOTAL COLLECTIONS	MONTH TO DATE FISCAL 2010-2011	FISCAL 2009-2010	JULY 1st TO DATE FISCAL 2010-2011	FISCAL 2009-2010	% CHANGE FISCAL YTD
SALES TAX	$235,353,430.72	$228,318,489.03	$2,094,327,820.93	$2,050,577,372.48	2.13%
WITHHOLDING TAX	132,931,986.16	123,684,103.78	1,165,551,832.80	1,133,330,525.05	2.84%
CORPORATE TAX	33,495,931.54	31,418,714.26	423,915,395.14	402,334,936.72	5.36%
USE TAX	23,015,882.83	21,560,276.39	202,955,606.82	207,359,177.13	-2.12%
INSURANCE PREMIUM TAX	42,999,251.13	42,219,686.06	141,791,447.21	142,356,560.00	-0.40%
TOBACCO TAX	12,505,750.75	14,258,451.99	132,106,414.04	129,628,341.09	1.91%
BEER TAX	2,725,278.21	2,799,547.33	25,246,233.87	24,949,111.86	1.19%
OIL SEVERANCE TAX	8,246,865.78	5,041,822.09	64,730,928.84	54,235,823.47	19.35%
GAS SEVERANCE TAX	1,542,713.78	1,993,694.51	16,934,159.05	17,389,284.60	-2.62%
ESTATE TAX	0.00	14,976.00	63,235.15	44,553.82	41.93%
CASUAL AUTO SALES	1,041,169.94	1,087,437.97	7,774,118.22	8,444,751.50	-7.94%
INSTALLMENT LOAN TAX	1,752,091.67	1,305,693.85	7,428,062.24	5,511,763.81	34.77%
MOTOR VEHICLE TITLE FEE	1,164,353.84	384,009.54	7,147,872.58	3,759,866.02	90.11%
NUCLEAR PLANT IN LIEU	0.00	0.00	20,000,000.00	20,000,000.00	0.00%
HAZARDOUS WASTE	4,755.00	2,844.93	2,818,844.53	3,974,586.80	-29.08%
GAMING FEES & TAXES	23,024,506.22	22,738,706.98	234,266,277.20	237,196,985.24	-1.24%
STATEWIDE PRIVILEGE TAX	102.56	28.25	701,647.79	629,231.27	11.51%
AMS SETTLEMENT FUND	0.00	0.00	0.00	0.00	0.00%
ATV/ MOTORCYCLE FEE	95,410.00	73,290.00	775,523.00	818,475.00	-5.25%
FREEPORT WAREHOUSE TAX	393,549.16	0.00	3,142,126.18	0.00	0.00%
AD VALOREM	10.00	0.00	7,776.96	1,130.00	588.23%
MOTOR VEHICLE PRIV. TAX	12,939,065.97	12,214,290.86	96,369,834.24	93,909,373.69	2.62%
PETROLEUM TAX	35,864,250.33	35,010,439.46	344,118,675.52	318,966,125.42	7.89%
TIMBER SEVERANCE TAX	270,414.10	318,467.30	2,729,954.59	2,500,882.05	9.16%
RAILROAD, UTIL.,& MUN.GAS	49.55	10,784.90	8,775,314.31	8,766,356.12	0.10%
RAIL CAR IN LIEU	0.00	31.36	4,454,558.95	4,378,335.49	1.74%
M.V.RENTAL SALES TAX	588,966.00	512,186.00	5,132,883.87	4,331,164.55	18.51%
CITY UTILITY TAX	36,278.16	119,283.48	632,075.42	664,158.51	-4.83%
TVA IN LIEU	2,144,982.42	2,064,340.78	21,418,918.34	23,617,205.17	-9.31%
SPECIAL COUNTY TAX	5,359,674.67	5,148,091.39	48,406,556.61	46,581,975.32	3.92%
PHONE 911 SURCHARGE	135,520.68	148,995.78	1,389,659.54	1,471,372.73	-5.55%
TIRE DISPOSAL FEE	260,633.25	(17,261.85)	1,868,375.30	1,785,273.25	4.65%
OCCUPANCY TAX	91,449.00	79,999.92	712,333.43	668,893.87	6.49%
ALCOHOLIC BEVERAGE TAX & PROFIT	6,672,082.47	6,815,621.06	72,549,581.48	72,697,091.56	-0.20%
ABC PERMIT & FILING FEES	214,685.00	445,585.00	4,331,860.00	4,520,470.00	-4.17%
TOTAL COLLECTIONS	$708,861,048.29	$654,833,690.73	$5,457,916,584.00	$5,299,878,156.23	2.98%

Based on the chart, sales tax, withholding tax, use tax, insurance premium tax and petroleum tax all exceed gaming taxes. So why can't others on this chart be raised to account for the loss of income, when casinos suffer losses?

Maybe our legislators should raise the gaming taxes if we have to cut state agency budgets every time the casinos have a bad year. As a matter of fact, I am going to give you a television headline that addresses that issue. I have to applaud Representative George Flaggs for this headline:

(24 January 2011) Legislator considers casino tax increase

But wait, let's make sure we understand. This is "a legislator" -- not "the legislature". Guess what else, this legislator George Flaggs, Jr. of Vicksburg who not only represents a casino town, but is also on the Gaming Committee in the Mississippi Legislature. And he wanted to raise their taxes.

http://www.wlbt.com/story/13900583/lawmaker-considers-casino-tax-increase?clienttype=printable

The same night on another station the Chairman of the Mississippi Legislative Gaming Committee came to the rescue and was quoted by another TV station.

(24 January 2011) No tax increase for Miss. Casinos, chairman says
Bobby Moak said he expects no "serious effort" in increase casino taxes this year.

http://www.wlox.com/Global/story.asp?S=13898648

These guys are supposed to be on the same team in the gaming committee. I want to make one point before I move on to the tax issues with regards to Mississippi casinos. The point is that I have researched the Mississippi Secretary of State (SOS) campaign finance reports for the last election, and have found many campaign donations to gaming committee members, but especially to Chairman Bobby Moak. I found where the representative in my own district, Mark Baker, had taken donations from the casino industry. However, he is no longer on the committee. Could that be just a way for casinos to circumvent the law to give a "legal" payoff? You will see more on that later.

Judith Phillips, a research analyst at the John C. Stennis Center compared Mississippi to other states with commercial casinos such as Louisiana and Illinois. Her findings were as follows:

Mississippi casinos are taxed at the 12% rate with eight percent going to the state and four percent to local governments. By contrast, Louisiana taxes its casinos at the rate of 21.5% and Illinois 20%. The MGC opposes taxing our casinos more. Why would they do that if they weren't just catering to the industry?

Let's compare Mississippi with Indiana. Bloomberg Business Week says:
Indiana surpasses Mississippi in gaming revenues (2009) with their $2.58 billion compared to Mississippi's $2.46 billion. We were third place (to Las Vegas and Atlantic City) but Mississippi now ranks 4th. Maybe we could learn something from the way Indiana taxes the industry. Just look at the percentages they charge as opposed to what we charge. I realize they have different types of gaming, but the percentages, even for Riverboat gambling aren't even close.

Do you want to know why we were third compared to Las Vegas and Atlantic City? It was just as the FBI informant said in the 1996 PEER Report. He said there were no rules or laws in Mississippi, and that the mob could do anything they wanted. The fact was the laws had already been in effect. They just weren't being enforced and still are not being enforced. For more information, look at the official PEER Reports by clicking on, or typing in these links. Excerpts from them will be provided throughout the book with these sites listed individually that correspond to the subject matter.

http://www.peer.state.ms.us/reports/rpt344.pdf

http://www.peer.state.ms.us/reports/rpt363.pdf

http://www.peer.state.ms.us/reports/rpt420.pdf

http://www.peer.state.ms.us/reports/rpt522.pdf

This chart shows the different fees and taxes imposed on gaming in other states.

STATE	CASINO TAX	USE OF REVENUE
Mississippi	Riverboat gaming—wagering license fee: 4% on the first $50,000 of monthly gross revenue 6% on the next $84,000 of monthly gross revenue 8% on all monthly gross revenue more than $134,000 A city or county may impose a license fee of 0.4% to 0.6% to 0.8% along the same monthly gross revenue scale as above. Many local governments also impose an additional 3.2% tax on monthly gross revenue.	$3 million or 25%, whichever is greater, of the state monthly revenue share goes to retire bonds until 2012. Any amount in excess of $3 million but less than 25% goes to the state Highway Fund until 2012. The remainder goes to the state general fund. All of the state revenues go to the general fund after 2012.
Indiana	Riverboat gambling—admissions tax for dockside and cruising boats: $3 per person Riverboat gambling—wagering tax for dockside boats: 15% of the first $25 million of adjusted gross receipts 20% of adjusted gross receipts in excess of $25 million but not exceeding $50 million 25% of adjusted gross receipts in excess of $50 million but not exceeding $75 million 30% of adjusted gross receipts in excess of $75 million but not exceeding $150 million 35% of all adjusted gross receipts in excess of $150 million Riverboat gambling—wagering tax for cruising boats: 22.5% of adjusted gross receipts	Admissions tax: $1 to the city where the riverboat is docked $1 to the county where the riverboat is docked $0.10 to the county tourism promotion fund $0.15 to the state fair commission $0.10 to the division of mental health $0.65 to the state horse racing commission. Riverboats operating on Patoka Lake have separate revenue distribution provisions. Wagering tax: 25% to the riverboats' home cities and counties, up to $33 million (the total local distribution level for 2002) 75% to the property tax replacement fund and the Build Indiana Fund lottery and gaming surplus account.

If you want to know the state of the MGC, ask these questions:

1. How many casino operators have been arrested since 1992?
2. How many owners?
3. How many managers?
4. How many bingo arrests were made prior to August 1, 1998?
5. How many bingo arrests were singularly made after 2001?
6. What law gives you a regulatory <u>and a law enforcement requirement?</u>
7. Do you only arrest employees/patrons when the casino is the victim?
8. How much money did you pay <u>enforcement officers</u> 2000-2010?
9. How many agents have you "put in a closet" with no job, for fear of what they know?
10. How many licenses have been issued after waiving a regulation and at least two laws?
11. How many machines are in the bingo halls that have never been tested by the labs?
12. How many machines are in the casinos that have never been tested by the labs?
13. How many "unannounced" inspections have bingo agents made to account for paper?
14. What happened to the money MGC once gave to the state for gaming addiction?
15. Provide the names of bingo halls that operated in the last 10 years, without giving the required percentage of funds to the charities (60/40 rule) but were allowed to operate.
16. What is the maximum salary for charity director of Class A halls?
17. Please provide any recommendations by agents for non-licensure that were licensed.
18. Please provide disciplinary records showing why the 2000-2004 bingo division director's computer was taken off the network, and his office key and cell phone taken away.
19. Provide any policy you have given to agents preventing them from going to the FBI.
20. Provide the qualifications of the current deputy director, when appointed.

Go to this site for MGC's prescribed form for requesting information through public records.

http://www.mgc.state.ms.us/cgd/cgd.html

It is about the only thing on that site that I have found worth going to. There is too much misrepresentation, and not enough archival information on it. A local law firm (Watkins, Ludlam, Winter, and Stennis) has the best site I have ever seen that can keep you informed about what is going on at the MGC, as well as the industry in headlines and lawsuits. Those guys are real professionals. The MGC should just link their customers to the lawyers' site.

http://msgaminglaw.com/

The MGC is very concerned about getting their tax dollars from gambling. They do enforce the law on the mom and pop country stores and gas stations by shutting down the old electronic games that you see behind curtains or in back rooms. I'm talking about on average one or two machines. They will sometimes make a raid across several counties. The business owner never tells them anything about where they came from so they just seize them, charge the store owner with a misdemeanor fine, and then go back to Jackson. Why is MGC management (not by agents' choice) enforcing those laws? Because they want to force the players to go to the casinos or bingo halls to play so they get their cut from taxes; again catering to the MGC by sending them business that they might have otherwise lost.

I know a bar owner that had one of those machines. Law enforcement officers came in last year and seized it. They took the money in it and he had to pay a $500 fine. Another person I know asked him about it and he laughed it off. He said, "They got $3 thousand out of that machine, and it hadn't been long since I had emptied it. I'll make back that money lost and the fine in another month." You know what? He was right and that is the mentality. You can go back to just about any of those old stores and find another machine in its place a month or so later. But bigger than that, casino owners have exactly the same mentality. The MGC occasionally charges a casino an administrative fine, and they pay it gladly. It is just the cost of doing business for them, just like that old country store owner of a single machine. If it is a bingo violator, their charity is now authorized by a law created by the legislature to pay their fines, so they have no reason to comply with the law.

Even though illegal machines themselves fall under gaming laws, in my opinion, the MGC needs to keep their eyes on the sites they have jurisdiction over like casinos and bingo halls. They are quick to whine about not having enough manpower or being overworked. The local sheriffs and/or police officers that stop in those stores for a coke and a donut need to be arresting the owners of those single machines. They see them every day.

In the novel *God Bless the Child*, James Colbert quoted former bingo king Robert Malone, who in the early 1990s was working with then bingo queen Sue Hathorn, on at least three occasions saying the fines meant nothing and were just a cost of doing business. For a real background on bingo and enforcement, it is a good book to read. Publisher's Weekly described it this way:

A woman's campaign against child abuse, a courtroom drama and political infighting over Mississippi's gambling laws are elements in this stirring report. Its focus is Sue Hathorn, who sought funding for a center for abused children that she opened in Jackson. Despite her adherence to Baptism, which frowns on gambling, Hathorn became partners with Robert Malone, owner of a bingo parlor, who faced racketeering charges for allegedly running a high-stakes racket under the guise of a charitable organization. Mississippi's attorney general Mike Moore--portrayed here as politically ambitious and overzealous--held that bingo, being a type of lottery, was illegal under the state constitution, but the Mississippi Supreme Court disagreed and cleared Malone in 1990.

Attorney Mike Farrell of Jackson won the case against Moore which forced the State Supreme Court into making a decision about gambling that was probably the precursor to legalized (casino) gambling soon to follow.

In a recent interview with Malone, he told me that he was both a distributor and a bingo hall operator when Mike Moore "came after" him. He said he believed he was being used as a pawn because he felt that Moore really wanted the lottery system, as did Ray Mabus who openly made his desires for it known. Malone said they couldn't get the legislature to act on gaming so Moore charged him with a violation of the constitution knowing Malone would appeal to the Mississippi Supreme Court when the lower courts ruled against him.

In *God Bless the Child*, Malone had indicated that Mike Moore froze all his bank accounts and seized his cash from the halls making him unable to pay his bills, even his attorney fees. However, Mike Ferrell insisted that Malone always paid him on time. When confronted about that discrepancy, Malone said his bills were paid by somebody bigger with a strong interest in getting a gaming law passed in the legislature. Although he would not say who paid the bills, he eluded to the fact that one casino on the coast was waiting to open its doors and was very helpful to him. Malone said his case was decided just before Christmas and the road was paved for gambling that following session with gambling doors opened shortly thereafter.

So the casinos moved forward after that and bingo took the sideline to be overlooked. Years later after first telling the Clarion Ledger that I was correct that the MGC had not made any arrests of bingo operators for eight years after I left, Executive Director Larry Gregory then furnished information to State Representative Mark Baker, claiming they had "assisted" in about a dozen arrests over that eight or nine year period. These were bingo cases that they had absolute jurisdiction over. They should not have been "assisting other agencies" in making arrests. It is the other way around by law. That would be like a heart doctor assisting a veterinarian. Even if the crimes were false pretense, embezzlement, or whatever, outside the bingo laws, the agents have the powers of arrest.

The bingo law requires all law enforcement agencies to assist gaming enforcement agents in enforcing the law. (See the statutes below.) They have jurisdiction on crimes outside the bingo laws due to their statutory status as a "peace officer". However, the Chairman of the Gaming Committee in the Mississippi Legislature, Bobby Moak, proposed a bill that would have only given them that status as it applied to bingo. Look at the agents' powers in the next statutory excerpt, followed by the requirement of other agencies to "assist them". It is not as MGC's Director Larry Gregory said that they were assisting the other law enforcement agencies. He was only being a puppet to the legislature, Governor Barbour, Lieutenant Governor Bryant, or a particular legislator that tasked him with doing something. When they said, jump," he just wanted to know how high. Please refer to the following excerpt:

97-33-197- Defines Commission's functions, duties and
RESPONSIBILITIES to include:
denial of licensure for violators of 51-203
    a. monitor licensees for compliance with laws and regulations
through:
        (1) routine
        (2) scheduled
        (3) unscheduled
            (a) inspections
            (b) investigations
             (a) Audits
h. **enforce laws** and assist other law enforcement officers in doing so
 as peace officers
i. to establish classes of halls limiting amount of prizes consistent with
respective class

Section 109 continued:
- All departments, commissions, boards, agencies, officers and
  institutions of the state and all subdivisions thereof **shall** cooperate with
  the commission on carrying out its **enforcement** responsibilities.
- It is the DUTY of the Sheriffs, Deputy Sheriffs and Police Officers of this
  state in the enforcement of the provisions of the Charitable Bingo laws
  and TO ARREST AND COMPLAIN against any person violating those
  laws "IF" REQUESTED TO DO SO BY THE COMMISSION

    I sent this information to scores of legislators, and not a single one
responded to me. I contacted the representative in my district. He helped get some
of the materials quickly for me from the MGC. I sent the information to all three
commissioners, and only got a limited response from one -- Commissioner John
Hairston. I sent a letter to the governor and I know he had already read about it
on the front pages of The Jackson Free Press, and The Clarion Ledger. I have no
doubt he was briefed about this and I know Lieutenant Governor Phil Bryant
knew because I told him myself face-to-face in early November 2009.

Chapter Five

THE GOVERNOR AND HIS CONNECTIONS TO THE PAST

"Why waste your money looking up your family tree? Just go into politics and your opponents will do it for you."

Mark Twain

It sure looked suspicious when, while the governor was considering a race for the presidency, he released two black females from prison on armed robbery charges. He then jumped quickly on the bandwagon to approve money for a civil rights history museum, at a time when our legislators were unable to come to an agreement on the state's budget or redistricting. Could his actions have been ploys to win the black vote if he did decide to run?

Public exposure of his questionable and possibly personal use of the state aircraft likely would have resulted in firing of any state employee accused of the same. That doesn't take into account his absence while the legislature was in session – time when he was being paid to be our governor, but instead was flying around the country hoping to elevate himself to a higher position by becoming President.

I believe that he knew, or should have known, that the MGC -- while tasked with the obligation of conducting investigations, making arrests, and regulating the industry -- was not making arrests at all for years, even though our tax dollars funded MGC law enforcement officers. I know that because I used to work there, and made 46 arrests in two years before resigning in disgust after the director told me the legislature was giving him a great deal of pressure and, as a result, we couldn't arrest anybody else. The MGC is required to send annual reports up the chain, specifically by statute to the lieutenant governor, who would share it with the governor.

In the early 1990's, the legislature spent our tax dollars writing a Gaming Act which included about 70 criminal violations that the MGC was tasked with making arrests for. Well, I take that back, what really happened is somebody in the gaming industry (probably a lobbyist's secretary), most likely edited a nationally accepted template of similar state laws, and gave it back to the legislator and the lobbyist when they returned from the steak house/bar. It was most likely a sleazy gaming distributor who pushed it, and paid the lobbyists since supposedly, charities can't use charitable funds to pay lobbyists. halls, and doesn't have to give any money to charity.

But that is another issue. Bottom line is, a governor approved it, and the current one hasn't repealed it, so he must intend for its contents to stand. However, the laws are strictly being ignored, and there is a reason. So why did we pay the legislators to pass that bill, and why have they not repealed it if they don't want arrests, just regulation? Would the public stand for it knowing they are exempt from laws?

I do have one ironic story about our current governor. He went on TV, and made the comment that he was a distant relative to Greenwood Leflore. That was about the time the Indians were trying to get approval for a casino in Jones County, and Barbour was against it. I guess he wanted to reveal that he was blood brothers with the Indians and show that he was really on their side.

If you were kin to Greenwood Leflore, it certainly would not be something to brag about. Aside from the fact that a county and city are named after him, he turned his back on his nation of Choctaws. Later, he turned his back on the South during the Civil War and aided and abetted the North. He supplied the North with men and supplies that would be used against the South. I am going to give you a REAL history lesson so you will understand. It is germane to this book because of the insight you gain into Mississippi politicians, their misleading legacies, and why Barbour doesn't need to be remembered just by his state of the state addresses. You need to know the REAL truth.

Greenwood Leflore's father, Louis Lefleur, kept the French spelling of his last name. Louis fought with Andrew Jackson in the War of 1812 as an officer of the US Army – he was commissioned by Jackson. Afterwards, Louis Lefleur had a trading post near the site of the Old State Capitol. He later moved the trading post to French Camp, MS. The mail was delivered in a stage coach from Nashville to French Camp along the Natchez Trace by a well-respected man from Nashville, Mr. John Donly. (Several spellings are found of Donly.) Seeing that young 14 year old Greenwood couldn't read, and could not understand English very well, Mr. Donly plead the case of his welfare with Louis and took Greenwood to live with him in Nashville to see that he got a good education.

Greenwood Leflore committed his first act of contempt for others by taking one of Mr. Donly's young daughters without his consent, leaving the state, and marrying her. This caused great dissent in the Donly family. (This daughter died several years later, and Greenwood then married her sister.)

Louis Lefleur maintained his friendship with Andrew Jackson, who retained many connections with the Indian leaders -- including all the district chiefs -- after commissioning them as Colonels in the US Army. They got little, to no, public credit for their bravery against the British in the Battle of New Orleans.

Jackson often made the stage coach trip to French Camp, and stayed at the Inn, visiting with his old acquaintance Louis Lefleur after that war.

Greenwood Leflore was already serving as a Regional Chief at only 21 years of age. Then, when he was only 22 years old, and although he had only one-quarter Indian blood, he was made Chief of the entire Choctaw nation. At that time, if the Indians put someone in charge that the US didn't approve of, the US would not recognize their appointment, and would not negotiate with the Indians. They knew Jackson would approve of Louis Lefleur's son, young Greenwood.

Greenwood Leflore was chosen to represent the Choctaw at the Treaty of Dancing Rabbit Creek in 1830, but the event turned out to have what some described as a "carnival-like atmosphere." No religious leaders were allowed, but whiskey was present. There's nothing like fire-water to lift the spirit of cooperation.

Most disturbing though, was the man sitting on the sidelines during the debate. Andrew Jackson sent his Secretary of War to the treaty negotiations. What would you conclude Jackson's intentions were from that? These regional chiefs had fought with Jackson before. They saw him kill massive numbers of Indians. They saw him take land even from those who had served with him. They saw the might of the US Army, and knew they would be slaughtered if they didn't comply. The Secretary of War was there to make sure they did comply.

Greenwood Leflore was rewarded with money and land for his negotiation efforts, and his family members were as well. Within a few years, he had accumulated more than 10,000 acres in the rich Mississippi delta and owned hundreds of slaves to work the land. There are arguments as to why the Civil War was fought, but it is indisputable that slavery was at the core.

Leflore built a mansion known as "Malmaison." He decorated it with only the finest furnishings direct from Paris. You can see the mansion at this site:

http://www.vaiden.net/malmaison.html

But what happened to the people -- his people -- the ones he represented at the treaty signing?

The Indians were not notified in advance exactly when they would be relocated. In the late fall of 1831, Army-contracted wagons just showed up at their doors. The contractors ordered them to gather only their necessities and load them on the wagons. If they weren't infants or crippled, they had to walk 1,000 miles to Oklahoma. On November 1, 1831, after one of the largest rainfalls in history and in record bitter cold, the first unfortunate party started out. The Army contractors lost their way due to their reliance on lakes and streams as landmarks. The rivers overflowed out of their banks and it was impossible to tell one body of water from another. The trip took longer than expected and the food and supplies diminished. Many died on that journey that would later be called, "The Trail of Tears". Meanwhile, Greenwood Leflore enjoyed his life of luxury in his mansion filled with fine French furnishings and with many slaves and housekeepers at his beck and call.

Some of the Indians had said they would rather have died fighting than give up their land. At least they would have gone out in a fight for what was theirs. I don't think there is any question that Leflore played both sides of the fence for financial gain.

About ten years later (early 1840's), Greenwood Leflore started his service in the legislature, first as a representative for two terms, and a senator for another term. The City of Greenwood was named after him in 1840. The County of Leflore was expanded to its current size from land annexations of other counties in 1871.

At the onset of the Civil War, even though he was close friends with Jefferson Davis, Leflore chose not to join the Confederacy. Instead, he offered his allegiance to the Union. He reportedly would remain neutral there at his mansion. However, that didn't happen either. Again, he turned his back on his people, the state, and the legislature where he was sworn to uphold the laws of Mississippi.

His own family members have written passages that appear in the Chronicles of Oklahoma stating that he would invite some of his former statesmen, turned Confederate Officers to his mansion for dinner, but he would require them to remove their gray jackets before entering. At the same time he was selling goods to Union forces. Again, playing both sides, he likely served as a spy for the North and elicited information from his half-dressed Confederate comrades. This link is a must-read for more details given by his own family members, who, like Barbour, are proud of him.

http://digital.library.okstate.edu/Chronicles/v005/v005p371.html

Leflore openly provided supplies, and equipment, as well as slaves to be used as Union soldiers against the South. Leflore temporarily refused payment for the 24 slaves he "sold" to the Union in early 1864. He kept the rest as slaves even though the North ordered release of them.

He planned to file a single claim at the end of the Civil War and would receive a large lump sum for all the damages, supplies, and slaves. The damages, and many of his losses, would be blamed on the Confederate Army. After the war, he would accuse the US of failing to honor the treaty that would have protected him from enemies both foreign and domestic. He insisted that the government pay for what he called a "broken promise." It was as if he expected Union forces to surround his compound on a 24/7 basis, and protect him individually. The full Congressional report makes it clear that was a farce. He claimed his losses were in the hundreds of thousands of dollars. He also wanted pay for the 24 "slaves" he turned over as Union soldiers to fight against the south.

It didn't quite work out the way he planned though. He died at the end of the Civil War willing most of his assets to his family, but reserving $10,000 earmarked for a memorial to himself. He left nothing for his fallen people. His son and son-in-law were made the executors of his estate, and they proceeded with his claim of losses, along with their own alleged losses.

They sought reimbursement for among other things, 24 slaves at $800 "a head" from Congress. However, Congress particularly noted that this was a man who had pledged his allegiance to the Union, headed by President Abraham Lincoln. Lincoln had issued the Emancipation Proclamation freeing the slaves. By law Leflore should have released his slaves at that time. Congress said if anybody at all deserved any compensation, it would be the black slaves that were sold to the Union Army and who served as fighters against the rebels. Again, Leflore was playing both sides of the fence, and receiving financial gain for his efforts. Please see the excerpts from the Congressional Report.

REPORTS OF THE COMMITTEES

OF THE

SENATE OF THE UNITED STATES

FOR THE

FIRST SESSION OF THE FORTY-THIRD CONGRESS.

1873-'74.

IN FOUR VOLUMES:

Volume 1......No. 1 to No. 280, inclusive.
Volume 2......No. 281 to No. 478, except Nos. 307 and 453.
Volume 3......No. 307, parts 1 and 2.
Volume 4......No. 453, parts 1, 2, and 3.

WASHINGTON:
GOVERNMENT PRINTING OFFICE.
1874.

43D CONGRESS, 1st Session.	SENATE.	REPORT No. 314.

IN THE SENATE OF THE UNITED STATES.

APRIL 29, 1874.—Ordered to be printed.

Mr. MITCHELL submitted the following

REPORT:

The Committee on Claims, to whom was referred the petition of John D. Leflore and James C. Harris, executors of the last will and testament of Greenwood Leflore, deceased, having had the same under consideration, beg leave to submit the following report:

It is insisted on the part of petitioners that Greenwood Leflore, head chief, reposing, as is claimed, on the faith of this treaty, elected to remain and did remain in the State of Mississippi, received his reservation, (which was, by the way, of itself a princely gift,) became one of the largest land-holders and wealthiest planters in that State, was found faithful among the faithless. From wealth exceeding one million dollars at the beginning of the war he found himself at its close stripped of everything save his land and his life; and that, therefore, in consideration of these facts, and in pursuance of the provisions of the treaty quoted, the Government of the United States should make full compensation to his executors and heirs; and in this connection petitioners pray that, if *their* construction of said treaty is in the judgment of Congress correct, that then a direct appropriation be made of such sum as to Congress may seem just and proper; but if such construction of said treaty be doubted or denied, then they pray the passage of a joint resolution giving jurisdiction of the subject-matter to the Court of Claims.

It is further stated in the petition that, at his own request, made shortly before his death, the four grandchildren of Greenwood Leflore placed the United States flag over his body, in the coffin, and it was buried with him. It is also averred that he contributed voluntarily and largely to the success of the arms of the United States; that in February, 1864, when the United States Army, or a part of it, came into the neighborhood of his plantation, he voluntarily turned over to the officer in command (Colonel Osband) twenty-four of his negro men, and had them regularly enlisted in the Army of the United States, and mustered into service in the First Regiment of Mississippi Cavalry of African descent; that the officer in command then offered to pay him the bounty of $300 each, amounting to $7,200, for the enlistment of the negroes, but he refused to receive it, alleging that the rebels would take it from him, and that he would get it afterward from the Government; that the officer gave him a certificate of the enlistment of the negroes, and a duplicate original of which, dated March 15, 1864, is filed in this case. At the same time, it is alleged, Greenwood Leflore turned over for the use of the United States Army twenty-four mules and three horses, all alleged to be of the value of $4,725.

1 gin-house and stand, worth	$4,000
170 bales of cotton, worth	38,250
A dwelling-house and smoke-house, worth	8,500
Also, that the rebels took from him and carried away—	
1 mare and 14 mules, worth	2,250
2 wagons and 5 yoke of cattle, worth	700
34 head of cattle, worth $40 each	1,360
Also, bounty on 14 negroes alleged to have been put into the United States Army	4,200
101 slaves emancipated by the proclamation of the President of date January 1, 1863	80,800
Total losses of James C. Harris	141,060

In a summary contained in the petition it is claimed that the losses of Greenwood Leflore and his family were as follows:

Greenwood Leflore	$339,245
John D. Leflore	196,800
Mrs. Rebecca C. Harris	141,060
Total	677,105

In addition to this the statement is made in the petition that said
Greenwood Leflore was in his life-time the owner of 10,000 acres of land,
then of the value of $400,000; and that the same, now owned by his
said children, is entirely unsalable; also, that the petitioners, John D.
Leflore and James C. Harris, are, as executors of Greenwood Leflore, in-
debted in the sum of $60,000, a part of which is in judgment in the
United States court in the State of Mississippi; that said land is subject
to the lien of such judgment, and liable to be sold at any time.

It will be observed that the whole of the losses for which compensation is prayed by petitioners fall under the four following classes:

1. Mules and horses furnished the United States Army.
2. Property destroyed and taken by the rebels.
3. Slaves liberated by the emancipation proclamation.
4. Bounty for negroes alleged to have been furnished by petitioners to
the United States Army, and who enlisted therein.

In reference to the first claim, namely, for mules and horses furnished
the United States Army, it is only necessary to say that it appears.
from the papers in the case, that for this petitioners have already received their pay.

The only remaining question is as to the right of petitioners to recover
some $12,300, claimed as bounty on negroes alleged to have been fur-
nished by them, severally, and by Greenwood Leflore to the United
States Army and enlisted therein. It is difficult to determine on what
principle this claim is made; if it is on the ground that these negroes
were the slaves of these claimants, it is a sufficient answer to say that
these enlistments took place on the 13th of March, 1864, over fourteen
months after the date that African slavery in America had, by both the

**moral sentiment of the country and the force of the President's proc-
lamation, which under the circumstances must be accorded all the force
of law, ceased to exist. If any bounty, therefore, is due from the Government on account of these enlistments, it is due the negroes who enlisted in the Union Army and aided in fighting its battles. Your committee are, therefore, on a consideration of the whole case, of the opinion
that every portion of petitioners' claim should be disallowed. Nor is
there anything in the case, in the judgment of your committee, to justify
its reference to the Court of Claims; and they therefore report back the
petition, and ask to be discharged from its further consideration.**

The politically-incorrect historians painted Leflore as a great man for which
a town and county were named. As Paul Harvey would say, "Now you know the
rest of the story" about a man who turned his back on the man who befriended
him, and saw to it that he was educated. He fled Tennessee for the safety offered
by his family in Mississippi. He turned his back on his nation of Indians by
agreeing to what fits the criteria of Ethnic Cleansing. He turned his back on his
friends and fellow statesmen. He not only refused to defend the state for which he
had served as a member of the legislature, but he openly sold goods and supplies
to the enemy that probably caused the deaths of some of yours and my ancestors.

If that's the man Governor Barbour wants to brag about having as a relative,
so be it. It is amazing Leflore wasn't hanged for treason, aiding and abetting the
enemy, or some charge of that nature, and that Malmaison didn't become a delta
headquarters for the Confederate Army. In addition, if the real truth had been
known, the city of Greenwood might have been renamed. I put my stock in the
few Indians that survived and have had to live in poverty because of men like
Leflore and politicians like we have. I hope they prosper in all their endeavors.

The Leflore family's friend Andrew Jackson was responsible for wholesale
slaughter of Indians, and used other Indians – including Leflore -- to assist in this
slaughter. He would then take their lands -- as he did first with the Creeks in
Alabama, the Seminole, Chickasaw, Cherokee and Choctaw. His actions might
make him a terrorist by today's standards. Research the US Archives and you will
find he was responsible for far more deaths of Americans than Osama Bin Laden.

Those people were Americans in the most basic sense, but were seen with about as much respect by "the invading Immigrant-Americans" as stray dogs.

Just for your knowledge, I want to define a few terms for you, and have you reminisce about Leflore, and his dear friend Andrew Jackson for which our Capitol is named. I encourage you to go beyond the history books, as I have, and look at research that has been done recently, as thousands of historical documents have been made available in microfilm or digital formats to researchers that are now telling the real truth, and the whole truth. Please consider this when you think about how we really settled this land:

Ethnic Cleansing: The expulsion, imprisonment, or killing of an ethnic minority by a dominant majority in order to achieve ethnic homogeneity (Merriam-Webster).

Genocide: The deliberate and systematic destruction of a racial, political or cultural group (Merriam-Webster).

Terrorism: The unlawful use of force or violence against persons or property to intimidate or coerce a government, the civilian population, or any segment thereof in furtherance of political or social objectives (FBI).

The bottom line was, Jackson wanted the Indians' land, and he wanted them off the land. The east coast was already becoming over populated by the standards of the day. Immigrants were pouring in, and the desire to move west was taking hold. Some settlers departed the eastern states, and settled on Indian land west of the eastern cities, often causing skirmishes. The Indians appealed to congress to try and stop the trespassing. It fell on deaf ears, and, when the Indians had enough, they attacked. When they attacked, Jackson rode in, with other Indians on his side, and attacked the "trouble makers."

If payments and offers of other land were cheaper and possible, Jackson used those techniques, but he didn't worry about the threats, coercion, or failed promises. If nothing else worked, we would go to war. That was the mentality. It amounts to eminent domain now.

We would attack other countries today (and have) for the same practices we allowed our leaders to do in the early to mid-1800's. The offices we work in, the land we live on and the churches we worship in are the fruits of Jackson's labors, assisted by Greenwood Leflore. Although I am glad for what we have, I am ashamed of how we got it, and find it hard to look a Choctaw in the eye.

I give you all this history so you will understand Haley Barbour's role and how politicians like him will bring up their friendship or kinship to make it appear they are on your side. Barbour fought the Choctaw from every angle to keep them from building a casino in Jones County but he was unsuccessful.

I'll just give you a few headlines from various media sources found in Mississippi:

June 22, 2010, Barbour asks Tribe to halt Jones casino.
(He sent a letter to the Chief asking them to stop, and asked AG for help)

http://neshobademocrat.com/main.asp?SectionID=2&SubSectionID=297&ArticleID=21293

July 15, 2010 Governor Barbour asks Federal Indian Gaming Chairwoman to Halt Construction of Slot Parlor
(Claiming it would strain state and local resources that would respond)

http://www.gulfcoastnews.com/GCNnewsGovWantsChoctawSlotParlorHalted071510.htm

July 17, 2010, AG: No reason to halt Choctaw casino
(Barbour furious the AG made that known to the Indians, would seek outside attorney)

http://neshobademocrat.com/main.asp?SectionID=2&SubSectionID=297&ArticleID=21481

July 26, 2010, Mississippi Governor says he'll sue to block tribe's casino
(Other statewide elected officials oppose development including Lieutenant Governor Bryant, Secretary of State Hoseman, State Auditor Pickering, United States Senator Wicker and United States Representative Harper.)

http://www.businessweek.com/ap/financialnews/D9H6VU9O0.htm

July 29, 2010 Governor Speaks at Neshoba County Fair
(Barbour says **all** Choctaws should vote on Proposed Casino (claims of kin to Leflore)

http://www.youtube.com/watch?v=QRcTsl5SgzA

August 10, 2010 Barbour asks EPA to block casino construction in Jones County
(Claims there are problems with wastewater treatment)

*http://neshobademocrat.com/main.asp?SectionID=2&SubSectionID=297&Article
ID=21813*

December 19, 2010 Controversial casino opens in Jones County
(Casino officials said Barbour's previous claims were just not true)

http://www.wapt.com/r/26189907/detail.html

Is that any way to treat the kinfolks you are so proud to have? Barbour first asked the Indians to stop. He then went to the Federal Indian Gaming Commission. When he didn't like their answer, he went to the attorney general.

He didn't like what the attorney general told the Indians, so he chastised him. Then he said he would sue them, and rallied all his politician buddies to agree with him. He then made it an issue for political campaigns by raising it at the Neshoba County Fair. That didn't work either. He said he would go to a federal agency (headquartered in his old stomping grounds at Washington, DC). That didn't work either.

He wanted more money for the state, and that's commendable, but after what we took from the Indians, after all the casinos, and income we have from them, how could anybody be so greedy? The state has casinos all over Tunica (Indian name), all over Natchez (Indian name), Greenville, Vicksburg, and the entire Gulf Coast. It is a total of 30 casinos. The Choctaws have two in Neshoba County, and wanted one in Jones County. Was this really going to hurt the Mississippi economy? We don't get tax revenues from them, so the politicians take issue with them getting some public services without contributing their sovereign taxes. Does this have the appearance of greed to you?

Are you opposed to the Indians opening up casinos anywhere they want on their sovereign territory? They bought the old Malmaison home site, and it has been rumored that the purpose was for opening a casino there. Opponents have already aired their opinions, especially in Carroll County. But some say we can never repay the Indians for what we have done to them. After the way their so-called leader treated them, while living a life of luxury, wouldn't you think it fitting for them to open a fourth casino right over the top of Leflore's old home site, even if they make billions of dollars? They are a sovereign nation, and neither the Mississippi Governor nor the Mississippi Legislature can regulate them.

Just because the name Leflore may be in Governor Barbour's family tree doesn't necessarily mean that he was related to Greenwood Leflore. I have read that his mother was a Leflore, and he said at the Neshoba County fair, that his great, great, great uncle was Greenwood Leflore. I do see similar traits in them. But Haley Barbour chose to make that issue public about the time he was incensed over the Mississippi Band of Choctaw Indians announcing they were going to build the casino in Jones County, Mississippi. You can pick your friends, but you cannot pick your relatives.

Chapter Six

PUPPETS AND PUPPETEERS

"When people learn no tools of judgment and merely follow their hopes, the seeds of political manipulation are sown."

Stephen Jay Gould

In 1996, the state's Performance, Evaluation and Expenditure Review commission (PEER) provided this information to the legislature after a review of MGC.

The perception of Mississippi as an industry-friendly state was not limited to academicians and the many casino owners choosing to locate in Mississippi. An affidavit from the FBI dated November 1993 requesting authorization for wire taps of organized crime figures suspected of racketeering and later convicted of conducting a blackjack scam at Mississippi's President Casino in Biloxi noted that the FBI had "documented the intent of several LCN (La Cosa Nostra) families from around the country to infiltrate the legalized gambling industry in Mississippi." In attempting to explain this intent, the affidavit included the following quote from a conversation between a "known" La Cosa Nostra associate and underboss." In Mississippi there's no regulations, no laws, there's not nothing, you can do anything you want to do."

The fact is there were laws and regulations, and had been for several years. The problem is, they weren't being enforced, they still aren't, and the perception of that individual was true.

In 2001, PEER again conducted a review of MGC, and this time they warned MGC of potential crimes being committed by both patrons and casino operators.

Criminal Risks

- Increase in white collar and organized crime—The cash-intensive casino environment is conducive to crimes such as embezzlement and money laundering.

They went on to tell the legislature in their report that this was another state agency that had not only broken the law in the past, but continues to break the law. They were allowing criminals to work in this all cash business without conducting background investigations. Here's verbatim what they said:

MGC continues to violate the law *because its procedures allow issuance of permits to employees before their background checks are complete. This practice continues to result in employment of individuals with charges or convictions of felonies or prohibited misdemeanors in a small percentage of cases—for example, at least thirty-nine of 18,084 cases in 2000. The statutory violations have occurred as outlined below:*

In calendar year 2000, MGC enforcement agents submitted 157 work permits cased to the MGC legal department to determine whether the permits should be revoked. PEER staff examined a sample of more than half of these cases (ninety-one) and found that thirty-nine revocation cases occurred because the applicants had been issued a gaming permit before their background checks revealed that they had been charged with or convicted of felonies or prohibited crimes—21 felonies and 9 misdemeanors. Nine other permits were revoked because applicants had lied on their applications about being charged with felonies. The crimes included theft, embezzlement and drug-related charges. PEER analysis determined that these thirty-nine gaming employees had worked eight and a half months (258 days) on average in casinos before their permits were revoked due to their criminal histories. (The 258 days included 186 days between issuance of the permit and notification to attend revocation hearings and seventy-two days between notification of hearings and the final disposition of the hearing.)

The 2001 PEER report also pointed out to the legislature that MGC had BOTH a regulatory responsibility and a LAW ENFORCEMENT responsibility.

The enforcement division is responsible for the regulation of gaming in accordance with the Gaming Control Act and MGC regulations. This responsibility embodies both law enforcement and regulatory functions. The Enforcement Division is responsible for performing these specific tasks.

In my small division of less than 10 agents, they stopped enforcing the law altogether that same year – a year after I resigned for not being allowed to make arrests due to pressure from the legislature to stop. Most of the agents' time was spent investigating backgrounds for licensure each year. However, MGC changed it to three year licenses. Only investigating their backgrounds once every three years, and not making any arrests, leaves me wondering what the heck the agents are doing. Gregory claimed they stopped arrests due to staff shortages. WRONG. Below is a record of arrests received by the charitable gaming division.

BINGO

	1993-1994	1995-1996	1997-1998	1999-2000	2001-2002	2003-2004	2005-2006	2007-2008	Totals
Management/Employees	0	*0	21	23	2	0	0	0	46
Patrons (None)	0	0	0	0	0	0	0	0	0
TOTALS	0	0	21	23	2	0	0	0	46

* 1 made in mid 1990's dismissed

There were no arrests in 1997 (before my appointment), and none in 1998 until mid-year. I was employed from August 1, 1998 until I resigned effective August 1, 2000. All but one of the 46 arrested was convicted in local courts. Our cases were worked so well, we only had a couple that required a hearing. The rest admitted guilt, and took their punishment.

One case was destroyed by the Hinds County "Political Machine," and we couldn't get it prosecuted with the "help" of then District Attorney Ed Peters. He sent us an assistant to supposedly help but we believed she was not only hostile to us, but loyal to the defendants. The case "mysteriously" made it over to the FBI office, and they prosecuted it, sending a former top cop and Hinds County Deputy, plus his wife to federal prison. They served about two years for embezzling charity money.

There were four investigations pending when I left, and the defendants were arrested in 2001. Only two were convicted. The commission allowed those two arrests for fear of my replacement quitting. There were no arrests in 2002, 2003, 2004, 2005, 2006, 2007 or 2008.

I doubt if there have been any since then. However I am tired of trying to get information through public record requests when their lawyers can't seem to interpret my requests, or want to bankrupt me by hiring people to search the records. I would encourage you to submit a public records request for 2009-2011.

Notice those eight listed in the bottom of the chart. These were what MGC called "assist cases" where the bingo halls (licensees) signed the charges themselves with information from the agents, but the arrests were made by local sheriffs' departments. I would not have even counted them myself. My state representative received the below chart in a letter from the executive director of the MGC:

Individual	Licensee	Violation	Date	Disposition	Court
Charged by MGC:					
Jeffery Walker	Youth Hope Ministry	97-33-75 (2) (a)	04/18/01	Plead Guilty & Paid Fine	Hinds County Justice Court
Bernice Ray Pope	Petal Moose Lodge	97-33-75(2) (a)	05/01/01	Dismissed	Hinds County Justice Court
Ian Deveraux	His Way Homes	97-33-75 (2) (a)	08/06/01	Remanded to the File	Hinds County Justice Court
Michael Williams	Magnolia Veteran's Assocation	97-33-69(3)	07/20/01	Plead Guilty & Paid Fine	Hinds County Justice Court
Charged by Licensee:					
Katrina Y.Thompson	His Way Homes Supervisor	97-23-19	07/05/01	Plead Guilty & Paid Fine	Lee County Justice court
Shirley Simpson	Mississippi Paralysis	97-33-75 (2) (a)	06/06/02	Plead Guilty & Paid Fine	Grenada County Justice Court
Jack Wilson	Mississippi Paralysis	97-33-75 (2) (a)	06/06/02	Plead Guilty & Paid Fine	Grenada County Justice Court
Valerie Morgan	His Way, Inc Supervisor	97-23-19	01/02/04	Plead Guilty & Paid Fine	Lee County Justice Court
Kathy Ashley	Ms Breast Foundation	97-23-19	11/22/05	11/12/2008 trial date set	Lee County Circuit Court
Steve Dihl	Moose Lodge 2472	97-23-19	07/08/07	Plead Guilty & Paid Fine	Forrest County Circuit Court
Fedelia Crosby	VFW 4272	97-23-19	02/14/08	November Trial Date	Lownes County Justice Court
Joe Lang	Fine Arts Institute of MS	97-45-7	04/04/08	Desoto County D.A. would not prosecute	Desoto County

Below is a chart showing the arrests made from the huge enforcement, and investigative divisions on the casino side of MGC. Notice they have never arrested a manager, supervisor, operator, or owner of a casino. They cater to the industry, and only make arrests when the casino is the victim. I don't know how many of these were convicted. Look how their number of arrests has steadily declined since Gregory took over in December 2001.

				CASINO					
ARRESTS	1993-1994	1995-1996	1997-1998	1999-2000	2001-2002	2003-2004	2005-2006	2007-2008	Totals
Management/Supervisors (None)	0	0	0	0	0	0	0	0	0
Patrons/Employees	29	46	55	66	71	69	50	33	419
TOTALS	29	46	55	66	71	69	50	33	**419**

I have shown you their performance. Now I will show you what authority they have by law when inspecting bingo halls:

Section 97-33-109 of the Mississippi Code:

Commission may inspect bingo business on a routine, scheduled or unscheduled basis to:

   a. Ensure compliance
   b. Assess premises
   c. View equipment and supplies
   d. Seize, remove and impound equipment/supplies in violation pursuant to a court order.
   e. Access books and records to determine compliance with bingo laws and regulations.
   f. Conduct IN-DEPTH audits and investigations.
   g. Verify internal controls required by the Commission are in place.
   h. Determine whether or not to assess fines, suspicions and/or criminal penalties against the organization or any person(s) responsible.

All the bingo laws can be accessed here; the number 109 shown above is this section. They are listed by title (97) - chapter (33) - Section 109.

http://www.michie.com/mississippi/lpext.dll?f=templates&fn=main-h.htm

Now I will show you what the law requires of them in performing their duties and responsibilities. I will use the governor's words, and say, "*our law requires it, as required by law, the law gives me little latitude, the Mississippi code orders me, and laws mandate.*"

Section 97-33-109 of the Mississippi Code

Defines Commission's functions, DUTIES and RESPONSIBILITIES to include:

Denial of licensure for violators for 97-51-203

a. Monitor licensees for compliance with laws and regulations through:

1.   Routine
2.   Scheduled
3.   Unscheduled

      (a)   Inspections
      (b)   Investigations
      (c)   Audits

SKIP TO SUB-PARAGRAPH h. OF THE SECTION

h.   Enforce laws and assist other law enforcement officers in doing so as peace officers.

i.   To establish classes of halls limiting amount of prizes consistent with respective class

http://www.michie.com/mississippi/lpext.dll?f=templates&fn=main-h.htm&cp=mscode

Now I will show you the requirement for other agencies to ASSIST THEM in carrying out their duties if requested.

Section 109 continued:

• All departments, commissions, boards, agencies, officers and institutions of the state and all subdivisions thereof **shall** cooperate with the commission on carrying out its **enforcement** responsibilities.

• It is the DUTY of the Sheriffs, Deputy Sheriffs and Police Officers of this state in the enforcement of the provisions of the Charitable Bingo laws and TO ARREST AND COMPLAIN.

Against any person violating those laws "IF" REQUESTED TO DO SO BY THE COMMISSION.

http://www.michie.com/mississippi/lpext.dll?f=templates&fn=main-h.htm

Now I will show you some of the laws they are mandated (just like the governor) to enforce with applicable penalties.

Any person, association or corporation violating any provision of sections 97-33-51 through 97-33-203 or any rule or regulation of the commission shall be subject to a fine imposed by the commission and to suspension or revocation of its license.

(1) Any person who commits any of the following acts, upon conviction, shall be fined not more than Five Thousand Dollars ($5,000.00) or imprisoned for one (1) year, or both:

    (a) Making any false statement in any application for a license under Sections 97-33-51 through 97-33-203, or in any official report to the commission;

    (b) Holding, operating or conducting any bingo game without a license;

    (c) Knowingly falsifying or making any false entry in any books or records, with respect to any transaction connected with the holding, operating or conducting of any bingo game;

    (d) Refusing to allow the commission access to any premises where a game of chance is being conducted or to any book, record or document relating to such conduct;

    (e) Intentionally causing, aiding, abetting or conspiring with another to cause any person to violate any provision of Sections 97-33-51 through 97-33-203;

    (f) Possessing, displaying, selling or otherwise furnishing to any person any pull-tabs, except as provided for in Section 97-33-77.

Now I will show you admissions that they haven't done their job in years. The Jackson Free Press (Reporter Adam Lynch) did an excellent, very detailed story in 2008, on the issue of stopping the arrests. I strongly encourage you to read the full article at:

www.jacksonfreepress.com/index.php/site/comments/blind_eye_easier_times_for_bingo_crimes

"At the very end, when I left, there was a person in Hattiesburg we were getting ready to arrest, and Larry Gregory came in and said, 'You're not going to be able to arrest this person.' I said, 'Why not,' and he said, 'His friend is a former legislator, and I've been getting calls from legislators and we've got too much pressure on this. We've got to back off from it.'"

Gregory, the Mississippi Gaming Commission Executive Director since December 2001, said he did tell Ward to back off, but only because the crime didn't fit the treatment. He also said he had never gotten any pressure from a member of the legislature. If it wasn't the legislature, the governor had to be the culprit, but I personally received snide remarks from legislators.

Larry Gregory knows we treated everybody the same and the accused in this case had done exactly what others had done. Larry's problem was that he wanted the executive director's job, and he needed support from the legislature since Chuck Patton was leaving for medical reasons. Larry listened to lawyer Bill Jones from Petal who said later that I had made a "poor ass" decision when, in my opinion, he made a poor ass decision because he said he helped write the law. In that case, he should have known our responsibility to enforce the laws. That is likened to an off-duty cop speeding down the highway, and being stopped only to tell the patrolman, "Hey man, I am a cop." He might get this response, "Okay, then you should have known that speeding is a violation of the law."

But Larry would never anger a member of the legislature, a former member like Jones, or even a future member. He would brown nose them in every way he could, and it didn't matter what party they were from. That's how he was a survivor all those years in a politically appointed position, being a puppet to the legislature, and most likely the governor. Somebody didn't want those laws enforced, or any negative publicity to come out on the gaming industry.

Larry would take that responsibility because he is a "yes man" that would take the bullet for the boss (right or wrong). He would never have made those decisions by himself, and interfere with arrests, any more than the Mississippi Game and Fish Commission would, even though they have regulations too. I believe this is a clear case of obstructing justice where the would-be arresting officer is intimidated, or threatened if he makes, or plans to make an arrest. That shot was called from on high. It could have been the Chairman of the Gaming Committee in the Mississippi Legislature, lieutenant governor, or the governor. I don't know for sure who did it, but it could only have been one or more them.

On September 28, 2008, Jerry Mitchell from the Clarion Ledger wrote a front page story after interviewing the executive director of MGC, and others (no longer available online, but on microfilm at the Eudora Welty Library). It said:

"The state MGC doesn't believe in arresting bingo violators any more, commission officials concede."

Well....Isn't that special? What if the Mississippi Commissioner of Public Safety told his troopers that he doesn't believe in arresting drunk drivers anymore? What if the Director of MBN told his agents he doesn't believe in arresting drug dealers anymore? How much wildlife would we still have if the head of the Mississippi Department of Wildlife and Fisheries just told the game wardens not to charge any illegal hunters, or fishermen with a crime anymore? What if our police chiefs and sheriffs told their officers from this point on, just give administrative warning tickets, and don't charge anybody with a crime? Most of all, what if Haley Barbour said, I don't believe in balancing the budget anymore, so I won't worry about the law that requires it, you know the one I told you about, and hope you read, in several state of the state addresses? Why is he protecting criminals in the gaming industry? I know they are there. I went to MGC on August 1, 1998, and only one arrest had occurred in 4 years but it was thrown out of court. In the next two years, I charged 46 people with crimes and all but one pled guilty.

Did they just suddenly stop committing crimes the day I walked out exactly two years later? Why is the SOS going behind the MGC cleaning up their mess, citing people administratively, and naming the criminal offenses in their order committed under the bingo laws, that should have led to arrests? There is a reason at the top of our state government for this obstruction of justice. Although our government is full of ignorance, and incompetence, this issue is not caused by either of those. It is intentional. We need to know why.

Another quote in that article said, "Rick's beef is we're not making any arrests, and it's true," Gregory said.

Well no kidding Sherlock! Rick pays taxes that pay for gaming agents, who are certified law enforcement officers costing more than administrative regulators, and they haven't made arrests in years. Shouldn't Rick have a beef with that? Shouldn't you? Shouldn't every taxpayer in the state? Would you live in a town where not one, but every police officer is told not to obey the law, and not to ever make any arrests? What action would you take?

Section 97-33-103 of the Mississippi Code

Commission SHALL prepare/provide COMPREHENSIVE annual report, rules/regulations to:

Lt. Governor
Speaker of the House
Chairman of the House and Senate, Judiciary Committees
Chairman of the House Ways and Means Committees
Chairman of the Senate Finance Committee

So look who is at the top of the chain that gets the bingo annual report to review what they have done (or not done) each year. The report should include the number of applications for licensure received, the number of background investigations completed, the number of applicants charged with falsifying applications, the number of agents assigned, agents' responsibilities in accordance with the law, number of arrests, number of pleas, number of cases gone to court, and the number of defendants found guilty, as well as the amount of administrative fines, sanctions imposed, and the dollar amount of fines imposed by the courts. That information is needed to determine their efficiency just like I am sure MHP does, with drunk driver arrests or tickets. They need that information to document their performance for performance based budgets. Oh, but in the second extraordinary session of 2009, the governor took MGC out of that spotlight. They now support themselves through revenue they take in, and are exempt from approved budgets, or across the board cuts. They can now do what they want without legislative oversight.

Why doesn't the MBR do that? The Department of Wildlife, Fisheries and Parks gets fees from licenses, boat registration, fines from violators, and so on. Why don't they do the same? It is because MGC is special. Remember when Barbour talked about making mandated cuts across the board? Well, he decided to give more money to the MBR. He gave over 90 new patrolmen to the MHP that didn't come free. He ordered recruitment of many more MBN agents. He gave MGC all the money they could use, and cut everybody else – no sacred cows?

You may not think the bingo business is that big. However, they took in over $1.6 million in 2009 and for the years 2000-2009, they made almost $1.2 billion (billion with a "B") dollars. Keep in mind, a good many of them are not honest, and don't report everything they make. However this money is all cash, and there is too much temptation to trust people who lie on their applications with that money. MGC just denies them a license now "IF" they catch them lying. They have convinced PEER that it is a better method. Even PEER didn't address the fact that when the legislature drafted the bingo laws, they considered different levels of crimes committed. They chose "falsifying an application" to be placed in the more serious category of crimes committed. Why and how could MGC ignore that requirement, and choose to ignore the law? Remember, the governor said even he can't do that. Gregory alluded to the fact that to make arrests would just tie up the courts more.

What a joke. During my tenure 45 of 46 cases pled guilty without taking up the court's time. Then he went on to say they didn't have sufficient manpower to do that. When I was there, the vast majority of time was spent on background investigations of applicants each year. When I left, they changed the licenses to be in effect for three years. That one action cut agent responsibilities by two thirds. Not allowing them to make arrests, as they did during my tenure, cut their responsibilities, and time consumed even more.

I received this e-mail from Commissioner Hairston after sending him the information.

RE: NEW LAWS   Back to messages

John Hairston   10/01/08
To rickward47@hotmail.com   Reply

Mr. Ward, thank you for the message. While I respect your interest, it would be inappropriate for a Commissioner of a regulatory body to address your question outside the public process. You are accusing State of Mississippi employees of behavior which lies somewhere between negligent and criminal; those accusations are of a nature which clearly are improper to discuss by email.

My suggestion would be for you to discuss your complaints with the Mississippi Attorney General's office. The AG's office has a full-time attorney imbedded within the Mississippi Gaming Commission to insure that actions of the Commission occur within the framework of State and Federal law. If Counsel from the Attorney General disagrees with you and elects to take no action, I hope you will take comfort that an independent body charged with great authority and discretion took the position that your difference of opinion with Director Gregory's management is just that, a difference of opinion, rather than illegal or criminal behavior. I trust the Attorney General will aggressively follow up action should they concur with you.

Given the nature of your message, I respectfully suggest that the two of us have no further direct dialogue on the matter. I don't wish to offend you, and I sincerely respect your right to voice concerns. But at the same time your accusations are such that it would be completely unethical for me to discuss them with you privately.

With respect,

Hairston

I appreciate Mr. Hairston's response. I completely agree with him on all but one thing. At least he did write back though. Some 40 legislators, the lieutenant governor, and the governor chose not to and completely ignored me, as did the chairman of the commission. The one thing I disagree with Mr. Hairston about is that this issue is just a difference in opinion between Larry Gregory and me. What he means is that Gregory is a manager, and has discretionary authority.

Just like Mr. Hairston can exercise discretionary authority at Hancock Bank, but he can't violate the law, or fail to comply with statutory requirements in that exercise. I don't agree with that statement on its surface. However, discretion is used in special circumstances, if there are extenuating circumstances, not across the board. Once it is done across the board, it is no longer discretionary, but rather Policy. He also has the right to set policy. But policy cannot conflict with the law any more than Hancock Bank's policies can conflict with either state law, or the federal laws that apply to his chosen profession in banking. Mr. Hairston knows that. Nolan Canon knows as a farmer he can't trespass on other people's property, he can't use unlawful pesticides to spray crops, or falsify records having to do with federal crop programs in his chosen profession as a farmer. Jerry St. Pe' knows he had to follow federal regulations, and contract law as well as navy regulations in building ships. He had no authority to mandate disobedience of the law in the shipbuilding business.

These men are all professionals. They aren't stupid. They are following orders from the person that appointed them when they take action this serious. And just like the governor said, he does not have the right to ignore, or disobey the law. So why does he allow this department head to do it? Why does he task this department head with doing it?

Matt Steffey, professor at the Mississippi College School of Law, told the Clarion Ledger's Jerry Mitchell, unless there's a statute that allows the commission to do that, "that would normally be understood to be outside the authority." He compared it to a law requiring a nuclear plant to meet eight requirements before being built, and the Nuclear Regulatory Commission saying six is good enough.

The governor is not operating in a vacuum. There are people on his staff that review and provide clippings that might bring him some embarrassment. The three commissioners that preside over MGC are appointed by the governor. Surely at least one of them, most likely Chairman St. Pe' would brief the governor as a duty to keep him informed. PEER reports citing MGC continually violating the law went to the governor, lieutenant governor, and the legislature. The arrest stoppage was admitted on the front page of two Jackson papers that I am sure the governor reads. I wrote the governor a letter myself -- somebody read it, and at least briefed him on the meat of the problem. So, why has he not taken action? He can't plead ignorance. Well maybe he can, but as we all know, ignorance of the law is no excuse.

He claimed over and over in his annual state of the state addresses that he had to abide by the law. Why then, doesn't he act on a director's failure to do so?

There is something hidden, and well-protected by powerful people, about gaming, including casinos and bingo. There is something very wrong with this picture.

Chapter Seven

POLITICIANS AND CONNECTIONS TO BINGO

"In order to become the master, the politician poses as the servant."

Charles de Gaulle

For some reason, politicians, law enforcement, prosecutors, politicos, and/or their associates are attracted to bingo and bingo funds. When I started making arrests for bingo violations, they came screaming. Some of them including Hinds County Sheriff Malcolm McMillin, Senator Terry Burton, then Lieutenant Governor Amy Tuck, and a black female state representative were all on boards of charities that were funded by bingo. Senator Burton went on later to open his own bingo hall in Canton with the Police Chief as the Security Guard, and the Chief's wife as the bingo hall manager. During my tenure we arrested a county supervisor, two former justice court judges, a police Lieutenant, and two deputies from different counties. A district attorney had been on one of the boards as executive director. Former State Senator, current Madison County Supervisor, and now candidate for Transportation Commissioner, Tim "Elvis" Johnson remained on the payroll of a bingo hall recently accused of fraud, misrepresentation, and using charitable funds for non-charitable purposes. See the link below:

http://onlinemadison.com/main.asp?SectionID=1&subsectionID=1&articleID=22162

His brother Rudy Johnson is Executive Director of the Golden Triangle Planning and Development District in Columbus, MS which is, among other sources, funded by a bingo hall.

He is currently running for a political position against my long-time friend Oktibbeha County Sheriff Dolph Bryan. Rudy's hall is consistently the highest grossing charity in the state that is somewhat funded by a bingo hall. It is not uncommon to see gross receipts in excess of $15 million dollars a year.

Sheriff Malcolm McMillin returned to the bingo industry after his first bout with Sue Hathorn's operation as a board member in 1998. According to Mississippi Court of Appeal documents, he became President of "His Way Homes" in June 2002. It was formerly operated by Cynthia "Cindy" Brunson, with the assistance of the charity's lawyer Scott Levanway, a lobbyist and attorney from

71

the coast. In October 2002, the board under McMillin's leadership decided to increase its size. Suddenly, McMillin's long-time pal and right hand man in his sheriff's office for many years, William "Bill" Gowan (now a judge in Hinds County) appeared, and was "elected" as a new board member along with one other. Then, McMillin and friends had majority control, and in November of 2002, the new board voted to oust Cynthia Brunson, leaving the charity and its money to be disposed of in any way they chose.

Brunson said her lawyer and the sheriff turned against her at some point, and claimed there were no papers showing her as a board member. She says she was locked out of the safe and building that contained the papers she needed to prove her side of the case. She said McMillin denied that. Unable to provide that proof, the court left the charity in the hands of Sheriff McMillin, and company. She said the charity had over $2 million dollars in cash and other assets when she left. Cindy said she has no idea how that money was disposed of.

I was unable to find any transactions for those years on "His Way Homes" or "His Way" through IRS 990 filings that charities provide the IRS to show the distribution of their funds. Cindy says the disposition of the funds, and other assets are anybody's guess. To read further about this civil action, please go to:

http://www.mssc.state.ms.us/Images/Opinions/CO28403.pdf

I recently looked at IRS 990 forms on certain other bingo funded charities, and viewed their last three years. Click the Guidestar link below, register (quick and easy), and enter the name of the charity in the white space in the middle of the page. Enter MS Children's Advocacy Center which runs the largest bingo hall in the Jackson area. Brenda Luster is the executive director, and receives about $132 thousand dollars a year, plus a car allowance. Her brother, the late Jimmy Dixon, and I worked together at the MGC. He assisted me in interviewing Brenda about her connections with Sue Hathorn and this bingo hall/charity back then. Both of us suggested she seek other employment. Jimmy was a fine person, and a retired Jackson police officer who would give you the shirt off his back. I had no reason to believe Brenda was any different. But she later returned to the organization, and soon headed it.

I looked into the charity recently, and was surprised to learn that she, and her two immediate subordinates/assistants, made over $100 thousand each. The other two employees made over $50 thousand dollars each. The hall operator makes almost $75 thousand a year. For a five man charitable business, at least on the surface, that may sound unreasonable. It even looks more awkward with three of the employees related to Brenda, or her assistant. One board member was Trent Lott's daughter. There were three years of the IRS 990 forms listed. Read them, and you will see who gets paid what. Because these are charities, this is public information -- names, addresses, income, expenditures, board members, assets, etc. You can obtain this information by law directly from the charity upon request. You may also get it at the local IRS office, or order it online in disk format from the IRS in Ogden, Utah, but the fastest and free way is to go to:

http://www2.guidestar.org/

In order to track suspicious activity on any charity, it is best to see what that charity is supporting. In other words, "follow the money." Sometimes it is difficult for you to see where it goes, but you don't see anything wrong. I investigated one scheme when I was at the MGC where an executive director was sending money to her husband's charity in a business name. It didn't look suspicious until I looked at the husband's charity filings, and found out who the incorporator was. Sometimes people will put things in their other family member names, or hire a married daughter with a different last name, and funnel money through them. Sometimes they use maiden names or sisters with a last name that you wouldn't recognize.

Before I go any further with this story I want to point out that my complaints have been non-partisan. I don't care what party is doing wrong. If they are doing wrong, they need to pay the fiddler. By the same token, I may look at friends, or acquaintances, that are in the business if for no other reason than making sure I don't get accused of siding with somebody who is doing wrong. If my friend is wrong, he too, needs to pay the fiddler. In the case I am about to bring up, I have no reason to believe these gentlemen are doing wrong. However, as I look more into it, there seems to be a lot of issues regarding different names, and family members that concern me. That is one reason I bring this one up. The other is just like I said before, for some reason, politicians seem to have vicarious relationships with these bingo halls, and either they, or their office in some way, may benefit from this relationship. So, you and I need to make sure they are okay.

"Bingo Baby," a bingo hall operated in Cleveland, MS by the Mississippi Delta American Legion Post #1776, was opened during my tenure at the MGC by an associate I knew from Attorney General Mike Moore's office named Morgan

Shands. He is a well-known politico in Mississippi and is much sought after by politicians seeking office. I tried to talk him out of opening it because of the perception eleven years ago. He said he was doing it to support Boy's State.

Morgan Shands and Steve Guyton (another well-known politico) are the incorporators/adjutant and post commander respectively of Mississippi Delta American Legion Post # 1776, Inc. The Articles of Incorporation were filed with the SOS's office on February 10, 2000 with Stephen Lufkin Guyton as the registered agent and Morgan Price Shands as an additional incorporator. On November 11, 2000, St. Ambrose Leadership College was formed with Morgan P. Shands listed as the registered agent and Steve Guyton as an additional incorporator. It makes one wonder why they incorporated Mississippi Delta American Legion Post #1776, Inc. using their full names and then incorporated St. Ambrose Leadership College using only Shands' first name and middle initial and Guyton's shorter first name version of Stephen with no middle name or initial. Of note, Donna Echols, former wife of Jim Mabus, another political operative and a cousin of former Governor Ray Mabus, was listed in a news article as being "on the steering committee of St. Ambrose Leadership College".

http://webcache.googleusercontent.com/search?q=cache:MB49V5Ry2roJ:findartic les.com/p/articles/mi_qa5277/is_200401/ai_n24274542/+donna+echols+%22top+ 40+under+40%22&cd=4&hl=en&ct=clnk&gl=us&source=www.google.com

Ms. Echols, a well-known lobbyist at the Mississippi Capitol, lists among her clients Penn National Gaming, the Beau Rivage Casino and Resort, the Mississippi State Troopers Association, the Mississippi Association of Chiefs of Police, the Hinds County Board of Supervisors, and St. Ambrose Leadership College. The link to her website is below.

http://www.theecholsgroup.com/clients.htm

"Bingo Baby" gave over $396 thousand in years 2007 and 2008 to the "St. Ambrose Leadership College" according to the Form 990's filed with the Internal Revenue Service. Other than a corporate filing with the SOS in the name of Morgan Shands, I am unable to find any information on a St Ambrose Leadership College, but their physical address is listed as 1004 Breeden Place. This appears to be a residence owned by Shands in Bay St. Louis. On State Senate Pro Tem Billy Hewes' July 8, 2011 campaign finance report for lieutenant governor it indicates he has paid Maverick Political Solutions $55 thousand as of June 15, 2011 for "campaign management". According to the SOS's website, Maverick Political Solutions was formed on February 13, 2008. The only incorporator is Morgan P. Shands of 1004 Breeden Place, Bay St. Louis.

https://business.sos.state.ms.us/imaging/30825639.pdf

St. Ambrose also has a post office box in Drew. In 2009, they gave $257,000 to the "St. Ambrose Leadership Academy". In their Form 990 filing dated August 09, 2010, the accounting firm listed was Accounting Support, Inc. of Marion, AR. Why would they have an Arkansas CPA? According to the Arkansas SOS's website, Accounting Support, Inc., located at 326 Southwind Drive in Marion, AR had its corporate status revoked on December 31, 2009 – seven months before the filing of Shands and Guyton's IRS Form 990. Why would the CPA corporation do the report after having been revoked by the Arkansas SOS, but still operating as a corporation? The link to the Arkansas SOS's documentation is below.

http://www.sos.arkansas.gov/corps/search_corps.php?DETAIL=224803&corp_ty pe_id=&corp_name=&agent_search=bosch&agent_city=&agent_state=&filing_n umber=&cmd=

I can find no documents filed with the Mississippi SOS's office in regard to "St. Ambrose Leadership Academy". I searched for associations, and found that Morgan's wife's maiden name is Angel Ambrose, but this may be coincidence. David Ambrose, possibly an in-law of Morgan Shands, appears on the roster as the Chaplain for the organization listed in Cleveland, MS, but has an address in South Mississippi. There is also a gentleman listed in Cleveland as the operator of the bingo hall whose name is Paul Buser. Again, an association search found a Rachel Shands Buser, believed to be Morgan Shands' sister and Paul Buser's wife.

According to a former Cleveland police officer and his wife familiar with the bingo hall, it is their belief that the hall is not run by Paul Buser, but rather a female from the local area. There is nothing on the surface that appears criminal on the part of this operation. However the association of US Senators, US Congressmen, two state top politicos, family member involvement possibly on both sides of one of the politico's families, questionable names in the organization as well as multiple addresses involving Hattiesburg, Bay St Louis, Madison,

Cleveland and Drew are clear examples of potential problems worthy of investigation. The sub organizations to the American Legion including Boys State and St Ambrose Leadership College as well as St Ambrose Academy make it next to impossible for the MGC to follow the money since the line is drawn limiting their authority under the American Legion organization. Rachel Shands-Buser was also found on a Facebook search of Steve Guyton's page.

RECENT ACTIVITY

"Billy Hewes is everywhere!" on Donna Carole Echols's photo.

Steve Guyton changed their profile picture.

"Hoddy-toddy!" on Billy Hewes's link.

Steve Guyton
I recommend the pancakes!

Breakfast with Billy Hewes
Location: Howell's Restaurant
Time: 8:00AM Friday, June 17th

31

June 17 at 12:58am · Share

Rachel Shands Buser I bet Steve-o eats the most pancakes!
June 17 at 8:36am

Steve Guyton Fluffy yet filling. Bye
June 17 at 12:08pm · 👍 1 person

Steve Guyton via **Billy Hewes**

Billy Hewes Campaign - Can't Decide
www.youtube.com

Our son Gardner has narrowed his choice of colleges down to four. Where do you think he should go? Click here to vote.
http://billyhewes.com/index.php/gardne...

June 16 at 11:08am · Share

These funds are supposed to be used to teach leadership skills to boys that would groom them for appointments to the military academies. So "Bingo Baby" in Cleveland, MS is licensed to politicos, major campaign managers, and current/former staff assistants to four US Congressmen and a United States' Senator. The charity is said to be on the Gulf Coast, and grooms young, sharp leaders for our US Congressmen to nominate for admission into the academies.

Shands, former Executive Director of the Mississippi Democratic Party, was the 2007 campaign manager for former State Representative and State Senator Mike Chaney's successful campaign for State Insurance Commissioner. In 2007, Shands was paid $26,250 from "Bingo Baby" and another $20,750 from the Mike Chaney campaign. He also worked on Senator Roger Wicker's campaign. Until recently, he worked on Senator Wicker's staff on the Gulf Coast, but resigned to run the state campaign for State Senate Pro Tem Billy Hewes (R), who is currently running for lieutenant governor. Steve Guyton served with former Fourth District Representative Mike Parker for 10 years. He has also worked for Congressmen Chip Pickering and Roger Wicker, and continues to work for now Senator Roger Wicker, and Congressman Gregg Harper. Oddly enough in 2007, while on the Congressional payrolls of both Congressmen Pickering and Wicker, Guyton was paid $2,000 by the Chaney campaign for "GOTV". In political circles "GOTV" stands for "Get Out The Vote".

http://www.sos.state.ms.us/PDF-Out/000000054319.pdf (see page 4).

Having run the bingo hall for 11 years, they know how to get money from bingo, and they know how to get money from congress. They save the senators and congressmen a lot of time by screening applicants for the military academies.

Shands and Guyton received a $200 thousand dollar grant from congress for their St. Ambrose Leadership College for restoration of a historic building near Co-Lin Community College. I guess this could be seen as suspicious, but I know Morgan, and never suspected him of wrong doing. I just wanted to show you all the connections between bingo and politicians that I am aware of -- being careful to mention good and bad issues. The problem is, with the bingo business, and all the cash money, you never know who is connected to whom, or what their motivations are. You also never know if ALL the money that is intended for the charitable purpose goes for that charity, or if somebody is trying to provide financial support to family members. Large pots of cash and untraceable money can corrupt the best of people.

PEER noted in 1996 that there was a problem with the MGC's authority in following the money. If you would like to read the PEER report from 1996 in its entirety, please go to:

http://www.peer.state.ms.us/reports/rpt344.pdf

The PEER Committee made this comment in their first report in 1996:

> **Weaknesses in controls over bingo operators'finances.** Mississippi law does not regulate or establish maximum limits on income derived from bingo, maximum payback percentage for total dollars wagered, or income requirements to donate to charity, nor does it require full accountability for use of the charity-bingo-generated funds. The only provision within the law requiring financial accountability for bingo organizations is Section 97-33-52 (2), which requires that licensees donate "all net proceeds" to be "expended only for the purposes for which the organization is created."
>
> Some bingo licensees advertise themselves as sponsoring and donating proceeds to a specific local charity, do not give any money to the charity, but still operate within the law. For example, in FY 1995, one Mississippi bingo licensee earned $141,010 in gross revenues, but made no distribution to its designated charity. Many representatives of the bingo industry think that the state of Washington has the most structured bingo laws and regulations in the nation. Thirty-one of Mississippi's bingo licensees donated less than the 4.5% minimum required by Washington. Of the eight top-grossing licensees, seven did not make the minimum contribution based on Washington's standards.
>
> **Commission's limited authority over bingo.** The Gaming Commission's authority is limited to enforcement of the Charitable Bingo Law on licensed bingo operations. Bingo enforcement agents may review expenditures and disbursements of bingo licensees, but do not have the statutory authority to follow the flow of funds generated to verify that they are ultimately used to support charitable activities.

I have always believed that most of the veteran-related bingo halls and the Catholic Church-run operations are on the up and up. However, most (although not all) of the rest just seemed to me as low class, white trash establishments and I never could understand why respectable people would associate with them. We had already closed the Cleveland hall once during my tenure (when it was run as

Firehouse Bingo) for funds embezzling. It did not have a good reputation. Shands and Guyton looked so out of place to me in that business, I compare it to seeing a Ku Klux Klansman in full dress walking down the streets of Harlem. That's not to say though that Steve Guyton and Morgan Shands, nor his family members or in-laws shown on the documents, have done anything wrong. The same goes for Brenda Luster, her sister-in-law, her assistant's two nieces, or Trent Lott's daughter. However, the IRS rules with regards to family members deal primarily with excessive benefit and they can hold the board members responsible for excessive salaries.

I would like to show you an example of a real bingo hall that I served a search warrant on in 1998. I mentioned it earlier but saved this information for later. The current executive director had been a member of the organization back then, and moved up when the previous director pled guilty to charges we made, and got her out of the business forever. It still operates under the same name, and the bingo hall that supports it is still the same hall, in the same place it was in then in South Jackson. She had Sheriff Malcolm McMillin on her board, and she had a member of the legislature on her board. After we conducted the search warrant, one of the first visits I got was from McMillin. The first phone call I got was from the attorney general (my previous boss) Mike Moore, who could not believe what I had done.

Within about a week, Assistant Attorney General Pat Flynn gave a very negative interview to the Clarion Ledger about me going after what they saw as Mother Theresa. When those little tidbits of intimidation didn't bother me, it wasn't long before members of the legislature started inquiring. So I had the Hinds County Sheriff, the Mississippi Attorney General, his Assistant Attorney General, and a member of the legislature contact me all upset over my actions. None of them intimidated me. I kept right on going, and worked with the defendant's attorney, reducing some of the more serious charges down to minor charges, and she pled guilty. After that, the industry made fun of me having convicted her of such minor charges. A member of the legislature made an issue out of that. But, the legislature was the body that made those minor charges. Those were the tools they gave us, then they didn't want us to use them.

I was disappointed with Attorney General Mike Moore's call because he was the very first one to call me early that morning after the search warrant was finished in the wee hours of the morning. I was upset because when I worked for him, one day the Chief Investigator (the late Bill East) told me that Mike was raving about the gaming machines that were in the country stores and gas stations in the delta. Bill said Mike wanted us to get a big truck, go around to all those stores, load up the machines, and bring them back to Jackson. Bill said Mike was convinced that the person behind them would be the first to squeal and then we would know who owned them and could go after them.

I don't remember what happened or why, but we never actually did that. Mike had not had much success in previous years dealing with machines on the coast, or closing down Robert Malone's bingo hall in Jackson. Malone hired Jackson Attorney Mike Farrell who appealed the case to the Supreme Court. They ruled against Moore, and Malone continued to operate. At any rate, when I answered the call from Mike that morning, and he was upset about this lady being arrested, and her bingo hall searched, the first thing I thought of was him saying the offended party on the machine deal would be the first to scream. He was the first to scream in this case. I don't know what that means if anything. I just thought it was ironic. Later when I wanted to return to the AG's office on a part-time basis only to retain my law enforcement certification, Bill said he couldn't talk Mike into hiring me. He said it was because I didn't know when to back off. Bill said he told Mike, "Mike, that's what you liked about him. You gave him an award for that the year after he came here." Bill said he could only surmise he wanted me to back off Sue Hathorn.

Anyway, next is a real bingo charity snapshot. This is the same hall I talked about earlier, but these tax records came about eleven years later. These are all public records that don't require a law enforcement officer, or auditor to access. Anybody can do it from the comfort of their own home by going to:

http://www.guidestar.org/

You will need to go through a short, no-cost registration process to actually see the records, but it's easy.

Form **990**		**Return of Organization Exempt From Income Tax**	OMB No. 1545-0047
Department of the Treasury Internal Revenue Service		Under section 501(c), 527, or 4947(a)(1) of the Internal Revenue Code (except black lung benefit trust or private foundation) ► The organization may have to use a copy of this return to satisfy state reporting requirements	**2009** Open to Public Inspection

A For the 2009 calendar year, or tax year beginning 05/01/09, and ending 04/30/10

B Check if applicable	Please use IRS label or print or type. See Specific Instructions.	**C** Name of organization MS Children's Advocacy Center, Inc.		**D** Employer identification number
☐ Address change		Doing Business As		64-0788869
☐ Name change		Number and street (or P O box if mail is not delivered to street address) P. O. Box 720716	Room/suite	**E** Telephone number 601-371-0980
☐ Initial return		City or town, state or country, and ZIP + 4 Byram MS 39272		**G** Gross receipts $ 5,741,832
☐ Termination ☐ Amended return ☐ Application pending		**F** Name and address of principal officer		**H(a)** Is this a group return for affiliates? ☐ Yes ☒ No **H(b)** Are all affiliates included? ☐ Yes ☐ No If "No," attach a list (see instructions)

I Tax-exempt status ☒ 501(c) (3) ◄ (insert no) ☐ 4947(a)(1) or ☐ 527

J Website: ► N/A   **H(c)** Group exemption number ►

K Type of organization ☒ Corporation ☐ Trust ☐ Association ☐ Other ►   **L** Year of formation   **M** State of legal domicile MS

Part I Summary

1 Briefly describe the organization's mission or most significant activities: PREVENTION OF CHILD ABUSE			

2 Check this box ► ☐ if the organization discontinued its operations or disposed of more than 25% of its net assets.

3 Number of voting members of the governing body (Part VI, line 1a)	**3**	5	
4 Number of independent voting members of the governing body (Part VI, line 1b)	**4**	0	
5 Total number of employees (Part V, line 2a)	**5**	20	
6 Total number of volunteers (estimate if necessary)	**6**		
7a Total gross unrelated business revenue from Part VIII, column (C), line 12	**7a**	59,559	
b Net unrelated business taxable income from Form 990-T, line 34	**7b**	-5,963	

		Prior Year	Current Year
8 Contributions and grants (Part VIII, line 1h)		105,135	120,603
9 Program service revenue (Part VIII, line 2g)			
10 Investment income (Part VIII, column (A), lines 3, 4, and 7d)		53,329	36,193
11 Other revenue (Part VIII, column (A), lines 5, 6d, 8c, 9c, 10c, and 11e)		458,092	956,045
12 Total revenue – add lines 8 through 11 (must equal Part VIII, column (A), line 12)		616,556	1,112,841
13 Grants and similar amounts paid (Part IX, column (A), lines 1–3)		49,245	
14 Benefits paid to or for members (Part IX, column (A), line 4)			
15 Salaries, other compensation, employee benefits (Part IX, column (A), lines 5–10)		742,413	726,992
16a Professional fundraising fees (Part IX, column (A), line 11e)			
b Total fundraising expenses (Part IX, column (D), line 25) ►			
17 Other expenses (Part IX, column (A), lines 11a–11d, 11f–24f)		252,416	211,572
18 Total expenses Add lines 13–17 (must equal Part IX, column (A), line 25)		1,044,074	938,564
19 Revenue less expenses. Subtract line 18 from line 12		-427,518	174,277

		Beginning of Current Year	End of Year
20 Total assets (Part X, line 16)		1,626,694	1,798,617
21 Total liabilities (Part X, line 26)		27,909	25,558
22 Net assets or fund balances Subtract line 21 from line 20		1,598,785	1,773,059

Part II Signature Block

Under penalties of perjury, I declare that I have examined this return, including accompanying schedules and statements, and to the best of my knowledge and belief, it is true, correct, and complete. Declaration of preparer (other than officer) is based on all information of which preparer has any knowledge

Sign Here	► *Brenda Luster, Executive Director*	1/4/11
	Signature of officer Date	
	Brenda Luster, Executive Director	
	Type or print name and title	

Paid Preparer's Use Only	Preparer's signature ► *D. Kyle CPA*	Date 12/16/10	Check if self-employed ► ☐	Preparer's identifying number P00037798
	Firm's name (or yours if self-employed), address, and ZIP + 4 Lyle, Walker & Co., P.A. P.O. Box 2596 Ridgeland, MS 39158			EIN ► 64-0744038 Phone no ► 601-981-0207

May the IRS discuss this return with the preparer shown above? (see instructions) ☒ Yes ☐ No

RECEIVED 2011 OGDEN, UT

SCANNED JAN 21 2011

Part III   **Gaming.** Complete if the organization answered "Yes" to Form 990, Part IV, line 19, or reported more than $15,000 on Form 990-EZ, line 6a.

	(a) Bingo	(b) Pull tabs/instant bingo/progressive bingo	(c) Other gaming	(d) Total gaming (Add col (a) through col (c))

Look at the machine rent/facility cost. Divide it by 12 for the monthly cost.

		(a) Bingo	(b)	(c)	(d)
3	Noncash prizes				
4	Rent/facility costs	735,254	243,474	2,947	981,675
5	Other direct expenses				
6	Volunteer labor ☐ Yes ☒ No				
7	Direct expense summary. Add lines 2 through 5 in col				4,628,991)
8	Net gaming income summary. Combine line 1, colum				742,647

This is the net that goes to the charity after all the expenses of the bingo hall are paid.

16   Gaming manager information:

Name ▶ Timothy Berryhill

Gaming manager compensation ▶ $ 72,800

This is how much they pay their bingo supervisor.

Description of services provided ▶ Charitable Bingo compliance

☐ Director/officer   ☒ Employee   ☐ Independent contractor

● List all of the organization's **former directors or trustees** that received, in the capacity as a former director or trustee of the organization, more than $10,000 of reportable compensation from the organization and any related organizations. List persons in the following order: individual trustees or directors; institutional trustees; officers, key employees; highest compensated employees, and former such persons.

☐ Check this box if the organization did not compensate any current officer, director, or trustee.

This is how much the director and her controller gets per year.

(A) Name and Title	(B) Average hours per week	(C) Position (check all th...			(D)	(E)	(F)
Tom Hudson CHAIRMAN	1.00				0	0	0
Tyler Lott Armstrong VICE CHAIRMA	1.00				0	0	0
Rett Crowder SECRETARY/TR	1.00				0	0	0
Angie Williams DIRECTOR	1.00				0	0	0
Brenda Luster EXECUTIVE DI	40.00	X			131,486	0	0
ALISA SMITH CONTROLLER	40.00		X		109,977	0	0

Part V-A	Current Officers, Directors, Trustees, and Key Employees (List each person who was an officer, director, trustee, or key employee at any time during the year even if they were not compensated) (See the instructions)		(B) Title and average hours per week devoted to position	(C) Compensation (If not paid, enter -0-.)	(D) Contributions to employee benefit plans & deferred compensation plans	(E) Expense account and other allowances
(A) Name and address						
Brenda Luster 112 Wildwood Drive	Madison MS 39110		EXECUTIVE DI 40	132,378	0	0
Tom Hudson P.O. Box 106	Brandon MS 39110		CHAIRMAN 1	0	0	0
Tyler Lott Armstrong 104 Trailwood Cove	Brandon MS 39216		VICE CHAIRMA 1	0	0	0
Rett Crowder 905 Keswich Court	Madison MS 39110		SECRETARY/TR 1	0	0	0
Angie Williams 3702 Old Canton Road	Jackson MS 39216		DIRECTOR 1	0	0	0

This is how much the director got paid another

Total Payroll, note that 3 out of 5 employees make over a hundred thousand dollars a year.

Part I	Compensation of the Five Highest Paid Employees Other Than Officers (See page 1 of the instructions. List each one. If there are none, enter		(b) Title and average hour per week devoted to posi			
(a) Name and address of each employee paid more than $50,000						
ALISA SMITH 3875 KIMBELL ROAD	TERRY MS 39170		CONTROLLER 40	105,959	0	0
CATHERINE DIXON 1631 N OLD CANTON ROAD	MADISON MS 39110		CLINICAL DIR 40	105,508	0	0
BRIAN ERVIN 163 GREEN FOREST DRIVE	CLINTON MS 39056		CLINICAL COO 40	62,365	0	0
MECHELLE PHILLIPS PO BOX 114	STAR MS 39167		BOOKKEEPER 40	58,954	0	0

$ 465,164 Total Salaries

When you only have some $ 700,000 left for the charity after the bingo expenses and the salaries of 5 people amount to almost $ 500,000 what is left for the charitable programs? Some $ 200,000 from a gross of almost $6 million dollars.

But who approves these kinds of expenditures for a "charity?" Excerpt from the following IRS form.

Form 990, Part VI, Line 15a - Compensation Process for Top Official

The Board has to approve all salary issues related to the Executive

Director, Clinical Director and Comptroller.

Form 990, Part VI, Line 15b - Compensation Process for Officers

The Executive Director determines all other employees' salaries/wages, with

SCHEDULE O (Form 990) Department of the Treasury Internal Revenue Service	Supplemental Information to Form 990 Complete to provide information for responses to specific questions on Form 990 or to provide any additional information. ▶ Attach to Form 990.	OMB No 1545-0047 **2009** Open to Public Inspection
Name of the organization MS Children's Advocacy Center, Inc.		Employer Identification number 64-0788869

Form 990, Part III, Line 4d – All Other Achievements

Depreciation

Form 990, Part VI, Line 2 – Related Party Information Among Officers

Brenda Luster ────────────▶ Catherine Dixon

Exec. Dir. ────────▶ Clinical Dir

Sister-in-law ────────

Alisa Smith ────────────▶ Shelia Jasper

Comptroller ────────▶ Clinic Asst

Niece by marriage ────────

Alisa Smith ────────────▶ Sandy Smith

Comptroller ────────▶ Clinic Asst

Niece by marriage ────────

So the charity has five board members and they are related to the top three. They set the salaries but three is a majority in a five man board. What are the odds they will be disapproved?

MSCHILD MS Children's Advocacy Center, Inc.
64-0788869   **Federal Statements**
FYE: 4/30/2010

Form 990, Part IX, Line 11g - Other Fees for Service (Non-employee)

Description	Total Expenses	Program Service	Management & General	Fund Raising
Janitorial	$ 9,488	$ 7,496	$ 1,992	$
Total	$ 9,488	$ 7,496	$ 1,992	$ 0

Form 990, Part IX, Line 24f - All Other Expenses

Description	Total Expenses	Program Service	Management & General	Fund Raising
Auto allowance	$ 7,400	$ 3,900	$ 3,500	$
Miscellaneous	4,525	4,525		
Business meals	1,361	1,075	286	
Bank charges	873		873	
Printing	563	563		
Contract Labor	539		539	
Total	$ 15,261	$ 10,063	$ 5,198	$ 0

Again, the charity has five board members, and the top three are related by kin. They set the salaries but three is a majority in a five man board. What are the odds they will be disapproved?

The executive director makes over $132 thousand, plus car allowance, her two assistants both make over $100 thousand, the other two make over $60 thousand and $50 thousand respectively and the operator of their bingo hall which requires no formal education makes almost $75 thousand. It is just outside my comprehension that a local charity would operate with salaries in those ranges. I think of a small office in a strip mall at best with an executive director making under $40 thousand, driving a 10 year old Ford with faded paint, a cracked windshield, the muffler hanging down, and having a couple of assistants that are volunteers dressed in second-hand clothing.

I'm overwhelmed when I see charity directors making well over a $100 thousand a year, driving a Mercedes, wearing designer clothing, fresh from the beauty shop with nails done to match each pair of shoes, French perfume, individually earning almost three times the annual mean income of a Hinds County family, and rarely darkening the door to oversee the bingo business. They are out there.

Below are just some of the schemes I remember seeing in only two years of employment as Division Director for Charitable gaming at the MGC 1998-2000:

Land purchase for charity from the director of the charity, who sets the price.

Police officer working part-time in bingo hall; records show him at work as policeman.

Male divorcee running bingo hall using charity funds to pay for child support.

Deputy Sheriff running halfway house pays personal credit card bills by charity funds.

Director rents hall for $2,000 a month but pays the owner $5,000 a month.

Building owner gives director $2,000 kickback and pockets an extra $1,000.

Former Justice Court Judge convicted by feds on loan sharking denies arrest for license

County Supervisor and wife embezzled tens of thousands from Shriner's charity.

Avid hunters form bogus charity to feed hungry, buy land, trucks, 4-wheelers, guns.

Operator opens five bingo halls under one shell corporation earning millions of dollars

Operator rents a huge building for a bingo hall, divides it in half, but pays the entire rent from charity money, utilizing the other side for other purposes.

A couple of equestrian lovers paying expenses by charity, bringing underprivileged kids in occasionally to "bring smiles to their little faces" reaping the benefit of their hobby.

A state senator opened his own bingo hall and did not pay the appropriate share to the charity, eventually forcing him to close. (The charity gets its money last. First of all, incoming gross earnings pay all the bingo hall expenses. Then the charity gets a portion of what is left. The commission set the standard using a 60/40 percent rule but has often waived it for certain charities, and not for others.)

A charity made up of people with disabilities is notified to close, for not meeting the 60/40 rule, since their bingo operator was only giving them about 10 percent. Charity members show up at a commission meeting to oppose shutting down. They influenced the commission by bringing in a lady with mechanical arms, a blind person with a seeing-eye dog, a quadriplegic in a wheel chair, and so on. They told the commission that ten percent of something was better than a hundred percent of nothing. They were allowed to continue to operate while others giving a higher percentage were not.

Some bingo charities will try to justify their amount of payment by the number of people they serve, the amount of money they take in, and so forth. However, when your salary is set higher than the state's governor, it could clearly come into question as Brenda Luster's was. But, some people are skillful enough to hide excessive benefit through kick-backs, and other means. The charitable reports are subject to scrutiny by anybody, and open to the public. That's what happens when you get into the public eye, or charitable work. More information on this issue in plain English from a non-lawyer can be found at:

http://www.sharinglaw.net/npo/ExcessBenefits-UserFriendly.htm

PEER's second report addressed that issue as well in the text below:

> Under current law, both well-intentioned and unscrupulous organizations could transfer funds to charities which are related parties because of common directors or key management. If the licensee is a well-intentioned organization, such transfers may not be a problem. However, such transfers could serve unscrupulous organizations by obscuring the audit trail of funds and could be an attempt by the licensee to remove funds from any potential oversight by the Gaming Commission. The commission should have authority to determine how such funds are utilized by a related party organization and trace funds until an unrelated organization is the recipient (i.e., an organization without material financial ties or without a key manager or director common to both). Granting the Gaming Commission greater authority to determine how charities' funds are expended would benefit legitimate charities by empowering the commission to detect abuses and rescind the licenses of unscrupulous organizations.
>
> To illustrate how bingo funds can flow between related organizations, PEER provides the following example. While PEER does not use actual names in this example, this is an actual case of funds transferred between entities. The flow of funds between the related parties presented below is not illegal and does not imply improper actions on the part of the organizations involved. The purpose of this information is to show how easily large amounts of funds may be transferred between related parties without oversight by the Gaming Commission.

http://www.peer.state.ms.us/reports/rpt363.pdf

Please review the PEER chart next to understand how the money flows, and how they warned the governor and legislature numerous times, years ago, of the need to correct this problem by new laws, but it never happened.

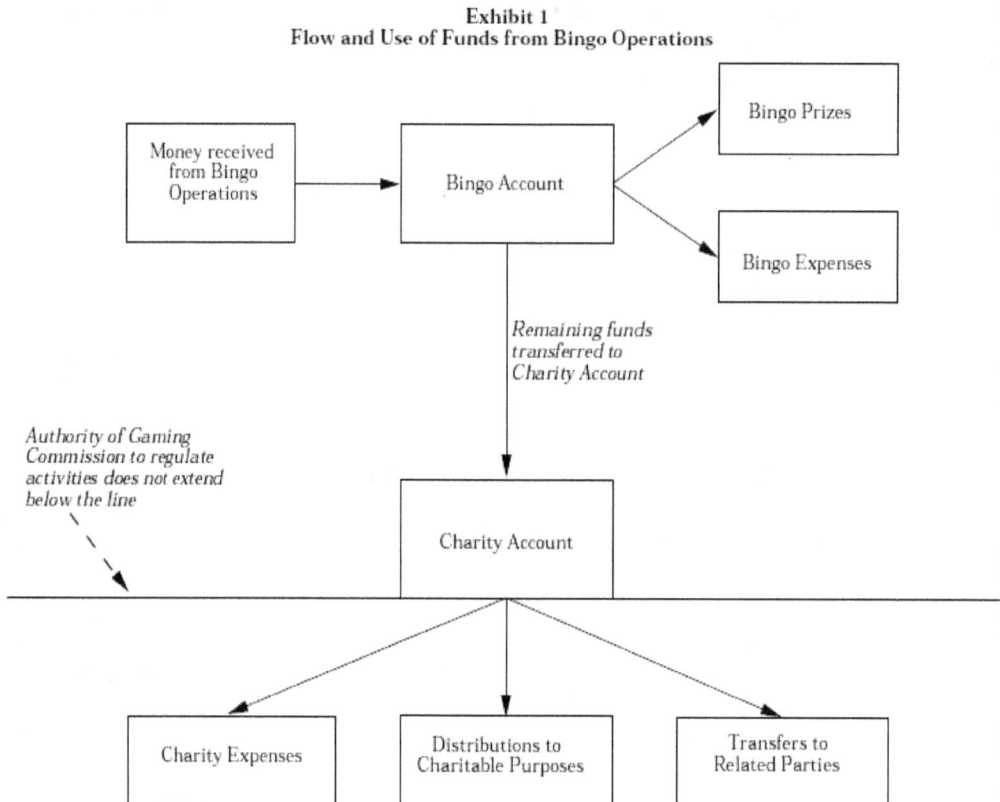

Exhibit 1
Flow and Use of Funds from Bingo Operations

```
┌─────────────┐                                      ┌──────────────┐
│Money received│         ┌──────────────┐            │ Bingo Prizes │
│ from Bingo  │────────▶│ Bingo Account│───────────▶ └──────────────┘
│ Operations  │         └──────────────┘
└─────────────┘                │         ───────────▶┌──────────────┐
                               │                     │Bingo Expenses│
                               │                     └──────────────┘
                               │
                        Remaining funds
                        transferred to
                        Charity Account
                               │
Authority of Gaming            ▼
Commission to regulate  ┌──────────────┐
activities does not extend│            │
below the line          │Charity Account│
                        └──────────────┘
─────────────────────────────────────────────────────────────────
         ┌──────────────┐  ┌──────────────┐  ┌──────────────┐
         │Charity Expenses│ │Distributions to│ │ Transfers to │
         │              │  │Charitable Purposes│ │Related Parties│
         └──────────────┘  └──────────────┘  └──────────────┘
```

SOURCE: PEER interviews of Gaming Commission officials.

Those charities listed below the line of the MGC's authority can be any phony name they come up with to funnel money back to family members. This issue was pointed out to the governor in 1997 and is more of a problem today than ever since the industry knows that nobody is going to arrest them. This is a common example of the PEER Commission doing great job finding the problems, but having no teeth to mandate a solution. They can only recommend, while MGC says, "*Yeah, yeah, yeah, Mr. Tiger with no teeth, send me the report and we will respond; then stay out of my hair until the next time.*" That was absolutely the attitude from the Director's Office during my tenure. This is just another waste of mine and your tax dollars while the industry gets more and more corrupt.

PEER went back in 2001, and did another review. This was a year after I left. I am enclosing their first page. If you would like to read more, please go to the link. However, notice that MGC is not doing what it should to protect the public. They are only concerned with protecting the industry.

A Management Review of the Mississippi Gaming Commission

When PEER first reviewed the Mississippi Gaming Commission (MGC) in 1996, the agency had begun licensing gaming establishments before its regulatory infrastructure was fully in place to address the economic, criminal, social, and other risks of legalized gambling. MGC has since improved in some areas, such as increasing its efficiency in conducting criminal background checks of casino employees. However, five years after PEER's initial review, MGC still does not have all of the components in place to protect the public effectively from the risks of legalized gambling.

The agency still issues work permits to employees before completing background checks and does not conduct thorough financial investigations of corporations applying to provide services in the gaming industry. Although MGC has established a routine compliance review program to determine whether casinos comply with internal control standards for safeguarding revenues, due to delays in implementation MGC has not yet conducted full compliance reviews of 12 of the state's 30 casinos.

The Enforcement Division has not developed a casino inspection program that specifies a checklist of steps that enforcement agents should routinely take to ensure that games are conducted in accordance with state law and MGC regulations. Also, MGC's enforcement agent training program does not ensure that agents have the necessary knowledge and skills.

Concerning oversight and control of electronic gaming devices, MGC does not thoroughly document the steps that it takes to approve electronic gaming devices and their modifications. Thus PEER could not verify whether the approval process is adequate to ensure that the devices comply with legal requirements (e.g., eighty percent minimum payout). Also, MGC does not test an adequate sample of proposed device modifications or provide adequate oversight through statistical analysis and machine verification checks.

MGC should establish criteria for each of its functional tasks through means such as analytical plans, checklists, audit steps, and a training manual; the agency should document its work to help ensure thoroughness and consistency through maintaining workpapers, inventories, and databases; and it should implement and comply with existing standards and mandates (e.g., federal regulations, state law, and its own policies and procedures).

July 10, 2001
http://www.peer.state.ms.us/reports/rpt420.pdf

Before I leave the issues identified by PEER, I want you to look at their last report done in 2009. Larry Gregory became the executive director in 2001 around the time the next to the last PEER report found its way to the governor. This report is a reflection of Larry Gregory's performance over the last nine years.

Enforcement

- The MGC's Enforcement Division still lacks a formal inspection program that would include a plan for conducting unannounced inspections of casino operations a pre-determined number of times to ensure adequate monitoring of the fair play of casino games.

- MGC does not provide adequate training for enforcement agents regarding MGC's regulations, table games, and electronic gaming devices and equipment. Thus MGC does not ensure that enforcement agents have the knowledge, skills, and abilities necessary to ensure that gaming is conducted honestly and competitively.

- MGC's management information system for enforcement does not maintain pertinent information related to enforcement activities and agents have no guidelines as to how to classify activities. As a result, MGC cannot effectively use the system as a managerial tool to monitor trends, target resources at specific risk areas, and assess the effectiveness of enforcement activities.

For all practical purposes enforcement doesn't exist at the MGC as other law enforcement officers would see it. That is not the fault of the many fine officers in that agency, but rather the expectation from our politicians that flows down the puppet strings of the commissioners and the executive director.

Oversight of Electronic Gaming Devices

- MGC now licenses independent testing labs that test electronic gaming devices. MGC's Gaming Lab reviews test results and reports submitted by the independent testing labs before approving gaming devices for use in the state.

- Although changes in the gaming industry suggest a need for increased focus on electronic gaming devices, the MGC does not aggressively monitor the integrity of such games through regular,

PEER Report #522   ix

I believe I mention later in the text that there is a need for verifying functionality and legality of these machines when I tell you about a technician jumping off the Golden Gate Bridge.

> unannounced inspections of electronic gaming
> devices and does not use proper methodology in its
> inspections.
>
> •   MGC has not ensured that its district offices have
>   the level of technical knowledge and expertise
>   needed to monitor the integrity of electronic
>   gaming devices prevalent in modern casinos.
>
> **Need for Additional Policies for Gaming Regulation**
>
> •   Even though the MGC staff state that they have
>   criteria for approval or modification of table
>   games, the MGC still has not developed written
>   criteria for approval or modification of table
>   games.
>
> **Monitoring Socioeconomic Risks of Casino Gaming**
>
> •   The MGC has not conducted a cost/benefit analysis
>   of the casino gaming industry in Mississippi.

I love the last finding. MGC has no desire to conduct a cost/benefit analysis of the gaming industry in Mississippi. Can you imagine what the costs of road construction, land purchase, lighting, and so on was in Tunica alone? How about Greenville? What about the additional police officers, deputies, firemen, fire trucks, police vehicles, additional state employees at MGC, MBR and so on? How much does it cost the state in services rendered, and loss of revenue during hurricanes and floods? The cost is probably immeasurable. We got more jobs, and more revenues, but when did (or do) we capture our expenses and realize a profit?

When gaming was just about to start in Mississippi, the choice was a lottery. I can't imagine that would have been a significant cost to taxpayers. It might be for convenience stores, but the lottery makes it worth their while. We wouldn't have needed all those overhead costs with a lottery. Ray Mabus pushed that issue back then and lost. I believe Mike Moore was in favor of it, but I don't remember him being as public about his opinion as Mabus was.

How much impact would it have on our state if all the casinos pulled up stakes and left? Policemen, fireman, city, county, and state employees would be without jobs. On the other hand, how much of an impact would it be on our state if we had elected the lottery system, and it closed down 10 or 15 years later? Do the math.

Every now and then I see a proposed bill in the legislature to bring in the lottery now to support higher education. That is what Georgia did, and it has paid for all Georgia residents' higher education for those who meet residency requirements, and grade point average. It has worked well for years. It is strapped now because so many more people have taken advantage of it, and it can't pay for all of them. Our current system can't keep our higher education fully funded now with casino money, and our residents still have to pay for their college educations. What is wrong with that picture?

I showed you the latest PEER report as it pertains to casinos, now I want to show you additional findings they reported with regards to bingo. You should recognize them as findings also pointed out many years before. The "tiger with no teeth" keeps reporting it, but the politicians continually ignore it when it is time to take action.

While data indicates that charitable bingo operations now contribute potentially more to the charities they support than in the past, state law does not adequately address the charity fraud risk because it does not authorize the Gaming Commission to track the flow of funds to determine whether charitable causes are being supported. Also, the commission lacks written policies for granting licenses of varying lengths, as well as a database to track pertinent information related to bingo hall inspections.

The following are specific follow-up conclusions regarding the Gaming Commission's regulation of charitable bingo.

Conclusions

Protection Against the Charity Fraud Risk

- State law does not provide the MGC with authority to inquire closely into the operations of charitable organizations and monitor their transactions to ensure that bingo halls are truly supporting charitable causes.

These are not all the problems they noted and I encourage you to read the full report at:

http://www.peer.state.ms.us/reports/rpt522.pdf

How many times does the state agency we employ (PEER), and pay for from our taxes have to tell the governor and his sidekicks about the same problems over and over? The below page is the same that goes out with each report. Note the committee members, and the people who get the report. They can't say they didn't know the problems exist.

The Mississippi Legislature

Joint Committee on Performance Evaluation and Expenditure Review

PEER Committee

SENATORS
GARY JACKSON
Vice Chair
CINDY HYDE-SMITH
Secretary
SIDNEY ALBRITTON
TERRY BROWN
MERLE FLOWERS
SAMPSON JACKSON
NOLAN METTETAL

TELEPHONE:
(601) 359-1226

FAX:
(601) 359-1420

REPRESENTATIVES
HARVEY MOSS
Chair
WILLIE BAILEY
ALYCE CLARKE
DIRK DEDEAUX
WALTER ROBINSON
RAY ROGERS
GREG WARD

Post Office Box 1204
Jackson, Mississippi 39215-1204

Max K. Arinder, Ph. D.
Executive Director

www.peer.state.ms.us

OFFICES:
Woolfolk Building, Suite 301-A
501 North West Street
Jackson, Mississippi 39201

August 11, 2009

Honorable Haley Barbour, Governor
Honorable Phil Bryant, Lieutenant Governor
Honorable Billy McCoy, Speaker of the House
Members of the Mississippi State Legislature

On August 11, 2009, the PEER Committee authorized release of the report entitled *Gaming Regulation in Mississippi: A Progress Report.*

Harvey Moss

Representative Harvey Moss, Chair

As I said before, politicians have often had some sort of hidden relationship with bingo hall operators. When I began the arrests in 1998, they jumped off those boards and other associations with the bingo halls like rats jumping off a sinking ship. As you saw from Barbour's state of the state addresses, he never mentioned gaming. Once a politician is exposed as having some sort of relationship with bingo, they usually bail out and want no more connections. A person running for political office could be severely hurt by a similar relationship. I think because of the known corruption in the business and the propensity for misuse of large amounts of cash, they would go to any end to keep that relationship secret. Has the mule left the barn?

I have shown you what PEER found in the MGC. These are not what Rick Ward, former employee and pissed off taxpayer says. It is what another professional state agency says with the concurrence of several senators and state representatives. As I said, the last PEER report covers almost the last nine years of current Executive Director Larry Gregory's reign. PEER has told the governor, the lieutenant governor, the speaker of the house, and other members of the legislature what is going on inside the MGC, and still it continues to be a problem for years. But how does the legislature deal with it? They don't.

HOUSE RESOLUTION NO. 148

1   A RESOLUTION COMMENDING THE SERVICE OF LARRY GREGORY,
2 EXECUTIVE DIRECTOR OF THE MISSISSIPPI GAMING COMMISSION, FOR HIS
3 MANY CONTRIBUTIONS, TIRELESS DEVOTION AND SERVICE TO THE STATE OF
4 MISSISSIPPI AND CONGRATULATING HIM UPON HIS RETIREMENT FROM PUBLIC
5 SERVICE.

6   WHEREAS, Larry Gregory has faithfully served in various
7   capacities of public service to the citizens of the State of
8   Mississippi for many years, and it is with appreciation that we
9   recognize his dedication and devotion upon his retirement; and
10   WHEREAS, a native of Jackson, Mississippi, Mr. Gregory served
11 four years in the United States Air Force and attended the
12 University of Southern Mississippi where he received a bachelor of
13 science degree in political science before continuing his
14 education at Mississippi State University, receiving a master of
15 public policy and administration, and he further received a
16 certificate of paralegal studies from Mississippi College; and
17   WHEREAS, during his time at the Mississippi Gaming
18 Commission, he helped to regulate a $2.9 billion industry,
19 managing a staff of 145 individuals who serve to regulate the
20 industry within the state; and
21   WHEREAS, Mr. Gregory has succeeded in instituting a strict,
22 but fair, regulatory approach within the industry, modeling the
23 state's free market approach of regulation after the model
24 employed by the State of Nevada; and
25   WHEREAS, as a guest commentator and speaker to numerous media
26 outlets, forums, conferences and civic clubs, he has attributed
27 the success of the gaming industry within the state to solid
28 regulation and a sound business approach; and

H. R. No. 148   ▮▮▮▮▮▮▮▮▮▮▮▮▮▮   N1/2
11/HR40/R1999
PAGE 1 (CAA\BD)

29   WHEREAS, most recently, in the wake of devastating Hurricane

30   Katrina, which Mr. Gregory cites as the source of his biggest

31   challenge as executive director, he helped move forward recovery

32   and reconstruction efforts for the state's gaming industries,

33   drafting regulations to direct rebuilding along the Mississippi

34   Gulf Coast; and

35   WHEREAS, he has been supported in his endeavors by his wife,

36   Mollie, and they live in Jackson, Mississippi, where they are

37   faithful members of Trinity Presbyterian Church; and

38   WHEREAS, it is the policy of the House of Representatives to

39   honor diligent state employees and elected officials, such as

40   Larry Gregory, whose career serves as an example to all citizens

41   of the State of Mississippi and whose legacy of service is

42   exemplified by initiative, fairness and good judgment:

43   NOW, THEREFORE, BE IT RESOLVED BY THE HOUSE OF

44   REPRESENTATIVES OF THE STATE OF MISSISSIPPI, That we do hereby

45   commend the remarkable career of Larry Gregory, express how his

46   leadership will be missed, congratulate him upon his retirement,

47   express deepest appreciation to him for the hard work and many

48   sacrifices he has made to serve the people of the state and extend

49   best wishes for continued success in all of his future endeavors.

50   BE IT FURTHER RESOLVED, That copies of this resolution be

51   furnished to Mr. Gregory and to the members of the Capitol Press

52   Corps.

See the original and dates/details of actions at:

http://billstatus.ls.state.ms.us/documents/2011/pdf/HR/HR0148PS.pdf

You might think because of all the many problems that still exist in the MGC, along with the ones I have reported, that Larry Gregory should have been fired by the governor. However, that is not the case at all. Larry has done a very good job. He has done exactly what they wanted him to do, and has not done any of the things they didn't want him to do. Bobby Moak says they want to "express their deepest appreciation to him for the hard work and many sacrifices he has made to serve the people of the state." I knew Larry as a friend and we had a mutual friend who knew him much better than I did. A couple of years ago, I asked that mutual friend why Larry misrepresented in the newspaper articles what was really going on, and why did he put up with the crap from the legislature being their puppet. His response to me was, "because he has to in order to keep his job." I know without a doubt that is absolutely true. If they called Larry tomorrow, and told him to start obeying the law, and put people in jail, he would have 12 people in jail by the end of next week. He is truly a public servant, and has had to give up his own morals, sacrificing his own soul to please somebody else that doesn't want to enforce the law for some strange reason. Larry could have quit like I did, the minute that became an issue. However, it would not have mattered. The legislature and governor would have filled his position with another yes man before the sun went down that day.

It should be evident to you in the next chapter why I think charities seek out corruptible politicians or corruptible politicians seek out bingo as a source of income for charities. I am not sure whether, or not politicians are corrupted by power, or the powerful are drawn to corruption.

Chapter Eight

BINGO AND ORGANIZED CRIME

"Organized crime constitutes nothing less than a guerilla war against society."

Lyndon Johnson

Almost anytime you find bingo corruption, no matter what state it might be in, you will find a politician and/or a lobbyist in the middle of it. The organization assembled to illegally obtain money almost always has a built in protective measure for the bad guys. That protective measure is usually a politician or law enforcement officer, and they often get a cut of the cash. There is so much cash that the organizations don't have to account for once the enforcement agencies get lax, that its free for the taking, and easily finds its way into political campaigns without any record.

The 1986 President's Commission on Organized Crime noted that:

the problem in defining organized crime lies not in the word 'crime', as society generally accepts certain behavior as criminal. The problem lies in what should be considered 'organized'. Some definitions of organized crime are very broad, encompassing any group of two or more individuals who conspire to commit a criminal act. Others limit the definition only to include La Cosa Nostra or the 'traditional' mob. What remains constant, however, are the characteristics that these organized criminal groups have in common: Their illegal activities are conspiratorial;

In at least part of their activities, they commit or threaten to commit acts of violence or other acts, which are likely to intimidate;

They conduct their activities in a methodical, systematic or highly disciplined and secret fashion;

They insulate their leadership from direct involvement in illegal activities by their intricate organizational structure;

They attempt to gain influence in government, politics and commerce through corruption, graft and legitimate means;

They have economic gain as their primary goal, not only from patently illegal enterprises such as drugs, gambling and loan sharking, but also from such activities as laundering illegal money through investment in legitimate business; They prey on otherwise innocent people who may be involved in low-level law breaking and are, therefore, afraid to go to law enforcement.

The FBI currently defines Organized Crime as:

"Any group having some manner of a formalized structure and whose primary objective is to obtain money through illegal activities. Such groups maintain their position through the use of actual or threatened violence, corrupt public officials, graft, or extortion, and generally have a significant impact on the people in their locales, region, or the country as a whole."

In summary and in comparison with bingo run activities, I will draw excerpts from the FBI definition:

Formalized Structure - (Board members with executive director, bingo manager, employees)

Objective is to obtain money through illegal activities - (skimming, theft, embezzlement, payoff)

Use of threats/violence - (threaten/intimidate enforcement officers through connection).

Corrupt officials - (Sit on boards for protection and/or receive funds/political mileage)

Have significant impact on their locales - (Fund children, veterans, disabled, programs in need)

Although Organized Crime may be difficult for local police to detect, especially in the large gaming industry, it is easy to see in bingo halls. Nobody ever recognizes that this "Little Old Gray Haired Lady" bingo business could be involved with organized crime. Some may even be involved in organized crime, and not know it. First of all there is no such thing as a "Little Old Gray Haired Lady" operation stamping paper sheets anymore. They primarily use gaming machines. Most of us could not distinguish between these gaming machines, and casino slot machines. I will give you an example going back to the characteristics of organized crime. Some derelict without a job has no income. (That is not to say that everybody without a job is a derelict.)

He takes the following steps:

Decides he has figured out a way to make big bucks, all cash in the bingo business.

Forms a "so-called" charity in MS because MS requires it to run bingo halls.

Secretly hides documents that would show real income, cash is taken from the pot

Charity appeals to politicians (children, drugs, disabled, indigent and veterans)

Starts a petting farm for underprivileged children to come and pet the animals.

Gets a Legislator, Sheriff, Deputy, Policeman, DA or judge to serve on his board.

They jump on it for the political mileage they get out of helping those groups.

Some members of those groups jump on it for other reasons (untraceable cash).

Pays himself as executive director of the charity $100,000 a year.

He pays for his expenses out of charity funds (car, computer and cell phone, etc.).

Gets spouse to form a charity without a bingo hall, and donates $100,000 a year.

Spouse pays herself $80,000 a year from the bogus charity.

If anybody attempts to arrest them, they will call their board members.

The board members apply pressure to either the legislature or MGC.

The "dogs" (gaming agents) are called off.

They are eventually dealt with through regulatory means and may pay a few fines.

That action most likely comes from the SOS if gaming can pass it off.

As an elected official, he's not subject to legislative intimidation, and MGC is glad.

The hall closes with several million dollars in their bank account, or stashed cash.

The charity stays intact and the money and interest continues to pay the director,

Here's what just happened in the previous scenario. An otherwise unemployed person gets rich paying himself and his spouse hundreds of thousands of dollars with amenities that bring their benefits to well over a quarter million dollars a year. I know it is hard to believe the possibility of a small Mississippi town involved in Organized Crime or that you would even consider this as Organized Crime. Keep in mind that Organized Crime is no longer reserved for fat mafia members with machine guns in fiddle cases, mirror sunglasses, fine Italian custom suits and big black Cadillac's with dark windows and New Jersey license plates.

During Prohibition, Organized Crime used hit squads. That continued for a couple of decades. This lingered on even recently with the top level mob bosses. However, during the 60's and 70's, mobs began to pay off police officers, or conduct shakedowns to continue their activities. But nowadays, the methodology is to appear to be legitimate, and gain respect. They donate to campaigns, and employ family members of important people. They get politicians and police officers on their payroll. They give substantial gifts to respectable families with influence. They throw huge "legislative feeds" with tables of expensive food fit for a king. They invite all members of the legislature and lobbyists to rub elbows. These are the people the charity (bingo hall) calls when heat comes down on the bingo hall. The agents are seen as overly aggressive and out of control. Then the arrests stop.

Their techniques have trickled down without physical harm to anyone. I will withhold my judgment and let you decide if this is "organized crime", but I will help you by underlining what occurred in my example:

They commit or threaten to commit acts of violence or **other acts, likely to intimidate;**

Conduct their activities in a methodical, systematic or **highly disciplined and secret fashion;**

Insulate leadership from direct involvement in illegal activities by intricate structure;

Attempt to gain influence in government, politics via corruption, graft, legitimate means;

Have economic gain as their primary goal, not only from patently illegal enterprises such as drugs, gambling and loan sharking, but also **from such activities as laundering illegal money through investment in legitimate business**;

Prey on otherwise innocent people who may be involved in low-level law breaking and are, therefore, afraid to go to law enforcement.

When it came time to license bingo machines, the law required the machines to be examined by the gaming lab before placed in use. The problem is the bingo industry was seen as the bastard child to the MGC when it was compared to casinos. Casino machines were a much higher priority. The lab was taking years to test a bingo machine, sometimes a year or more, even in the casino industry. So the MGC felt pressure to do something. They gave interim permits to be used until such time as their machines could be tested.

You probably have already guessed that the "interim" approval became permanent. Many of those machines were no longer being made. Only a couple of distributors were licensed to sell them. Parts were no longer available for them. They were like buying an old computer without new software that might have been manipulated by a whiz kid. To keep them running meant bastardizing from junk parts of other machines. Why not trash them?

Some of the machines were being updated. In 2000, a local distributor of California based Game Tech demanded they could not be manipulated. However, in September 2002 Game Tech employee Brett Keaton was under investigation for rigging their own machines in bingo halls. The night before Gaming Agents showed up at his job, he jumped off the Golden Gate Bridge. But how many people did he tell how to rig the machines before his big leap?

If the MGC cannot allocate enough of their budget to pay for additional machine testing staff to ensure legitimate play, the machines should not be authorized, temporarily or otherwise. The state does not allow us to put our cars in use without first showing they are safe enough to operate, and obtain a state inspection sticker. We owe the same to our citizens who play. That goes for the casinos as well as the bingo businesses. A sticker or certificate of approval should only be issued when the machine has actually been inspected.

In a 1996 report by the Chicago Crime Commission, former mob-bookie and gambling boss, William 'BJ' Jahoda, testified against the mob. He addressed the membership of the commission on the dangers of legalized gambling, stating that any politician who supports it is "uninformed, in someone's pocket or doesn't care." *Whether run by the government or run by the mob, the goal of organized gambling is to empty everyone's pockets and fill theirs.*

I don't necessarily agree that ANY politician who supports it falls into that category although I believe there are some that do. There are some that I am sure have a genuine interest in bringing tourism, jobs, entertainment, and increased revenue to the state for legitimate reasons. I am all for that, and not against gaming. I am only concerned that there is no enforcement to speak of, and when there is, it is only when the casino is the victim. I will give you some examples of corruption from other states:

According to *the New York Times* in 1990 the bingo industry was bringing in $31 million dollars a year in Tennessee. The FBI had started an undercover operation in 1986 after a member of the House of Representatives reported that a lobbyist approached him, offered him bribes and bragged about already doing so with other members. "Operation Rocky Top," as it was termed used the former top regulator of the gaming industry (turned lobbyist) and later an informant. He revealed his techniques of how he helped would-be bingo licensees obtain licensing when they were bogus charities. The bingo hall operators were funneling cash money back to legislators.

Over 50 people were convicted for their participation in the scheme, many of which were public officials, including the Secretary of State, and House Majority leader. The Secretary of State committed suicide after being called to testify in a federal grand jury for the third time.

A state representative also committed suicide after he was officially charged with bribery. The State of Tennessee responded by placing limits on campaign contributions and enacting more stringent lobbying laws.

One would have thought that the legislators would have learned their lessons in Tennessee after Operation Rocky Top. However in a second sting unrelated to bingo, the FBI arrested seven lawmakers and other officials on public corruption charges. On May 25, 2005 the FBI introduced legislators to a program they called, "Operation Tennessee Waltz." It began with the arrest of powerhouse Senator John Ford and ten others. In January of 2008, the *Commercial Appeal* newspaper reported that all twelve had either been convicted, or plead guilty with long-defiant Senator Kathryn Bowers being the last. Ford was also charged with telling FBI agents (after they gave him $55 thousand in bribes) that if they were really FBI agents, he would shoot them. Sentences handed out ranged from two to five years except for John Ford who received 66 months. The informant was given probation on an embezzlement charge.

It seems that anywhere you look, you find people entrusted with millions of dollars in the bingo (bogus charity) business that have sticky fingers. Many have been arrested. There have been repeated attempts by law enforcement agencies to warn the public and other agencies throughout the country of this threat. I will go back about 20 years, and give you some examples:

The Pennsylvania Crime Commission published a report in 1992 warning law enforcement officials of Racketeering and Organized Crime in the Bingo Industry.

The Virginia Pilot reported on November 20, 1997 that a baseball association bingo manager was convicted of illegal gambling and skimming hundreds of thousands of dollars from their charity.

On April 29, 2002, the *Chicago Sun Times* reported that the federal grand jury had indicted ten men who prosecutors said skimmed over $3.2 million dollars from the bingo hall.

On June 9, 2006, the *Rocky Mountain News* reported that ten people including a former city council member were facing 30 felony charges handed down by the grand jury. They were charged under the Colorado Organized Crime Control Act.

In August 2006, the State of Oregon issued a report titled, "Organized Crime in Oregon," in which bingo was listed, followed by public corruption. They concluded that they had learned from history that a significant presence of organized crime could lead to public corruption. They further stated that criminal enterprises may corrupt public officials in order to safeguard illegal money-making operations.

WCTV in Tallahassee, Florida reported in August of 2010 that two men, who operated a bingo hall there, were arrested on dozens of felony counts of Florida bingo laws. Agents told the TV station the men were responsible for skimming tens of thousands of dollars from charities.

On October 4, 2010, in Alabama, four legislators, three lobbyists, and four others were arrested by the FBI on indictments stemming from an undercover sting relating to bingo, and corruption. Bribes ranged from $5 thousand to $2 million for positive votes on bingo legislation.

In December 2010, the *Pocono Record*, Pocono, PA reported that the former fire chief, and his wife who was the secretary/treasurer of the volunteer fire department were arrested. They were described by others as a respectable couple. Court documents said they were siphoning cash from bingo fundraising events. The wife admitted opening sealed bingo money bags, taking out the deposit slip, and replacing it with a slip of less money, then retaining the funds. They skimmed at least $68 thousand, according to the court documents, leaving the fire department coffers empty.

You can look in just about any state that operates bingo and you will find instances of bingo operations generating funds for charities that were skimmed off the top by bingo hall operators. The rest of the majority of cases I worked were individuals lying on their applications, usually about prior arrests. Falsifying an application is an indication of dishonesty. If a person is dishonest to a state agency to get licensed, imagine what he might do if he were exposed to mounds of cash often up to several million dollars per year.

The MGC executives themselves contributed to unqualified charities obtaining a license. The agents have done an outstanding job in conducting background investigations. When an applicant is found to have falsified an application (most often lying about prior arrests) they now write an investigative report citing the violations that disqualify the applicant, and submit it up the chain of command to the executive director. He reviews it and makes his recommendation to the commission at the monthly meeting. During my tenure, I never knew of an agent recommendation being changed. Any violation of the law depicted in the report should have resulted in a recommendation by the executive director to the commission to not license the entity, and the individual who falsified the application should be arrested as the legislature intended by making that one of the more serious charges they passed in the bingo laws.

A couple of years ago, I filed a public records request in accordance with the law, asking MGC lawyers for a copy of the report from the agent on a charity that was disqualified on three counts. They never provided it, but tried to appease me and insult my intelligence with a copy of the minutes which showed only the executive director's recommendation to the commissioners. The truth lies in the records.

On May 7, 2008 Executive Director Larry Gregory first told a reporter from the *Jackson Free Press* that agents were making misdemeanor arrests for people putting the wrong address on applications during my tenure. He indicated in particular that the case ultimately resulting in my resignation was one of those. Confronted with that statement, I laughed, and gave the reporter information to the contrary.

He re-contacted Gregory who then admitted it wasn't for the wrong address, but in fact was for lying about a prior arrest record. He then started another excuse insisting it was a misdemeanor where the treatment didn't fit the crime. This case was being handled no differently than any other case. And oh, by the way, the legislature only passed misdemeanor laws in the Bingo Act. However, the Mississippi's Legislature made falsifying a gaming application a misdemeanor, but if you lie on an application to obtain a fishing license, it is a felony. Where is the common sense?

In addition, the reporter said he got a listing of all the arrests made in the last eight to ten years through a public request. The report indicated the division had not made a single arrest since 2002. However, when I asked for additional information through my state representative, he got a report within a few days showing 12 additional arrests that they had supposedly "assisted" other agencies in. If you saw the actual documents would you call this lies and deceit?

Chapter Nine

FAVORITISM, LIES AND COVER UPS

"We have the incredible privilege of serving in the highest offices in the state. We must prove ourselves worthy of our fellow citizen's faith. We must be trusted to always place the public's good above our own and to always choose fairness over favoritism."

Jodi Rell

During my tenure at the MGC over ten years ago, the commissioners added a regulation that required any charity applying for a license to conduct bingo as a means of charitable support to have a three year history of charitable activity. Waivers of that rule were rare, and probably didn't occur but once every couple of years when the requesting charity had many other things going for it.

There is a difference between a regulation and a law, as it pertains to the MGC. The commission has the authority to issue regulations that aren't specifically covered in the law. They are administrative and regulatory violations subject to administrative sanctions, and civil fines. Where the law is specific making a certain offense a violation of that law, those breaking the law are subject to criminal charges, and fines imposed by a criminal court judge. In this case a statutory requirement is a law enacted by the legislature that requires a charity to meet certain statutory requirements before they are issued a license.

Administrative sanctions may also be taken against the violator in addition to criminal prosecution, or in lieu of prosecution.

When I was there, our lawyers made sure we knew the difference and that those dual actions were not considered "double jeopardy" since that term only applies to judicial proceedings, and not administrative sanctions. They also made sure the commissioners knew if they acted in an "arbitrary or capricious" manner with no legal precedence, they (the lawyers) would not be able to defend their (commissioners') actions.

The Merriam-Webster dictionary provides one definition of "arbitrary" that says "marked by or resulting from the unrestrained and often tyrannical exercise of power, 'protection from arbitrary arrest and detention.'" It goes on to define "capricious" as "governed or characterized by caprice: Impulsive, unpredictable."

The commissioners used the laws, and regulations as they saw fit with no standardization. Fines were often imposed with no standards in place (usually applied to casinos). One of the PEER reports indicated the MGC should set a standard fine for a particular offense. That was to prevent the appearance of favoritism, or being too harsh on an organization they may not have liked. After all, if you get a traffic ticket for an offense, in almost all cases, you can call the law enforcement agency responsible, or the respective judge's clerk and they will tell you exactly how much the fine is, no matter who you are, or what they may think of you. Why isn't that possible in the MGC or through its attorney general embedded lawyers?

There are many cases that could fit the bill of arbitrary and capricious acts on the part of the MGC. I have documentation of more than I would like to look at. I don't want to bore you with a lot of information that may sound confusing. However, I will appeal to your better judgment, and give you one simple example. Simply put, the commission can waive a licensure requirement that they imposed through regulations as long as there is some basis without being arbitrary and capricious. However, they cannot waive a law the legislature passed. In one case, they did it twice without authority.

As I mentioned before, one of the regulations they adopted requires any charity applying for a license to have a three year history of charitable activity. That was adopted because we had people seeing big rolls of cash in the bingo business who wanted to open a bingo hall. However, state law requires an organization running a bingo hall to be a charity, civic or veteran organization. This regulation prevented everybody and their brother (to some extent) from opening a bingo hall for some purpose other than charity. Here it is:

§ 97-33-52. Organizations authorized to conduct bingo games; disposition of proceeds; records and reports

(1) <u>A bingo game may be conducted only</u>:

(a) When held <u>for the benefit of a charitable organization</u> that (i) is licensed pursuant to Section 97-33-55 or Section 97-33-59; (ii) is <u>domiciled in the State of Mississippi;</u> and

(b) <u>When the game is held by active members of such organization.</u>

While perusing the SOS site one day in early 2009, looking at listings of charitable organizations that received charitable funds from bingo operations, one in particular caught my eye. It showed something I had never seen before, and I was very familiar with all these reports from years gone by.

This particular report showed a charity organization with an address listed outside the State of Mississippi. See spreadsheet below:

Organization	State	Fiscal Year	Total Revenue	Total Expenses	Fundraising Expenses	Administrative Expenses
Benevolent And Protective Order of Elks Lodge 606 - Biloxi	MS		The charitable organization is currently exempted from annual finacial reporting requirements with the Mississippi Secretary of State's Office			
Benevolent and Protective Order of Elks Lodge 977 - Clarksdale	MS		The charitable organization is currently exempted from annual finacial reporting requirements with the Mississippi Secretary of State's Office			
Benevolent And Protective Order of Elks Lodge 978	MS		The charitable organization is currently exempted from annual finacial reporting requirements with the Mississippi Secretary of State's Office			
Coalition for Citizens with Disabilities	MS	2005	$ 1,890,428.00	$ 1,811,443.00	$ 1,290,990.00	$ 115,987.00
Disabled American Veterans #5 Robert Veal Chapter	MS		The charitable organization is currently exempted from annual finacial reporting requirements with the Mississippi Secretary of State's Office			
Fine Arts Institute of Mississippi	MS	2006	$ 1,295,541.00	$ 1,273,532.00	$ 1,210,422.00	$ 62,110.00
Generus Stepping Stones, Inc.	TN	2005	$ 3,562,206.00	$ 3,344,531.00	$ 2,413,011.00	$ 81,634.00
Golden Triangle Planning and Development District	MS	2006	$ 16,439,386.00	$ 15,916,355.00	$ 3,357,352.00	$ 6,156,539.00
Good Samaritan Center, Inc.	MS	2005	$ 6,572,208.00	$ 6,099,209.00	$ 5,140,625.00	$ 71,902.00
Greenwood Community & Recreation Center, Inc.	MS	2006	$ 1,757,835.00	$ 1,759,686.00	$ 1,659,072.00	$ 13,635.00
His Way, Inc.	MS	2006	$ 8,215,961.00	$ 8,011,254.00	$ 6,530,665.00	$ 43,972.00
Knights of Columbus - Father A.C. Dennis Council Kiln #7087	MS		The charitable organization is currently exempted from annual finacial reporting requirements with the Mississippi Secretary of State's Office			
Knights of Columbus - Lumberton #7211	MS		The charitable organization is currently exempted from annual finacial reporting requirements with the Mississippi Secretary of State's Office			
Knights of Columbus - Meridian #802	MS		The charitable organization is currently exempted from annual finacial reporting requirements with the Mississippi Secretary of State's Office			
Knights of Columbus - Picayune #6872	MS		The charitable organization is currently exempted from annual finacial reporting requirements with the Mississippi Secretary of State's Office			
Living Independence for Everyone, Inc.	MS	2005	$ 5,413,391.00	$ 5,234,726.00	$ 3,166,139.00	$ 222,615.00
Loyal Order of Moose - Jackson Moose Lodge 1426	MS		The charitable organization is currently exempted from annual finacial reporting requirements with the Mississippi Secretary of State's Office			
Loyal Order of Moose Lodge #1662	MS		The charitable organization is currently exempted from annual finacial reporting requirements with the Mississippi Secretary of State's Office			

It caught my eye because its address was in Tennessee. I looked further.

I reviewed their articles of incorporation to see who was behind it, and who the members were. Remember the law said it must be domiciled in the state, and the bingo hall had to be operated by members of the organization. As a memory refresher, Matt Steffey, law professor at Mississippi College who often advises the media, told the Clarion Ledger in September 2008, the commissioners had no authority to issue a waiver absent a specific law that said they could. He likened their action to that of a nuclear facility having eight statutory requirements but the Nuclear Regulatory Commission telling them it was okay that they only met six of the eight requirements. At any rate, here is what I found:

Business ID: 861826
Date Filed: 09/22/2004 12:00 PM
Eric Clark
Secretary of State

F0001 - Page 1 of 2

OFFICE OF THE MISSISSIPPI SECRETARY OF STATE
P.O. BOX 136, JACKSON, MS 39205-0136   (601) 359-1333
Articles of Incorporation 1247

729032 SEP 22 04

The undersigned, pursuant to Section 79-4-2.02 (if a profit corporation) or Section 79-11-137 (if a nonprofit corporation) of the Mississippi Code of 1972, hereby executes the following document and sets forth:

1. Type of Corporation

[ ] Profit   [X] Nonprofit

2. Name of the Corporation

Generus, Inc.

3. The future effective date is
(Complete if applicable)

4. FOR NONPROFITS ONLY: The period of duration is [ ] years or [X] perpetual

5. FOR PROFITS ONLY: The Number (and Classes) if any of shares the corporation is authorized to issue is (are) as follows

Classes	# of Shares Authorized	If more than one (1) class of shares is authorized, the preferences, limitations, and relative rights of each class are as follows	
			(See Attached)

6. Name and Street Address of the Registered Agent and Registered Office is

Name	Mildred Williams
Physical Address	1900 North West Street, Suite B
P.O. Box	
City, State, ZIP5, ZIP4	Jackson MS 39202

7. The name and complete address of each incorporator are as follows

Name	Samuel L. Begley
Street	123 N. State Street

Rev. 01/96

F0001 - Page 2 of 2   **OFFICE OF THE MISSISSIPPI SECRETARY OF STATE**
                              P.O. BOX 136, JACKSON, MS 39205-0136   (601) 359-1333
                              Articles of Incorporation

| City, State, ZIP5, ZIP4 | Jackson | MS | 39201- |

Name

Street

City, State, ZIP5, ZIP4

Name

Street

City, State, ZIP5, ZIP4

Name

Street

City, State, ZIP5, ZIP4

729032 SEP 22 04

8. Other Provisions   ☑   See Attached

9. Incorporators' Signatures (please keep writing within blocks)

Samuel Lee Bayly
9/22/04

Rev. 01/96

ATTACHMENT TO
ARTICLES OF INCORPORATION
OF
GENERUS, INC.

I.   **SPECIFIC AND GENERAL PURPOSES**

a.   The specific and primary purposes for which this corporation is formed are to operate for the advancement of charity including but not limited to senior citizens, at risk children, children who have medical or emotional difficulties, services for the visually impaired and for others who have developmental or medical conditions. We also provide residential healthcare services for the frail, homebound seniors.

b.   The general purposes for which this corporation is formed are to operate exclusively for such charitable purposes as will qualify it as an exempt organization under 26 U.S.C. § 501(c)(3) of the Internal Revenue Code of 1986 or correspondent provisions of any subsequent federal tax laws, including, for such purposes, the making of distributions to organizations which qualify as tax-exempt organizations under that Code.

c.   This corporation shall not, as a substantial part of its activities, carry on propaganda or otherwise attempt to influence legislation; nor shall it participate or intervene (by publication or distribution of any statements or otherwise) in any political campaign on behalf of any candidate for public office.

The above purposes shall be construed as both objects and powers, and the enumeration of specific powers shall not be held to limit or restrict in any manner the powers of this Corporation.

II.   **NO MEMBERS**

The Corporation will have no members.

729032 SEP 22. 04

Don't forget the spreadsheet I showed you earlier that indicated this corporation is domiciled in the State of Tennessee. Also remember that the domicile and requirement that the hall be operated by members of the organization are state laws that the commission has no authority to waive. Well, how can this charity say in its charter on file as a matter of public record with the SOS, that they will have no members, and are operating in Tennessee, but tell the MGC they operate in Mississippi, and still get a license from the MGC? What is wrong with this picture?

Here is the waiver the MGC issued on their regulation prohibiting a charity from gaining a license if they had no three year history of charitable activity. Notice that it only says they are receiving a waiver of the regulation from not having a three year history. Nowhere does it address the two laws that say it must be domiciled in the state, and it must be operated by members of the charity.

Minutes of the Mississippi Gaming Commission
March 17, 2005 Regular Monthly Meeting
Page 32

LARRY K. GREGORY,
EXECUTIVE DIRECTOR

ATTEST:

THOMAS H. MUELLER
SPECIAL ASSISTANT ATTORNEY GENERAL

There is no indication in the minutes that the lawyer for the attorney general gave legal advice to the commission that even though they were waiving a regulation requiring a three year history of charitable activity. There were also two statutory laws not complied with.

Minutes of the Mississippi Gaming Commission
March 17, 2005 Regular Monthly Meeting
Page 31

D.   RECOMMENDATION OF WAIVER – Requirement of three-year history of
        Charitable Activity

1.   Generus Stepping Stones, Inc.

John Carroll and Sam Begley, representing Generus Stepping Stones, Inc.,
presented the request to the Commission.

EXECUTIVE DIRECTOR'S RECOMMENDATION: "The
Executive Director recommends that Generus Stepping Stones, Inc.
be granted a waiver from the requirement of having a three-year
history of charitable activity"

Commissioner Canon: Motion to adopt recommendation
Commissioner Sanders: Second

RECORDED VOTE: Chairman St. Pe'   YES
                    Commissioner Sanders: YES
                    Commissioner Canon: YES

ITEM VI.

PUBLIC COMMENT

None.

ITEM VII.

ADJOURNMENT

There being no further business, the meeting was adjourned at 10:55 a.m.

JERRY ST. PE', CHAIRMAN

HOWARD R. SANDERS, COMMISSIONER

NOLEN CANON, COMMISSIONER

There is no indication from these minutes that the MGC Commissioners or executive director discussed the need to, or lack of authority to, waive the two required statutory laws, therefore that must have been discussed outside the meeting in violation of the public meeting laws. I am filing a violation notice with the Mississippi Ethics Commission. Let's see where that goes.

I decided to look into the history of these two laws, and see if it had ever been an issue before. I knew that if it had ever become a question of law the Mississippi Attorney General's Office would most likely have issued an opinion on the law's validity, and they did. Here is what I found:

DOMICLE & ACTIVE MEMBERS

Office of the Attorney General
State of Mississippi

Opinion No. 93-0500
August 10, 1993

Re: Organizations that may sponsor Bingo

Senator Amy Tuck Powell
Mississippi State Senate
2004 Pin Oak Drive
Starkville, MS 39759

Dear Senator Powell:

Attorney General Mike Moore has received your request for an opinion and has assigned it to me for research and reply. Your letter asks:

According to the wording of the gaming laws regulating bingo, a member of the group in charge must be present at the bingo game. My question is since the "Very Special Arts" group has no organized membership, can they sponsor a bingo game?

In response I refer to Section 97-33-52 of the Mississippi Code which states that:

A bingo game may be conducted only:

(a) When held for the benefit of a charitable organization that (i) is licensed pursuant to Section 97-33-55 or Section 97-33-59; (ii) is ◆domiciled◆ in the State of Mississippi; and

(b) Except as otherwise provided in this section, the game is held by active members of such organization. (emphasis added)

You are correct in the assessment that this statute requires any bingo game to be held by an active member of the organization; therefore, by definition, a group that has no active members may not sponsor a bingo game.

Very truly yours,

Mike Moore
Attorney General
By: Mike Lanford
Special Assistant Attorney General

Go to: http://government.westlaw.com/msag/ and type in 93-0500 in the search block, then, click on the line that says: Senator Amy Tuck Powell (in blue).

All the while I was digging up my own information I was making every attempt to get information from the MGC lawyers through the Public Records Act. I was getting the runaround every time I tried.

I wanted to know if the agents had done their jobs in the background investigation, and brought these issues to the attention of the executive director. I wanted to see what THEIR recommendation was to the commission because I had been told by an informant that the director had either changed it, or forced others to change it, not citing the applicable laws. I said that specifically in my request, but the MGC lawyers sent me a copy of the minutes which only showed the director's recommendation to the commission and the commission's action. They knew that was not what I was asking for. There is no doubt in my mind the lawyers were not being forthcoming in sending me exactly what I asked for. This was my response to the lawyers over their legal games.

February 9, 2009

Mr. Louis Frascogna
Special Assistant Attorney General
Gaming Division
Post Office Box 23577
Jackson, MS 39225.3577

Re: Your letter of January 29, 2009 responding to request for public records

Dear Mr. Frascogna:

I have received your response referenced above and copies of documents you believe to be those requested in my public records request. However, there still seems to be confusion as to what records I am seeking since your response did not provide all those records.

Although I have not had the pleasure of working with you in the past, I have dealt with others in your office over a period of months. The request is the same. I am looking for specific recommendations FROM THE AGENTS/SUPERVISORS regarding applicants. I am not looking for the recommendation imprinted on the minutes that the Executive Director made to the Commission at its meetings. Please note in my request for records I specifically said, "ANY AND ALL RECOMMENDATIONS" (for the applicants specified).

In the event you don't understand the process, I will try to explain it. The applicant applies for a license. The agent conducts a background check. The agent completes his investigation and submits a RECOMMENDATION to his supervisor. His supervisor either accepts the recommendation and endorses it before sending it to the Executive Director or makes his own recommendation to include with the agent's initial recommendation which could override the agent recommendation. Nonetheless it is still a part of the investigation. NEVER GOT IT

Please reconsider my request as the one responded to does not meet my expectations and provide me specifically with what I am asking for. So far what you have provided is the Executive Director's recommendation to the Commission. That does not meet the request of ANY AND ALL which should include the agents' recommendations and supervisors at each step.

Lastly, will you confirm that the memo from Larry Gregory regarding Generus Stepping Stones' Waiver Request is the only issue the Commission considered to determine their eligibility for licensure and that there were no issues other than residency/3 year history? Thank you.

I never got the records I requested. I got a memo that Eddie Williams (assistant director) sent to Larry Gregory about the agency approval written a month after they were already licensed. I am convinced, without a doubt, they were covering up the fact that agents were making recommendations against licensure, specifically citing the violations found in the law, and the leadership was changing the law enforcement officers' investigative reports, and/or recommendations before they got to the commissioners.

Since Mike Lanford was the "go-to-guy" in the new attorney general administration, and since he was the author of the opinion written during Mike Moore's administration, I contacted him for help. After failing to respond for three weeks he told me essentially that the attorneys in the MGC were doing what they were supposed to, and the commission had not broken the law. I had provided him with all the copies of the materials regarding the charity organization in question, and <u>he disputed his own position detailed in his opinion to Amy Tuck</u>. The law has not changed at all in that regard, and still reads the same today. So tell me, how can that be? I got this record after the fact (which I believe was written after the fact) as a means of damage control. Someday, one of these three people may have to answer for that.

Jerry St. Pe'
Chairman

Howard Sanders
Commissioner

Nolen Canon
Commissioner

Larry Gregory
Executive Director

MISSISSIPPI GAMING COMMISSION
Post Office Box 23577
Jackson, Mississippi 39225-3577
(601) 576-3800

Memo

To: Larry Gregory

From: Eddie Williams

CC: Don Howarth

Date: 04/14/2005

Re: Generus Stepping Stones Inc.

Generus Stepping Stones Inc. received waiver of the requirement of a 3 year history of charitable activity from the Commission at the March 17, 2005 regular monthly meeting. The application has been reviewed and the charitable gaming division feels confident that all proceeds will go to the Flowood, MS based organization and none of the proceeds will benefit Senior Citizen Services Inc., located in Memphis, TN that will assist in the operation of the Bingo.

Notice in the body of the paragraph Williams says they waived the three year history requirement. But he also says the proceeds will go to their operation in Flowood, MS, and that the people from the location in Memphis will assist in the operation of the bingo. This is highly irregular, and as best I can tell from the many name changes, addresses changes, and change to being a charity under another charity in Memphis called Meritan, the Flowood operation was simply an office. Other halls have been denied licensure for the same issue. I believe this document was done after the fact. If my memory serves me correctly, the Prostate Foundation was sending money to Louisiana and the commission revoked their license.

The FBI is currently investigating corruption of this type as evidenced by the recent Alabama arrests. They conclude that they will continue these type operations in other states. One may already be in the works here, and we may not even know about it for a few years. A case of obstructing justice could develop just from FBI agents interviewing some people within the MGC.

The law enforcement officers there are good people, and I am convinced they wouldn't lie, if for no other reason than not wanting to go to jail for lying to the FBI. Even if it goes to civil court, I don't think they will lie under oath. If it does, I will personally provide the FBI with the transcript showing all testimony, and I will make sure all the right people receive a subpoena -- lawyers (who were both participants and witnesses), legislators and current and former employees included.

Anyway, I contacted Mike Lanford through e-mails, and documented our dialogue.

Please read my e-mails, and the responses below:

From: rickward47@hotmail.com
To: mlanf@ago.state.ms.us
Subject: OUR DISCUSSION THIS MORNING
Date: Mon, 9 Feb 2009 14:16:45 -0500

Mike:

Thanks for talking to me this morning. I don't believe your
lawyers are doing anything wrong intentionally. I do believe MGC has
ignored the law and I knowing that during my tenure at MGC
management/commissioners often ignored advice from your lawyers. I
don't believe your office should have legal experts embedded there

knowing these type violations are taking place and amplified by PEER and private citizens without action. Please review my attached PowerPoint.

Rick

>>> <rickward47@hotmail.com> 2/16/2009 9:41 AM >>>
Mike:

You know who I am. I am not some "nut case" that thinks he got abducted by aliens. I am a registered voter and concerned citizen, career law enforcement officer/military officer who gave over 30 years to public service. I have a valid complaint. Why ignore me?

I am amazed how politicians will bend over backwards up until the day before election to talk to anybody that might vote for them but the next day, their insulation package goes into effect. Then they get anybody on their staff they can to run interference for them and avoid controversial issues at all cost. Finally it gets to a point that the buffer personnel don't even get back to you.

I have provided you proof that the MGC has ignored the law on two specifications with one licensee. In addition your lawyers embedded in the MGC signed off on the process which in turn showed a total disregard for an Attorney General ruling that you wrote yourself.

I would like to know what you (Jim Hood) intend to do about this and what we can expect to occur with the license of the organization that appears should never have been issued.

Mike, I have the utmost respect for you and Jim Hood, considering what little I know about him. However, I am not going to let this issue fade away into the sunset. Like me or not, if you ask Mike Moore what my greatest trait was, he will most likely tell you, tenacious bulldog, not willing to let go of a bite when he gets it. I haven't changed and I am due a response. Thanks,

Rick Ward

Date: Tue, 17 Feb 2009 09:53:07 -0600
From: MLANF@ago.state.ms.us
To: rickward47@hotmail.com

Subject: RE: OUR DISCUSSION THIS MORNING

 I am not ignoring you. Yours is not the only issue I am dealing with
 right now. Will get back with you asap.

From: rickward47@hotmail.cTo: mlanf@ago.state.ms.us
Subject: RE: OUR DISCUSSION THIS MORNING
Date: Tue, 17 Feb 2009 11:54:17 -0500

Mike:

Thank you for the response and I apologize for that comment. I have just been so frustrated lately
with the things I have seen. My doorbell, phone and mail box was overloaded just before election
with politicians wanted me to help give them the job they wanted and I am just finding that not a
single one is willing to even talk to me now.

Very Respectfully,
Rick

From: rickward47@hotmail.com
To: mlanf@ago.state.ms.us
Subject: RE: OUR DISCUSSION THIS MORNING
Date: Tue, 10 Mar 2009 17:53:24 -0400

Mike:

Your below e-mail indicated you were not ignoring me. You also indicated you would get back
with me ASAP. However you wrote that on February 17, lacking one week being a month ago. It
is now March 10th and still no response. I sent you the information a month ago yesterday. I have
no doubt you are busy but I think this is a very important issue and I just feel like it needs more
attention than it is getting. Could you please update me?

Thanks,
Rick

>>> <rickward47@hotmail.com> 3/10/2009 5:20 PM >>>

Mike:

In addition to the other concerns I already addressed, I have been trying for months to get a public record from MGC. First I was required to tell them who the record was on before they would even tell me if it would be public or not. I continued to re-try and ended up filing a complaint with the Ethic's Commission, which like everything else led to nothing.

I gave in in January and told them specifically who I was interested in and told them specifically that I wanted ANY and ALL recommendations to include agent, supervisor, etc. All they provided me was the minutes with Executive Director's recommendation. I wrote them back a month ago explaining the response to the public records request was lacking the records I requested (please see attached letter). I have not even gotten a response.

Again, these lawyers work for the AG as you do. Why can't the public get what it asks for and why can't your office deal with these subordinate lawyers when they fail to provide the public what it is entitled to by law, but they give the gaming industry anything it wants?

Rick Ward

From: **MIKE LANFORD** (MLANF@ago.state.ms.us)
Sent: Wed 3/11/09 10:41 AM
To: rickward47@hotmail.com

Rick,

I have reviewed the matters presented in your prior emails within our office and with our staff attorneys assigned to represent the MGC, including the public records issues. As I am sure you understand, I am
not at liberty to divulge the details nor the general nature of the privileged advice given by our office to our client agency. I can tell you that I believe that we have given and continue to give sound legal counsel and representation to the MGC.

I realize you may differ and that you may desire to take some action. However, we think the MGC is complying with the law as it is currently written. I am sorry that I am not able to assist you further.

Sincerely,

Mike

From: rickward47@hotmail.com
To: mlanf@ago.state.ms.us

Subject: RE: OUR DISCUSSION THIS MORNING

Date: Wed, 11 Mar 2009 13:20:08 -0400

Mike:

I was speechless when I first read your e-mail and overlooked your
comment that I may not agree and may want to take some action. I can't
help but comment on how funny that is. No wonder people up north think
we don't wear shoes in this good ole boy network.

Action? What action? You mean file a complaint with the Ethic's
Commission where your bosses brother is in charge? Give me a break.
No state agency is going to entertain, much less take action. You guys
have it sewed up in the state system. I am just hoping Obama will
hurry up and install a democrat US Attorney to start looking into some
of this crap. I will be beating his door down on day one.

By the way, did you see in the news where the Alabama Attorney General
is being investigated by the US Attorney and FBI for ....guess
what? Corruption and protection of none other than the gaming industry....
specifically bingo halls. Imagine that.

Have a great day.
Rick

How could Mike say the MGC is acting in accordance with the law when they have totally ignored two statutory requirements in approving Generus Stepping Stones? In addition, they waived their own regulation (which they have the authority to do). In order to show this was not arbitrary and capricious, records (minutes) would have to indicate they waived one regulation, and decided not to abide by two laws in licensing any previous organization. The minutes did not indicate that, and the action had to be taken outside the public setting with a phony memo issued afterwards.

My source told me it was just another example of the MGC showing favoritism to some, including lawyers that represent the casinos' interests. I don't know Mr. Begley, who signed the corporate document, and appeared before the commission on their behalf, but I doubt seriously if he asked for any favoritism from the MGC because of his representation of casinos. They would have provided it whether it is asked for or not.

The other issue hasn't even been addressed. The official minutes address only the recommendation for licensure with a waiver of the three year history requirement. That means the two statutory laws were not even discussed in the public setting. Larry Gregory apparently made that decision himself as it said in the memo from Eddie Williams to him. However, that memo (as bogus as I think it is) was sent after the fact almost a month following the commission granting the license. There was no reason for him to discuss the application with Gregory after that. The license had already been issued. But Gregory and Williams knew of the two statutory requirements. Did they tell the commissioners, and if so, why wasn't it in the minutes?

Somebody other than "the one with an axe to grind" needs to ask this question, "How could that organization get that waiver?" Minute Records will show there are other organizations that only needed one waiver, and the commission disapproved them.

I hope you can see through this. Again, I would like to say that I am not just showing you evidence of my difficulties with these agencies for the sake of showing you my personal issues. These are not personal issues. They are very public, and affect each and every one of us as taxpayers. My primary reason for making this public is for you to see the uncaring, arrogant, and pompous attitudes our public officials, and public servants employed under those officials have towards us, who dare question their motives. We can, and should remember these people when we go to the polls. I have shown you attitudes and actions of both Democrat and Republican.

This is a nonpartisan analysis of our state. I have shown you issues with the public official heads of these agencies, their lawyers, the directors, and on down to the lowest worker bees. The public officials heading the agencies set the tone, whether they are members of the legislature, or publically elected (or appointed) to head their respective agencies. We cannot allow ourselves to become so dependent on the gaming industry that we have to ignore the laws they break. We don't do it with any other industry.

Chapter Ten

CAMPAIGN CONTRIBUTIONS AND LACK OF ENFORCEMENT

"Successful politicians are insecure and intimidated men. They advance politically only as they placate, appease, bribe, seduce, bamboozle or otherwise manage to manipulate the demanding and threatening elements in their constituencies."

Walter Lippmann

Did you know that it is **not** against the law in Mississippi for a member of the legislature to accept campaign funds from an industry he regulates? I mean a person who is responsible for oversight, and laws that regulate or cause enforcement, or no enforcement, of that industry? Of all the other laws, you would think we would have one for that. But legislators aren't going to pass any laws against themselves. If a politician is going to run for office he has to have money. He has to get that money somewhere and there are limitations. I can "almost" see a person not yet in office accepting money from an industry he might, as a part of his job, regulate in the future. However, for a sitting lawmaker to accept money from the industry he regulates raises serious questions, especially when that industry gets protection from the laws. But I have been told by the Mississippi Ethics Commission that it is not a violation of the ethics laws either. (Members of the legislature sit on the board of the Mississippi Ethics Commission that is headed by Attorney General Jim Hood's brother, and members of the legislature passed these ethics laws.)

State Senator Billy Hewes claimed Tate Reeves had done the same in a Sun Herald article by saying, Reeves had received money "from lawyers, consultants and bankers who make millions in fees from government borrowing."

However, Hewes has made no effort to my knowledge in cleaning off his own legislative door steps to stop people like Bobby Moak from doing the same thing. It seems that it is only when it affects Hewes personally, that it becomes an issue that shouldn't be done.

Here's my point, Representative Bobby Moak, Chairman of the Gaming Committee in the Mississippi Legislature, introduces laws that can help or hurt the industry. He can write a law that could cause them to be placed in jail or fined or even put out of business. He communicates with the MGC Director of an agency that has never arrested a single owner, operator, manager or supervisor of

125

a casino and writes revisions of the bingo laws that are in favor of the industry, not the enforcement agencies and rarely the charity. In fact nobody is ever arrested in the casinos even from the manager on down unless that person is committing a crime against the casino. No arrests occurred in the bingo division in at least eight years after I left and probably have not since then. I would file a public request for the 2009-2011 records, but the lawyers at the MGC would want me to hire a new part-time, temp employee for them to pull the records.

I am not suggesting that Mr. Moak has violated the law. However, we need to enact laws that prevent this appearance of impropriety. I have no problem with casinos making all the donations they want, to people that aren't involved in regulating them. The law (as it is) allows it. We are the problem for not demanding that they pass legislation against such activities.

The governor appointed three commissioners to oversee the action of the MGC on a monthly basis. I sent all of them most of this information in a Power Point brief almost three years ago. I am confident that they brief the governor from time to time on things going on, especially the chairman. So if they all have knowledge of it -- but not one has done a thing to see that arrests are made for violations of the law -- why are they continuing to ignore the law? Who is to blame here?

In the following pages you will find campaign contributions from numerous members of Harrah's Casino -- and occasional donations by other casinos -- or their senior employees. The last contributors on this list are John and Rene Grisham. Moak shows off his friendship with Grisham on one of his web sites and often makes it known publically. Grisham served in the legislature with him in the 80's and they have remained friends.

This is also a great argument for term limits. Longevity builds power, and history has shown us that power has a tendency to corrupt. This gentleman has been in the legislature for 27 years, and is now running for Speaker of the House to gain even more power. I am not saying he is corrupt. However, until we get our hands around matters like this, we will be viewed as falling for anything and everything. It is of the utmost importance that the legislature hold its members accountable through new laws just as they hold us accountable.

2007 ELECTION CYCLE
CPR – SS 07-01

CANDIDATE REPORT OF 2007
RECEIPTS AND DISBURSEMENTS

RECEIVED
ONLY

2007

Elections Division,
Secretary of State

Name of Candidate _Bobby Moak_

Address _P.C. Box 242 Bogue Chitto_ County _Lincoln_

Telephone (Work) _800 585 6244_ (Home) _____ (Fax) _601 734 2563_

Contact Name _Bobby Moak_ Email Address _bmoak@lache.tiner_

Office Sought _State Representative District 53_ Political Party _Democrat_

☐ Check here if above is different from previous report

TYPE OF REPORT
▪ CHECK THE CATEGORY OF REPORT YOU ARE SUBMITTING ▪

___ May 10, 2007	Periodic Report (January 1, 2007, through April 30, 2007)	....	Mandatory
✓ June 5, 2007	Periodic Report (May 1, 2007, through May 31, 2007)	....	Mandatory
___ July 10, 2007	Periodic Report (June 1, 2007, through June 30, 2007)	....	Mandatory
___ July 31, 2007	Pre Election Report (July 1, 2007, through July 28, 2007)	....	Primary Candidates
___ August 21, 2007	Pre Election Report (July 29, 2007, through August 18, 2007)	....	Runoff Candidates
___ October 10, 2007	Periodic Report (July 1, 2007 through September 30, 2007)	....	Mandatory
___ October 30, 2007	Pre-Election Report (October 1, 2007, through October 27, 2007)	....	Mandatory
___ November 13, 2007	Pre-Runoff Report (October 28, 2007, through November 10, 2007)	....	Runoff Candidates
___ January 10, 2008	Periodic Report (October 28, 2007, through December 31, 2007)	....	Mandatory
___ Termination Report (Candidate will no longer accept contributions or make campaign expenditures and has no outstanding campaign debt or obligations.)		Required to terminate reporting obligations	

IMPORTANT

(1) Periodic reports are mandatory, even if no contributions or expenditures have occurred. In such case, the candidate shall submit a report indicating "0" (zero) for total amount of reported contributions and expenditures during this period.

(2) Until a candidate files a termination report, annual and periodic reports must still be filed in accordance with Miss. Code Ann. § 23-15-807 (b) (3) and (5).

(3) The appropriate office must be in actual receipt of the required reports by 5:00 p.m. on the reporting day. If the deadline falls on a weekend or a holiday, the office must be in actual receipt of the required reports by 5:00 p.m. on the first working day before the deadline. Faxed reports are acceptable.

(4) Contributions in excess of $200 received after the reporting period but more than 48 hours before 12:01 a.m. on the day of the election must be reported by FAX or otherwise within 48 hours of the contribution. Use separate form "48 Hour Report" to report such activity.

REPORTED CONTRIBUTIONS AND DISBURSEMENTS

Page 2 of 4

Name of Candidate or Committee _____ mark _____

Reporting period _____ through _____

ITEMIZED RECEIPTS

A. Source: ☐ Corporation ☐ PAC ☐ Individual ☐ Loan ☐ Other (please specify)_____	Date (Mo., Day, Year)	Amount of each receipt this period
Full name Southern Farm Bureau Life Ins Co	__/__/__	$ 500 00
Mailing Address	__/__/__	$
City, State, Zip Code Jackson, Ms	__/__/__	$
Name of Employer (Required)	__/__/__	$
Occupation (Required)	Aggregate year-to-date	$ 500 00

B. Source: ☐ Corporation ☐ PAC ☐ Individual ☐ Loan ☐ Other (please specify)_____	Date (Mo., Day, Year)	Amount of each receipt this period
Full name LuAnn Pappas	__/__/__	$ 1,000 00
Mailing Address	__/__/__	$
City, State, Zip Code Mays Landing, N.J.	__/__/__	$
Name of Employer (Required) Harrahs	__/__/__	$
Occupation (Required) Marketing Director	Aggregate year-to-date	$ 1,000 00

☐ Other (please specify)	Date (Mo., Day, Year)	receipt this period
Full name Frederick and Karen Sock	__/__/__	$ 1,000 00
Mailing Address	__/__/__	$
City, State, Zip Code Biloxi, Ms	__/__/__	$
Name of Employer (Required) Executive VP and Manager	__/__/__	$
Occupation (Required) Harrahs	Aggregate year-to-date	$ 1,000 00

☐ Other (please specify)_____	Date (Mo., Day, Year)	receipt this period
Full name Non-reportable	__/__/__	$ 600 00
Mailing Address	__/__/__	$
City, State, Zip Code	__/__/__	$
Name of Employer (Required)	__/__/__	$
Occupation (Required)	Aggregate year-to-date	$ 600 00

Name of Candidate or Committee _____ monk _____   Page __3__ of __4__

Reporting period _____ through _____

ITEMIZED RECEIPTS

A. Source: ☐ Corporation ☐ PAC ☐ Individual ☐ Loan ☐ Other (please specify)	Date (Mo., Day, Year)	Amount of each receipt this period
Gary Loveman / Kathleen Welsh	__/__/__	$ 3,000 00
Mailing Address	__/__/__	$
City, State, Zip Code	__/__/__	$
Name of Employer (Required) Harrahs	__/__/__	$
Occupation (Required) CEO	Aggregate year-to-date	$ 3,000 00

B. Source: ☐ Corporation ☐ PAC ☐ Individual ☐ Loan ☐ Other (please specify)	Date (Mo., Day, Year)	Amount of each receipt this period
Silver Slipper Casino Venture	__/__/__	1,000 00
Mailing Address	__/__/__	$
City, State, Zip Code Bay St Louis ms	__/__/__	$
Name of Employer (Required)	__/__/__	$
Occupation (Required)	Aggregate year-to-date	$ 1,000 00

C. Source: ☐ Corporation ☐ PAC ☐ Individual ☐ Loan ☐ Other (please specify)	Date (Mo., Day, Year)	Amount of each receipt this period
Full name Zeneca Services	__/__/__	$ 500 00
Mailing Address	__/__/__	$
City, State, Zip Code Wilmington, DC	__/__/__	$
Name of Employer (Required)	__/__/__	$
Occupation (Required)	Aggregate year-to-date	$ 500 00

D. Source: ☑ Corporation ☐ PAC ☐ Individual ☐ Loan ☐ Other (please specify)	Date (Mo., Day, Year)	Amount of each receipt this period
Full name Coca Cola Bottling Co	__/__/__	$ 300 00
Mailing Address	__/__/__	$
City, State, Zip Code Jackson, ms	__/__/__	$
Name of Employer (Required)	__/__/__	$
Occupation (Required)	Aggregate year-to-date	$ 300 00

07-02-2007 02:42PM FROM-   T-248 P 002/007 F-487

Page _____ of _____

Name of Candidate or Committee _____

Reporting period _____ through _____

ITEMIZED RECEIPTS

A. Source: ☑ Corporation ☐ PAC ☐ Individual ☐ Loan

	Date	Amount of each receipt this period
Full name *Ameristar*	__/__/__	$ 1,000 ⁰⁰
Mailing Address	__/__/__	$
City, State, Zip Code *Las Vegas, NV*	__/__/__	$
Name of Employer (Required)	__/__/__	$
Occupation (Required)	Aggregate year-to-date	$ 1,000 ⁰⁰

B. Source: ☐ Corporation ☐ PAC ☐ Individual ☐ Loan

☐ Other (please specify) _____

	Date (Mo., Day, Year)	Amount of each receipt this period
Full name *Non-Reputable*	__/__/__	$ 525 ⁰⁰
Mailing Address	__/__/__	$
City, State, Zip Code	__/__/__	$
Name of Employer (Required)	__/__/__	$
Occupation (Required)	Aggregate year-to-date	$

C. Source: ☐ Corporation ☑ PAC ☐ Individual ☐ Loan

☐ Other (please specify) _____

	Date (Mo., Day, Year)	Amount of each receipt this period
Full name *MS Dental PAC*	__/__/__	$ 1,000 ⁰⁰
Mailing Address	__/__/__	$
City, State, Zip Code *Jackson, MS*	__/__/__	$
Name of Employer (Required)	__/__/__	$
Occupation (Required)	Aggregate year-to-date	$ 1,000 ⁰⁰

D. Source: ☐ Corporation ☐ PAC ☐ Individual ☐ Loan

☐ Other (please specify) _____

	Date (Mo., Day, Year)	Amount of each receipt this period
Full name	__/__/__	$
Mailing Address	__/__/__	$
City, State, Zip Code	__/__/__	$
Name of Employer (Required)	__/__/__	$
Occupation (Required)	Aggregate year-to-date	$

ITEMIZED RECEIPTS

Name of Candidate or Committee _____

Reporting period_____ through _____

Page _____ of _____

A. Source: ☐ Corporation ☐ PAC ☑ Individual ☐ Loan
☐ Other (please specify)_____

	Date (Mo., Day, Year)	Amount of each receipt this period
Full name Jonathan / Lexi Halkyard	__/__/__	$ 1,000.00
Mailing Address	__/__/__	$
City, State, Zip Code Las Vegas, NV	__/__/__	$
Name of Employer (Required) Harrah's	__/__/__	$
Occupation (Required)	Aggregate year-to-date	$ 1,000.00

B. Source: ☐ Corporation ☐ PAC ☑ Individual ☐ Loan
☐ Other (please specify)_____

	Date (Mo., Day, Year)	Amount of each receipt this period
Full name Mary and Jeff Thoma	__/__/__	$ 750.00
Mailing Address	__/__/__	$
City, State, Zip Code Las Vegas, NV	__/__/__	$
Name of Employer (Required) Harrah's	__/__/__	$
Occupation (Required)	Aggregate year-to-date	$ 750.00

C. Source: ☐ Corporation ☐ PAC ☑ Individual ☐ Loan
☐ Other (please specify)_____

	Date (Mo., Day, Year)	Amount of each receipt this period
Full name Michael Silberling (Catherine)	__/__/__	$ 750.00
Mailing Address	__/__/__	$
City, State, Zip Code Omaha, NE	__/__/__	$
Name of Employer (Required) Harrah's	__/__/__	$
Occupation (Required)	Aggregate year-to-date	$ 750.00

D. Source: ☐ Corporation ☐ PAC ☑ Individual ☐ Loan
☐ Other (please specify)_____

	Date (Mo., Day, Year)	Amount of each receipt this period
Full name Marily G. Wian	__/__/__	$ 500.00
Mailing Address	__/__/__	$
City, State, Zip Code Las Vegas, NV	__/__/__	$
Name of Employer (Required) Harrah's	__/__/__	$
Occupation (Required)	Aggregate year-to-date	$ 500.00

Page _____ of _____

Name of Candidate or Committee _____

Reporting period _____ through _____

ITEMIZED RECEIPTS

	Date (Mo., Day, Year)	Amount of each receipt this period
A. Source: ☐ Corporation ☑ PAC ☐ Individual ☐ Loan ☐ Other (please specify) ____	__/__/__	$ 300.00
Full name ms Malt Beverage	__/__/__	$
Mailing Address		
City, State, Zip Code Jackson, ms	__/__/__	$
Name of Employer (Required)	__/__/__	$
Occupation (Required)	Aggregate year-to-date	$ 300.00
B. Source: ☐ Corporation ☐ PAC ☐ Individual ☐ Loan ☐ Other (please specify) ____	Date (Mo., Day, Year)	Amount of each receipt this period
Full name ms Petroleum Marketers & Convenience Stores	__/__/__	$ 300.00
Mailing Address	__/__/__	$
City, State, Zip Code Jackson, ms	__/__/__	$
Name of Employer (Required)	__/__/__	$
Occupation (Required)	Aggregate year-to-date	$ 300.00
C. Source: ☐ Corporation ☑ PAC ☐ Individual ☐ Loan ☐ Other (please specify) ____	Date (Mo., Day, Year)	Amount of each receipt this period
Full name Baker Donelson PAC	__/__/__	$ 1,000.00
Mailing Address	__/__/__	$
City, State, Zip Code Jackson, ms	__/__/__	$
Name of Employer (Required)	__/__/__	$
Occupation (Required)	Aggregate year-to-date	$ 1,000.00
D. Source: ☑ Corporation ☐ PAC ☐ Individual ☐ Loan ☐ Other (please specify) ____	Date (Mo., Day, Year)	Amount of each receipt this period
Full name Ameristar Vicksburg	__/__/__	$ 1,000.00
Mailing Address	__/__/__	$
City, State, Zip Code Vicksburg, ms	__/__/__	$
Name of Employer (Required)	__/__/__	$
Occupation (Required)	Aggregate year-to-date	$ 1,000.00

Page _____ of _____

Name of Candidate or Committee _____

Reporting period _____ through _____

ITEMIZED RECEIPTS

A. Source: ☐ Corporation ☒ PAC ☐ Individual ☐ Loan	Date (Mo., Day, Year)	Amount of each receipt this period
☐ Other (please specify) _____		
Full name _MS Bankers Assoc_	__/__/__	$ 1,000 00
Mailing Address	__/__/__	$
City, State, Zip Code _Jackson, MS_	__/__/__	$
Name of Employer (Required)	__/__/__	$
Occupation (Required)	Aggregate year-to-date	$ 1,000 00

B. Source: ☐ Corporation ☐ PAC ☒ Individual ☐ Loan	Date (Mo., Day, Year)	Amount of each receipt this period
☐ Other (please specify) _____		
John & Roochelle Payne	__/__/__	$ 3,000 00
Mailing Address	__/__/__	$
City, State, Zip Code _New Orleans, LA_	__/__/__	$
Name of Employer (Required) _Harrahs_	__/__/__	$
Occupation (Required) _Regional VP_	Aggregate year-to-date	$ 3,000 00

C. Source: ☐ Corporation ☐ PAC ☒ Individual ☐ Loan	Date (Mo., Day, Year)	Amount of each receipt this period
☐ Other (please specify) _____		
Full name _Sherri Pucci_	__/__/__	$ 500 00
Mailing Address	__/__/__	$
City, State, Zip Code _Memphis, TN_	__/__/__	$
Name of Employer (Required) _Harrahs_	__/__/__	$
Occupation (Required) _General Manager_	Aggregate year-to-date	$ 500 00

D. Source: ☐ Corporation ☐ PAC ☒ Individual ☐ Loan	Date (Mo., Day, Year)	Amount of each receipt this period
☐ Other (please specify) _____		
Full name _Charles Atwood_	__/__/__	$ 2,000 00
Mailing Address	__/__/__	$
City, State, Zip Code _Las Vegas, NV_	__/__/__	$
Name of Employer (Required) _Harrahs_	__/__/__	$
Occupation (Required) _Board Vice Chairman_	Aggregate year-to-date	$ 2,000 00

Page _____ of _____

Name of Candidate or Committee _____

Reporting period _____ through _____

ITEMIZED RECEIPTS

A. Source: ☐ Corporation ☑ PAC ☐ Individual ☐ Loan ☐ Other (please specify) ____	Date (Mo., Day, Year)	Amount of each receipt this period
Full name: ms Cable Telecommunter	__/__/__	$ 500.00
Mailing Address:	__/__/__	$
City, State, Zip Code: Jackson, ms	__/__/__	$
Name of Employer (Required):	__/__/__	$
Occupation (Required):	Aggregate year-to-date	$ 500.00

B. Source: ☐ Corporation ☑ PAC ☐ Individual ☐ Loan ☐ Other (please specify) ____	Date (Mo., Day, Year)	Amount of each receipt this period
Full name: Tyson	__/__/__	$ 500.00
Mailing Address:	__/__/__	$
City, State, Zip Code: Springdale AK	__/__/__	$
Name of Employer (Required):	__/__/__	$
Occupation (Required):	Aggregate year-to-date	$ 500.00

C. Source: ☑ Corporation ☐ PAC ☐ Individual ☐ Loan ☐ Other (please specify) ____	Date (Mo., Day, Year)	Amount of each receipt this period
Full name: Isle of Capri	__/__/__	$ 1,000.00
Mailing Address:	__/__/__	$
City, State, Zip Code: St Louis, mo	__/__/__	$
Name of Employer (Required):	__/__/__	$
Occupation (Required):	Aggregate year-to-date	$ 1,000.00

D. Source: ☐ Corporation ☐ PAC ☐ Individual ☐ Loan ☐ Other (please specify) ____	Date (Mo., Day, Year)	Amount of each receipt this period
Full name: Gulf States Toyota	__/__/__	$ 1,000.00
Mailing Address:	__/__/__	$
City, State, Zip Code: Houston, TX	__/__/__	$
Name of Employer (Required):	__/__/__	$
Occupation (Required):	Aggregate year-to-date	$ 1,000.00

ITEMIZED RECEIPTS

Name of Candidate or Committee _____

Reporting period _____ _____ through _____ _____

Page _____ of _____

A. Source: ☐ Corporation ☑ PAC ☐ Individual ☐ Loan ☐ Other (please specify)	Date (Mo., Day, Year)	Amount of each receipt this period
Full name: Electric Power Associations	__/__/__	$ 1,000 00
Mailing Address	__/__/__	$
City, State, Zip Code: Jackson, MS	__/__/__	$
Name of Employer (Required)	__/__/__	$
Occupation (Required)	Aggregate year-to-date	$ 1,000 00

B. Source: ☑ Corporation ☐ PAC ☐ Individual ☐ Loan ☐ Other (please specify)	Date (Mo., Day, Year)	Amount of each receipt this period
Full name: Penn National	__/__/__	$ 1,000 00
Mailing Address	__/__/__	$
City, State, Zip Code: Wyomissing, PA	__/__/__	$
Name of Employer (Required)	__/__/__	$
Occupation (Required)	Aggregate year-to-date	$ 1,000 00

C. Source: ☐ Corporation ☑ PAC ☐ Individual ☐ Loan ☐ Other (please specify)	Date (Mo., Day, Year)	Amount of each receipt this period
Full name: MS Realtors	__/__/__	$ 1,000 00
Mailing Address	__/__/__	$
City, State, Zip Code: Jackson, MS	__/__/__	$
Name of Employer (Required)	__/__/__	$
Occupation (Required)	Aggregate year-to-date	$ 1,000 00

D. Source: ☑ Corporation ☐ PAC ☐ Individual ☐ Loan ☐ Other (please specify)	Date (Mo., Day, Year)	Amount of each receipt this period
Full name: Beau Rivage	__/__/__	$ 1,000 00
Mailing Address	__/__/__	$
City, State, Zip Code: Biloxi, MS	__/__/__	$
Name of Employer (Required)	__/__/__	$
Occupation (Required)	Aggregate year-to-date	$ 1,000 00

Page _____ of _____

Name of Candidate or Committee _____

Reporting period _____ through _____

ITEMIZED RECEIPTS

A. Source: ☐ Corporation ☒ PAC ☐ Individual ☐ Loan ☐ Other (please specify)	Date (Mo., Day, Year)	Amount of each receipt this period
Full name: Mss Railroad Assoc	10/16/07	$ 500.00
Mailing Address: P O Box 22524	__/__/__	$
City, State, Zip Code: Jackson, MS	~~10/16/07~~	$
Name of Employer (Required):	__/__/__	$
Occupation (Required):	Aggregate year-to-date	$ 500.00

B. Source: ☒ Corporation ☐ PAC ☐ Individual ☐ Loan ☐ Other (please specify)	Date (Mo., Day, Year)	Amount of each receipt this period
Full name: Danny Cupit P.C.	10/16/07	$ 500.00
Mailing Address: P.O. 22829	__/__/__	$
City, State, Zip Code: Jackson, MS	__/__/__	$
Name of Employer (Required):	__/__/__	$
Occupation (Required):	Aggregate year-to-date	$ 500.00

C. Source: ☐ Corporation ☒ PAC ☐ Individual ☐ Loan ☐ Other (please specify)	Date (Mo., Day, Year)	Amount of each receipt this period
Full name: EN PAC	10/16/02	$ 250.00
Mailing Address: P.O. 1640	__/__/__	$
City, State, Zip Code: Jackson, MS	__/__/__	$
Name of Employer (Required):	__/__/__	$
Occupation (Required):	Aggregate year-to-date	$ 250.00

D. Source: ☐ Corporation ☐ PAC ☐ Individual ☐ Loan ☐ Other (please specify)	Date (Mo., Day, Year)	Amount of each receipt this period
Full name: John & Renee Grisham	10/16/02	$ 10,000.00
Mailing Address:	__/__/__	$
City, State, Zip Code: Charlottesville, VA	__/__/__	$
Name of Employer (Required):	__/__/__	$
Occupation (Required):	Aggregate year-to-date	$ 10,000.00

Please notice on the cover page, that this report is only for one month (May 2007).

The bottom of the last campaign finance report is very interesting to me, although it is not illegal. I had just read John Grisham's book *The Appeal* when I sought these documents. He mentioned, as he often does in his books, small Mississippi towns. In this case it was Bogue Chitto, which happens to be his friend Mississippi Representative Bobby Moak's town of record. I thought it was ironic in Chapter 20 that Grisham, through one of his characters, explains to the reader how to circumvent campaign donation limitations. Granted this is fiction, but it just shows the irony of how these things can really happen.

In the passage I am speaking of, a group was having a discussion about raising money for a campaign. The leader of the group told his followers that he wanted them to raise $100 thousand. One of the members remarked that the limit was $5 thousand. The leader admonished him by calling him a "smart son-of-a-bitch". He then began to add up his family members, office workers, and pleased clients, calculating that he could raise a hundred grand by the end of the week. At the end of the book, John Grisham thanks, among others, his old legislative friend Bobby Moak for advice. I can't tell who is advising whom.

At any rate, going back to the campaign finance reports, look at the Harrah donations in particular. Corporations are limited to $1 thousand donations, but look how many of those came from different high level employees of the casinos -- not only in Mississippi, but Las Vegas and New Jersey as well. Do those donations show an appearance of impropriety, whether it exists or not? Would you want your representative to do that? Do you think we need laws to prevent that type activity?

Let's look at the gaming committee's members during the last election, and see who accepted campaign contributions from the gaming industry. All this money was received during 2007. A few months later Bobby Moak introduced a bill in an extraordinary session that could have brought casinos to other counties. The senate also introduced their version which was passed in both houses, but went into conference and failed. Every member of the Gaming Committee in the Mississippi Legislature that you see below voted "yea" on Moak's bill. What does that tell you? Each of them received money from the gaming industry, and, only a couple of months after the last campaign finance report was due in, the house introduced HB # 5 that was modified by the senate as SB 2199, and according to the legislative docket room and www.votesmart.org all of these active members of the gaming committee voted yea, on the bill favoring the industry.

Willie Bailey (D) House district 49; member of House Gaming Committee
07-12-07 $250.00 from Harrah's Casino

Mark Baker (R) House district 74; member of House Gaming Committee
06-15-07 $250.00 from Isle of Capri Casino
07-11-07 $250.00 from Harrah's Casino

James Evans (D) House district 70; member of House Gaming Committee
07-31-07 $250.00 from Harrah's Casino

03-21-07 $1,000.00 from Bobby Moak (D), gaming committee chairman, House district 53
06-0-07 $200.00 from Casino World

* Daniel (Danny) Guice (R) House district 114; member of House Gaming Committee
07-13-07 $250.00 from Harrah's Casino

John Hines (D) House district 50; member of House Gaming Committee
06-26-07 $250.00 from Isle of Capri Casino
07-19-07 $400.00 from Bobby Moak Campaign (House Gaming Committee chairman)
07-20-07 $500.00 from Harrah's Casino

*Michael Janus (R) House district 117; member of House Gaming Committee
05-14-07 $1,000.00 from Gulfside Casino Partnership
06-01-07 $500.00 from Isle of Capri Casino
07-03-07 $500.00 from Harrah's Casino

John Mayo (D) House district 25; member of House Gaming Committee
06-26-07 $500.00 from Isle of Capri Casino
06-28-07 $500.00 from Harrah's Casino

* No longer in House of Representatives

Bobby Moak (D) House district 53; Chairman of House Gaming Committee
01-17-07 $1,000.00 from Isle of Capri Casino
01-26-07 $500.00 from Torguson Gaming Group
02-01-07 $1,000.00 from Beau Rivage Casino
02-01-07 $2,500.00 from Beau Rivage Casino (in-kind contribution)
02-14-07 $1,000.00 from Treasure Bay Hotel & Casino
06-08-07 $1,000.00 from Silver Slipper Casino Venture
07-10-07 $2,000.00 from Ameristar Casino
07-10-07 $12,000.00 from Harrah's Casino employees
07-31-07 $4,500.00 from Harrah's Casino employees
10-10-07 $1,000.00 from Isle of Capri Casino
10-10-07 $1,000.00 from Beau Rivage Casino

What's wrong with this picture? It is not a violation of our campaign finance laws (that the legislators passed), nor is it a violation of our ethics laws (that the legislators also passed). It sounds like we need more issues on the ballot as a referendum. Our hands are almost completely tied in that respect too without a constitutional amendment. If you want more information on this subject, or to see a shocking Mississippi report card, go to:

http://www.citizensincharge.org

Look closely at the statistics, and laws related to Mississippi. More information on the bills presented following the gaming committee's campaign donations can be found in the following documents:

MISSISSIPPI LEGISLATURE   FIRST EXTRAORDINARY SESSION 2008

By: Representative Moak   To: Gaming

HOUSE BILL NO.   5

```
 1       AN ACT TO AMEND SECTION 19-3-79, MISSISSIPPI CODE OF 1972, TO
 2   PROVIDE THAT LEGAL GAMING MAY BE CONDUCTED IN COUNTIES IN WHICH IT
 3   IS BEING CONDUCTED ON THE EFFECTIVE DATE OF THIS ACT, AND IN
 4   COUNTIES IN WHICH A NOTICE OF INTENT TO APPLY FOR A GAMING LICENSE
 5   HAS BEEN FILED BEFORE THE EFFECTIVE DATE OF THIS ACT AND EITHER A
 6   RESOLUTION HAS BEEN ADOPTED BY THE COUNTY BOARD OF SUPERVISORS
 7   STATING THAT NO PETITION HAS BEEN FILED TO REQUIRE THE CALLING OF
 8   AN ELECTION ON LEGAL GAMING IN THE COUNTY, OR AN ELECTION HAS BEEN
 9   CONDUCTED PRIOR TO THE EFFECTIVE DATE OF THIS ACT AND A MAJORITY
10   OF THE VOTERS VOTED IN FAVOR OF CONDUCTING LEGAL GAMING IN THE
11   COUNTY; AND FOR RELATED PURPOSES.
```

Take notice that this bill was proposed in an extraordinary session that doesn't get much public attention. It is the only bill that Moak introduced in the 2008 extraordinary session, only a few months after he, and other members of the gaming committee, received thousands of dollars in donations from casinos. This bill would have streamlined the casinos' efforts. Please see the following senate version of the bill.

MISSISSIPPI LEGISLATURE
2008 Regular Session
To: Finance
By: Senator(s) Yancey, Burton, Fillingane, Jackson (15th), King, Nunnelee, Ward, Carmichael, Clarke, Flowers, Frazier, Gordon, Hudson, Kirby, Lee (35th), McDaniel, Mettetal

Senate Bill 2199

AN ACT TO AMEND SECTION 19-3-79, MISSISSIPPI CODE OF 1972, TO DESCRIBE THOSE SPECIFIC COUNTIES IN WHICH LEGAL GAMING MAY BE CONDUCTED AND TO LIMIT LEGAL GAMING TO THOSE DESCRIBED COUNTIES; TO CONFORM THE PROVISIONS OF THE SECTION TO THIS ACT'S LIMITATION ON ALLOWING LEGAL GAMING ONLY IN CERTAIN SPECIFIC COUNTIES, BY DELETING THE REQUIREMENT OF AN ELECTION ON THE QUESTION OF LEGAL GAMING IN A COUNTY; AND FOR RELATED PURPOSES.

Either I have this very special gift that lets me see something that doesn't pass the smell test above all others, or nobody else has ever been involved with this, and just doesn't know. Stevie Wonder could see what's happening in our state. People feel it doesn't have a direct impact on them so they don't worry about it, or don't know what to do. It DOES have an impact on you, and it may become apparent too late if you don't get involved. I want to reiterate what PEER pointed out in 2001:

Criminal Risks

- *increase in white collar and organized crime*--The cash-intensive casino environment is conducive to crimes such as embezzlement and money laundering.

- *cheating on the games*--The risk exists that both patrons and the casinos will cheat on the games.

I also want to bring back the below table previously used for bingo discussions so you can see the number of arrests by Mississippi Gaming Commision Casino divisions, and notice that they are all employees or patrons. The casino is always the victim, and never a suspect.

CASINO

ARRESTS	1993-1994	1995-1996	1997-1998	1999-2000	2001-2002	2003-2004	2005-2006	2007-2008	Totals
Management/Supervisors (None)	0	0	0	0	0	0	0	0	0
Patrons/Employees	29	46	55	66	71	69	50	33	419
TOTALS	29	46	55	66	71	69	50	33	**419**

In case you would like to pose some of these questions to other members of the gaming committee in the legislature, you will find all the names of current committee members in Appendix II, near the back of this book. As far as the bingo industry goes, absent enforcement, there is no telling how much cash money passes through political hands almost daily – cash money that we will never know about.

Chapter Eleven

THE MISSISSIPPPI LEGISLATURE

"In my experience, only third-rate intelligence is sent to the legislatures to make laws, because the first-rate article will not leave important private interests go unwatched to go and serve the public for a beggarly four or five dollars a day, and a mi"

Mark Twain

I have to start this chapter off by showing you the mentality of some of our legislators. They often waste their time on stupid bills, or bills that have been tried every year and failed. My favorite example of a stupid bill is one introduced by Representative Bobby Moak of Bogue Chitto, Mississippi. I laugh any time I think of the name of that town. It is obviously an Indian name but a friend of mine says it comes from an Indian word meaning, "Bogus Cheater".

I doubt that's true, but at any rate, Moak introduced a bill in 1998 that would have allowed a judge to order the removal of a body part of any person who violated any part of the Controlled Substances Act (with no distinction between a misdemeanor, or a felony). The proposed bill would have allowed the defendant to work it out with the judge which body part would be removed. I know you don't believe that, so I have included a copy of this bizarre bill for you from the Mississippi Legislature's website and I have included a link to the site itself:

http://billstatus.ls.state.ms.us/documents/1998/HB/0100-0199/HB0196IN.htm

I can just imagine what may have prompted this one.

MISSISSIPPI LEGISLATURE

1998 Regular Session

To: Judiciary A

By: Representative Moak

House Bill 196

AN ACT TO AUTHORIZE THE REMOVAL OF A BODY PART IN LIEU OF OTHER SENTENCES IMPOSED BY THE COURT FOR VIOLATIONS OF THE CONTROLLED SUBSTANCES LAW; AND FOR RELATED PURPOSES.

BE IT ENACTED BY THE LEGISLATURE OF THE STATE OF MISSISSIPPI:

<u>*SECTION 1.*</u> *In lieu of any other penalty prescribed by law, the court may allow any person who is convicted for a violation of the Controlled Substances Law to have a body part removed. The convicted person and the court must agree on which body part shall be removed.*

SECTION 2. This act shall take effect and be in force from and after July 1, 1998.

How could such a stupid bill even receive any consideration? I will just give you one example of how these things happen, and later you will see the sheer volume of bills that are proposed as compared to those passed. Then you might agree with this scenario. This is just an example but it is a fact that these type things happen. They have happened to me twice.

Let's say old man farmer, who has ten kids (all adult voters) and family all around him, has a field out on the back forty where he finds a trace of trespassers - - growing some kind of big old, tall weed he ain't never seen before. He calls the sheriff, who in turn calls the MBN and they put a deer-surveillance camera on a tree. They come back and get the camera a few days later and there on the pictures are some old boys he tells the MBN agents he ain't never seen before. One had a water bucket in his hand, and the other was picking buds off. They are arrested, but all get nothing but probation, no prison time, really pissing off the old farmer. He calls up his state representative, who tells him "We need a new law." The farmer says, *"Ya damned right we do, and it ought to call for them having to get their arms or legs cut off if they don't want to go to prison. Then, by Golly, they wouldn't be able to walk out into them fields or pick no buds, not to mention watering them plants. That would fix 'em."* The representative says, "Why Mr. Farmer that is a great idea. I'm gonna do that just for you. By the way, have you ever been to the Capitol Building? Come on up Tuesday, and I'll show you around, and buy you lunch. When we get done, I'll give you a sticker to put on your car and a sign to go in your yard."

So the old farmer goes away happier than a pig in slop thinking his legislator is the greatest thing since sliced bread, and all members of the other party are his enemies.

Here are two other laws that will show you the legislators' priorities:

§ 97-33-75. BINGO LAWS MISDEMEANOR VIOLATIONS

(1) Any person, association or corporation violating any provision of Sections 97-33-51 through 97-33-203 or any rule or regulation of the commission shall be subject to a fine imposed by the commission and to suspension or revocation of its license.

(2) Any person who commits any of the following acts, upon conviction, shall be fined not more than Five Thousand Dollars ($5,000.00) or imprisoned for one (1) year, or both:

(a) Making any false statement in any application for a license under Sections 97-33-51 through 97-33-203, or in any official report to the commission;

(b) Holding, operating or conducting any bingo game without a license;

(c) Knowingly falsifying or making any false entry in any books or records, with respect to any transaction connected with the holding, operating or conducting of any bingo game;

§ 49-7-21. GAME AND FISH VIOLATONS

License certificates; hunting, trapping or fishing without license prohibited; penalties:

(7) Any person who obtains a license under an assumed name or makes any materially false statement to obtain a license is guilty of a <u>FELONY</u> and shall be subject to a fine of Two Thousand Dollars ($2,000.00) or may be imprisoned for a term not to exceed one (1) year, or both. (According to the AG at the time, if it says it is a felony, it is indeed a felony.)

So you can live in Louisiana, give your friend's address in Jackson to catch a few fish, and you can be convicted of a felony. You can lie about past convictions for embezzlement or theft to obtain a bingo license, be trusted with millions of dollars per year (IN CASH), and only be convicted of a misdemeanor for lying under gaming laws. (That is, if they were to arrest you, which won't happen.)You might ask, "WHAT IS WRONG WITH THIS PICTURE????"

That addresses the legislature's priorities -- choosing between millions of dollars in theft from charities as opposed to catching a mess of fish. I have never heard anyone say the Mississippi Department of Wildlife and Fisheries (MDWF) does a poor job, unlike comments about the MGC. However, I am trying to show you which one is more important to the legislature. By the way, the legislature gave the MDWF a Commission with regulations just like the MGC but that hasn't stopped the MDWF from understanding they have both an enforcement and regulatory responsibility. They still enforce the law, unlike the MGC.

So let's move on now to other laws the legislature has passed outside the gaming laws that depict poor priorities, or self-serving. Here's one:

Mississippi Code, 23-15-811 provides penalties for violating the Election Code:
Any candidate or any other person who shall willfully and deliberately and substantially violate the provisions and prohibitions of this article shall be guilty of a <u>misdemeanor</u> and upon conviction therefore shall be punished by a fine in a sum not to exceed Three Thousand dollars ($3,000.00) or imprisoned for not longer than six months or by both fine and imprisonment.

So we know how much emphasis they put on themselves and their other political associates violating the election laws. Our next law provides for minor punishment in the event an elderly person in a care facility is abused, neglected or exploited, and attendants or other witnesses fail to report it.

43-47-7. Reporting abuse, neglect, or exploitation; establishment of central register; confidentiality.

(1) (a) Except as otherwise provided by Section 43-47-37 for vulnerable adults in care facilities any person including, but not limited to, the following, who knows or suspects that a vulnerable adult has been or is being abused, neglected or exploited shall immediately report such knowledge or suspicion to the Department of Human Services or to the county department of human services where the vulnerable adult is located. (Misdemeanor up to $5,000 fine and/or 6 months in county jail.)
(2)

What if it was your mother or father being abused? Would you feel a misdemeanor was good enough? Do you value them more than a mess of fish? How about if your daughter ended up in an illegally operating abortion clinic without your knowledge, run by butchers? How serious do you think the state might want to prosecute the owners of the illegally operating clinic?

41-75-26 Abortion Facility, operating without a license; penalty; injunctions
(1) Any person or persons or other entity or entities establishing, managing or operating an abortion facility or conducting the business of an abortion facility without the required license, or which otherwise violate any provision of this chapter regarding abortion facilities or the rules, regulations and standards promulgated in furtherance thereof shall be subject to revocation of the license of the abortion facility or non-licensure of the abortion facility.

If convicted, it would be a misdemeanor and if so, they could get a fine not to exceed $1,000, and no jail time. Are you happy about that?

Let's move away for a moment from health related issues to sports. You might conclude that this law is "way out in left field." Bribing someone to throw a game is a very serious charge that could get you a felony, and up to 5 years imprisonment, but only a $100 to $1,000 fine, but it is okay if you bribe a wrestler:

§ 97-29-17. Bribery; participant in professional or amateur games or other athletic contests; wrestling excepted.

(1) Whoever gives, promises, or offers to any professional or amateur baseball, football, basketball, or tennis player, or any player who participates in or expects to participate in any professional or amateur game or sport, or any person participating or expecting to participate in any other athletic contest or any coach, manager, or trainer of any team or participant or prospective participant in any such game, contest, or sport, anything of value with the intent to influence such participant to lose or try to lose or cause to be lost or to limit his or his team's margin of victory in any baseball, football, basketball or tennis game, boxing, or other athletic contest in which such player or participant is taking part or expects to take part or has any duty in connection therewith shall be guilty of a felony and upon conviction shall be punished by imprisonment in the county jail for not less than six (6) months nor more than five (5) years in the penitentiary, or by a fine

of not less than one hundred dollars ($100.00) nor more than one thousand dollars ($1,000.00), or by both such fine and imprisonment.

(2) Any professional or amateur baseball, football, basketball, or tennis player or any boxer or participant or prospective participant in any sport or game or a manager, coach, or trainer of any   team   or   individual   participant   or prospective participant in such game, contest, or sport who solicits or accepts anything of value to influence him to lose or try to lose or cause to be lost or to limit his or his team's margin of victory in any baseball, football, basketball, tennis or boxing contest or any other game or sport in which he is taking part or expects to take part or has any duties in connection therewith shall be guilty of a felony and upon conviction shall be punished by imprisonment in the county jail for not less than six (6) months nor more than five (5) years in the penitentiary, or by a fine of not less than one hundred dollars ($100.00) nor more than one thousand dollars ($1,000.00), or by both such fine and imprisonment.

Back to one more serious issue that rates only a misdemeanor charge for violations affecting the mentally retarded, thanks to our legislature. Do you agree with this one?

41-19-155 Penalties for serious violations at the South Mississippi Regional Center for the Mentally Retarded.

Any person who: (1) under the provisions of Sections 41-19-141 through 41-19-157 knowingly and unlawfully or improperly causes a person to be adjudged mentally retarded; (2) procures the escape of a legally committed resident or knowingly conceals an escaped legally committed resident of the center; or (3) unlawfully brings any firearm, deadly weapon or explosive into the center or its grounds or passes any thereof to a resident, employee or officer of the center is guilty of a misdemeanor and upon conviction shall be punished by a fine of not more than two hundred dollars ($200.00), imprisonment for not more than one (1) year, or both.

We have all seen jackasses in the legislature but "real" jackasses are not allowed near church grounds on Sunday. They made the law themselves, and regardless of how old it is, it still exists on the books. All they have to do is vote to repeal it if they want to get rid of it. How long do you think it has been since this has been a problem?

97-29-57 (A criminal statute)

A person shall not keep a stallion or jack nearer than one hundred yards to a church, or in public view in an enclosure bordering on a public highway, or nearer thereto, than one hundred yards; nor shall any person stand such animals in open view of any public place, or negligently keep such animal or suffer it to run at large. Any such offender, upon conviction, shall be fined not less than twenty-five dollars, and shall be liable for all damages done by such animals so kept or running at large.

For years we have seen the bill trying to get district attorney investigators the authority to make arrests, or carry weapons. (It finally passed in the 2011 session.) We see repeated tries regarding the law that would allow the running of radar by county sheriffs as it is done in Lowndes County. We often see that sheriff's departments need civil service job protection for their deputies. These bills never pass but they keep getting presented.

I have done my best to make a point as to the legislature's priorities. The problem is, you and I sit at home, and expect our legislators to go to Jackson once a year for three months to vote on repealing, passing, or revising current laws, and introducing or co-sponsoring new laws, whichever is in our best interest. However, it has been my experience, particularly in the bingo business, that they contact only the bingo operators, distributors, manufacturers, lobbyists, or MGC. You and I may never know about a proposed bill. By the time we discover it, the bill has already passed. Very few people have time to go and sit at the legislature during the sessions.

I remember when Trent Lott first got elected to congress. He would send out a pamphlet before the session and address the laws he would be voting on. He would seek every voter's opinion regarding that law before he voted on it. You still see that somewhat with members of congress on their websites, but I have never seen it in our legislature.

Each one of them has a state-provided web page on the legislative site. How hard would it be for them to list those laws they are proposing, or voting on, so we could see and provide them our input? If they haven't been in close contact with their constituents, they vote the way they want, or the way they have been influenced. We may suffer the end result.

The Mississippi Legislature is composed of two houses, the Senate and House of Representatives. Our Senate has 52 members, and the House of Representatives has 120 members for a total of 172, state-elected people to represent us on matters of the law.

California has only 120 members. It is the third largest state in the union, with 163,696 square miles, and represents almost 40 million people, compared to Mississippi, which represents less than three million people, and has only 48,430 square miles. Might you ask, "What's wrong with this picture?"

Mississippi pays its legislators $10 thousand a year (for three months work) and at least another $10 thousand in per diem for travel, lodging, and food expenses. They are also paid for mileage. That $10 thousand expense-account is broken down into $116 per day. I used a 90 day session for comparative purposes, although they are often called back for special sessions. In 2005 alone, we had five extraordinary sessions, all dealing mostly with budget issues or other financial woes. That wasn't even mentioned in the state of the state address by the governor. That wasn't mentioned because the reason for the financial woes, and need for budget changes, was what Hurricane Katrina did to the gaming industry on the coast. The state plays down the significance of the money coming from that industry as a means of protecting them from undue publicity. In reality, they know darn well the significance of that money, and how it impacts the budget. They don't want to have to raise taxes, or anger the gaming industry.

Assuming there are no extraordinary sessions called, the expense fringe alone costs Mississippi taxpayers $1,795,680 per year. They don't even have to account for the expenses in a detailed voucher like Arizona, Arkansas, Colorado, Florida, Idaho, Maryland, Massachusetts, Michigan, New Mexico, Nebraska, and Wyoming. New Mexico legislators receive no salary and are only paid their per diem rate but they, unlike Mississippi legislators, have to submit vouchers. By the way, Missouri verifies roll call before issuing per diem payments. Connecticut, New Hampshire, Rhode Island, New Jersey and Ohio give no per diem at all. With the exception of Ohio, these other states are so small the legislators can commute without incurring expenses on behalf of the state. Some of the larger states give less per diem to those who live within a certain number of miles of the capitol. This could be true also for the outlying counties near Jackson. Even in the federal system, per diem is not authorized inside a 50 mile radius.

Because of the lobbying efforts, and no limit on what they can spend on legislators to influence their votes, many legislators never have to spend the per diem money because the lobbyists foot the bill for food, drinks, and even huge banquet style dinners overflowing with the finest food available. Could that be why they don't have to fill out vouchers? If a lobbyist paid for the meal, they would be falsifying a report by claiming it themselves. Did you know the SOS laws have no limit on how much a lobbyist can spend on a member of the legislature to influence legislation? They only have to report it.

If you want to see that in action, all you have to do is go to one or two of the finest restaurants in Jackson, or one of the adjoining towns, during the session. That includes lunch, and dinner, and the bar. If you had gone to one of the restaurants on County Line Road during the last session, I am confident you could have taken a Senate/House roll call, and obtained a quorum. Another restaurant on the I-55 frontage road had so many members at the bar you would have had to push your way through a crowd with free-flowing liquor. Were the legislators paying it from their state per diem, which is paid by Mississippi taxpayers, who would frown on liquor if it had to be on a state voucher?

The legislature must have exempted themselves from detailed vouchers, because I have worked for three state agencies, and all of them required the submission of very detailed vouchers for reimbursement. We didn't get a set number of dollars, rather up to a certain amount, but we were paid only by providing a detailed list of the expenses we incurred. They could not claim those meals and drinks paid for by lobbyists if they were required to submit detailed vouchers.

Why is this, an issue? It is an issue because almost every year, the legislature and the governor complains about not having enough money to fund the state agencies -- usually based on the gaming industry having a bad year. Therefore, the agencies can expect to cut their budgets by five percent or more. Then the legislature can't come to any agreement, so they put the state budget near the end of the session so they may have to stay longer, or be called back at our expense.

Aside from reducing the number of our legislators to save money, cutting out per diem for those within 50 to 75 miles from the capitol is another widely accepted option used by many states. However additional funds could be saved if the state would use, whenever they could, teleconferencing. The State of Kentucky conducted a study into that subject in the late 1990s to early 2000s.

http://www.e-archives.ky.gov/pubs/LRC/rr287.pdf

The State of Alaska already uses it as described in the following article.

http://w3.legis.state.ak.us/laa/lio/lio.php

It is widely used in many states now in both criminal and civil court proceedings. Mississippi law already allows the use of teleconferencing for ANY public meeting as described herein. It just hasn't been used for legislative purposes, but could save a lot of money.

Mississippi Code Section 25-41-5. Official meetings of public bodies

(1) All official meetings of any public body, unless otherwise provided in this chapter or in the Constitutions of the United States of America or the State of Mississippi, are declared to be public meetings and shall be open to the public at all times unless declared an executive session as provided in Section 25-41-7.

(2) A public body may conduct any meeting through teleconference or video means. A quorum of a public body as prescribed by law may be at different locations for the purpose of conducting a meeting through teleconference or video means provided participation is available to the general public at one or more public locations specified in the public meeting notice. Read the full statute at:

http://www.ethics.state.ms.us/ethics/ethics.nsf/PageSection/A_meetings_meetings_law/$FILE/Open%20Meetings%20Act.htm?OpenElement

What about the quality of our legislators? We will later look at members of the Mississippi Legislature based on their individual performance, and the legislature as a whole.

The legislature is mostly made up of businessmen, including lawyers. Ask yourself this question. "How could a successful businessman leave his practice and family for at least three months out of the year for $10 thousand?" You might surmise that they aren't much of a businessman, or lawyer and have to supplement their income. If they are that unsuccessful in their full-time profession, how adequate are they as legislators? We will see when we examine their number of bills introduced as compared to their number of bills signed by the governor. Maybe there is another reason they want to be there.

On Wednesday, April 6, 2001, Salon.com said Barbour was basically the governor of a failed state and, "Mississippi leads the nation in almost everything that a state doesn't want to lead the nation in. Mississippi is the poorest state in the union, with the highest poverty rate and the lowest quality of life. And the state government is ineffective and oblivious when it isn't just plain corrupt."
That just about sums up our legislature and its leadership.

http://www.salon.com/news/haley_barbour/index.html

This is a must see video about legislators:

http://www.youtube.com/watch?v=pqhD4-5gYaw

Chapter Twelve

LEGISLATIVE REPORT CARDS

"Ninety percent of the politicians give the other ten percent a bad reputation."

Henry Kissinger

I spent many hours putting these charts together from material found on the Mississippi Legislature's website for the 2011 session. I have made every effort to ensure its accuracy. While I might have missed a number or gained a number here and there, I don't think there are any glaring errors, or errors that would make any significant difference in the outcome. I encourage you to look on the site yourself. If there are any errors, please notify me by e-mail at rickward.com, and I will make corrections for the next publication. I found errors on the site myself regarding Senator Willie Simmons, and notified the docket room.

http://billstatus.ls.state.ms.us/2011/pdf/s_auth.xml

I am not trying to say one person is bad or the other is good. You may think that a person who submits a large number of proposed bills is doing a good job. However, somebody else may not think so if that person is not very successful in getting those bills passed. I have tried to assemble this information in such a way that you can determine how the average legislator performs in a certain category and how another member compares to the average performer.

My methodology takes into consideration that our legislator's primary responsibilities, other than dealing with their constituents throughout the year, are to attend the sessions for the first three months of the year. During those three months, they should be proposing new legislation, voting on changes in current legislation, co-sponsoring legislation in support of their colleagues (with their constituents in mind), and repealing legislation that is no longer needed.

I am aware that in reality, much of this legislation is agreed on, or at least considered after hours in bars and restaurants with lobbyists who often prepare their intended legislation on behalf of the legislator concerned. You don't have to be a lawyer to be in the legislature, you just need insight as to what would make our society better. Our cup runneth over with lawyers and lobbyists as well as administrative staff that do much of that work.

Name	Dis	Years	D/R	Auth or	Passed	Percent	Co-Author	Passed	%	Average	Attaboy	Co-Attaboy
Sidney Albritton	40	7	R	42	5	12%	25	4	16%	14%	4	19
David Baria	46	3	D	45	1	2%	12	3	7%	5%	3	29
David Blount	29	3	D	25	4	16%	22	8	16%	16%	5	41
Terry Brown	17	7-S /12-H	R	12	1	8%	16	6	42%	25%	1	20
Nickey Browning	3	15	D	4	1	25%	13	7	54%	40%	4	19
Hob Bryan	7	27	D	8	2	25%	4	3	75%	50%	3	16
Terry Burton	31	19	R	36	6	17%	29	13	45%	31%	5	75
Albert Butler	36	??	D	3	0	0%	15	7	47%	24%	0	30
Kelvin Butler	38	7	D	18	1	6%	22	9	41%	24%	2	177
Videt Carmichael	33	11	R	29	12	41%	11	6	55%	48%	8	39
Lydia Chassaniol	14	4	R	6	0	0%	24	9	38%	19%	1	28
Eugene Clarke	22	7	R	22	1	5%	17	6	35%	20%	0	43
Nancy Collins	6	1	R	1	0	0%	13	6	46%	23%	0	15
Doug Davis	1	6	R	18	1	6%	11	5	45%	26%	5	50
Deborah Dawkins	48	11	D	26	0	0%	7	2	29%	15%	5	38
Bob M. Dearing	37	31	D	60	7	12%	44	17	39%	26%	12	86
Tommy Dickerson	43	11/Break /8	D	12	5	42%	13	3	23%	33%	3	21
Joey Fillingane	41	4-S /7-H	R	67	2	3%	22	8	36%	20%	1	135
Merle Flowers	19	7	R	17	2	12%	19	7	37%	25%	2	18
Hillman Frazier	27	8-S/H-13	D	7	0	0%	15	5	33%	17%	4	89
Tommy Gollott	50	31-S/12-H	R	7	2	29%	18	10	56%	43%	2	21
Jack Gordon	8	27-S/12-H	D	8	2	25%	8	5	63%	44%	0	19
Alice V. Harden	28	23	D	57	2	4%	20	7	35%	20%	8	32

Billy Hewes	49	19	R	36	6	17%	14	4	29%	23%	18	29
W. Briggs Hopson, III	23	3	R	20	6	30%	11	5	45%	23%	1	42
John Horhn	26	18	D	30	3	10%	13	2	15%	13%	15	29
Billy Hudson	45	3	R	10	1	10%	24	11	46%	28%	2	18
Cindy Hyde-Smith	39	11	R	17	5	29%	13	8	62%	46%	6	44
Gary Jackson	15	7	R	9	3	33%	23	8	35%	34%	1	31
Robert L. Jackson	11	7	D	22	1	5%	27	8	30%	18%	10	103
Sampson Jackson II	32	19	D	24	1	4%	20	9	45%	25%	2	175
Kenneth Jones	21	3	D	5	0	0%	17	4	24%	12%	2	46
David Jordan	24	8	D	14	1	7%	27	8	30%	19%	2	38
Tom King	44	11-S/6-H	R	21	5	24%	19	9	47%	36%	4	36
Dean Kirby	30	19	R	40	13	33%	9	2	22%	28%	6	32
Ezell Lee	47	19-S/4-H	D	7	1	14%	12	6	50%	32%	2	23
Perry Lee	35	7	R	14	7	50%	38	7	18%	34%	4	61
Chris McDaniel	42	3	R	22	2	9%	32	11	34%	22%	6	37
Nolan Mettetal	10	15	R	19	0	0%	16	8	50%	25%	2	22
J. Walter Michel	25	12-S/4-H	R	16	1	6%	8	2	25%	16%	8	31
Tommy Moffatt	52	15	R	9	3	33%	13	5	38%	36%	1	33
Haskins Montgomery	34	3	D	2	2	100%	23	8	35%	68%	1	61
Eric Powell	4	3	D	22	1	5%	20	6	30%	18%	10	28
Derrick T. Simmons	12	1	D	0	0	0%	0	0	0%	0%	0	0
Willie Simmons	13	18	D	0	0	0%	0	0	0%	0%	0	15
Bill Stone	2	3	D	22	2	9%	15	8	53%	31%	10	56
Gray Tollison	9	15	D	51	8	16%	10	2	20%	18%	7	22
Bennie Turner	16	18	D	8	2	25%	7	4	57%	41%	0	36
Giles Ward	18	3	R	19	2	11%	24	9	38%	25%	6	39
Michael Watson	51	3	R	40	3	8%	37	8	22%	15%	4	59
JP Wilemon, Jr.	5	??	D	16	2	13%	19	12	63%	12%	2	36
Lee Yancey	20	3	R	25	1	4%	26	5	19%	12%	2	30
Totals Averages Effectiveness				1070 17%	139		917 51%	335		1318 25%	212 4	2272 52

My personal view is that we can look at these charts and determine how aggressive a member of the legislature is by how many bills they propose. We can evaluate their success rate to tell how worthy the legislation is by how many of those proposed bills get passed. We can gain some insight into whether or not they are a leader or a follower by comparing the number of bills they present themselves to the number of bills they co-sponsor.

By the same token, we can gain insight as to how good of a negotiator they are by the success shown in the number of co-sponsored bills that are passed. We could look at the number of "attaboys" they sponsor to see how well they are recognizing accomplishments within their districts. We can compare those numbers with the number of "attaboys" co-sponsored to see how much they want to please other members of the legislature. I make one exception to that argument, and that is the "attaboys" that are given posthumously, usually for our military personnel who have lost their lives in the line of duty. All of them deserve recognition, even though some politicians will gain political mileage from it. Using this information, we could establish a set of metrics to track progress of each senator. The areas of measurement could be:

- Production (how many bills they produce/propose)
- Success (how many bills they either propose or co-sponsor get passed)
- Leadership (how many bills they propose, compared to following the leader by co-sponsoring)
- Negotiation Skills (how many instances of getting colleagues to join them in co-sponsoring bills)
- Constituent Relationship (# commendations/resolutions they propose for constituents)
- Colleague Relationship (# commendations/resolutions they join their colleagues on)

The number of bills proposed, by person, was from 0 to 60. The number of co-sponsored bills by one person was as high as 126. The number of proposed "attaboys" went from 0 sponsored to 175 in the co-sponsored category. The charts show each member's own personal performance by looking at three primary areas:

a. The number of bills they proposed to include their success rate measured in percentile.
b. The number of bills they co-sponsored, including success rate measured in percentile.
c. How many "attaboys" they proposed, compared to how many they co-sponsored.

These charts allow you to draw your own conclusion, but let me tell you how to base your measurements as I did. By adding the total number of bills proposed by all members of the senate, (1,072) for example, we have a number divisible by the total number of senators (52).The answer is rounded up to 21 which is the average number of bills proposed by each senator -- knowing that some present far more and others present far less -- but this gives us a starting point to measure their performance.

From that 1,072, only 139 of those were passed which give us an average of their success rate by dividing 52 into 139. That answer is rounded up to three. So the average senator introduces 21 bills and only three of them are passed. I chose that number as the benchmark and anyone who introduced at least 21 bills with a minimum passage rate of three became the standard to measure their place on the chart as compared to their colleagues. I did exactly the same thing with co-sponsored bills. I omitted "attaboys" and appropriations bills, which are for the most part "rubber stamped."

At the end of my calculations, I determined the following Senators to be above average in both numerical performance and success rate on bills they proposed. They are listed in order by the percentage points depicting their success:

NAME	# PROPOSED	# PASSED	SUCCESS RATE
Carmichael	29	12	41%
Kirby	40	13	33%
Burton	36	06	17%
Hewes	36	06	17%
Blount	25	04	16%
Dearing	60	07	12%
Albritton	42	05	12%
Horhn	30	03	10%

The top performers who proposed successful legislation.

If you concur with this methodology, those eight people are the only ones of 52 that perform in the above average category for successfully getting their bills passed. They range from 10 to 41 percent effective. Although these are very good compared to the others, none of them would make it in a job that requires production level performance, using this methodology to measure their performance/success level on bills introduced. Would you employ someone who is only 41 percent effective? How about ten percent?

Now we will look at the top performers that were able to co-sponsor bills, and assist in their passage. There were 22 above the benchmark. That is almost three times as many who were above average on bill proposals. There were 917 instances of co-sponsoring with 335 bills successfully passed. The benchmark for co-sponsoring is rounded up to 18 with a passage score rounded down to six.

NAME	# PROPOSED	# PASSED	SUCCESS RATE
Wilemon	19	12	63%
Gollott	18	10	56%
King	19	09	47%
Hudson	24	11	46%
Burton	29	13	45%
Jackson, S.	20	09	45%
Butler, K.	22	09	41%
Dearing	44	17	39%
Chassaniol	24	09	38%
Ward	24	09	38%
Flowers	19	07	37%
Fillingane	22	08	36%
Montgomery	23	08	35%
Jackson, G.	23	08	35%
Hardin	20	07	35%
McDaniel	32	11	34%
Jackson, R.	27	08	30%
Jordan	27	08	30%
Powell	20	06	30%
Watson	37	08	22%
Lee, P.	38	07	18%
Blount	22	08	16%

The top performers who co-sponsored successful legislation.

These columns depict those people with the highest average percentile scores that combine both successful proposed legislation and successful co-sponsored legislation. The benchmark average is 25%, therefore 25 of 52 scored above average when combining the two scores on bills introduced and bills cosponsored (successfully).

NAME	AVERAGE PERCENTILE
Montgomery	68
Bryan	50
Hyde-Smith	46
Carmichael	48
Gordon	44
Gollott	43
Turner	41
Browning	40
King	36
Moffatt	36
Jackson, G.	34
Lee, P.	34
Dickerson	33
Lee, E.	32
Burton	31
Stone	31
Kirby	28
Hudson	28
Davis	26
Dearing	26
Brown	25
Flowers	25
Jackson, S	25
Mettetal	25
Ward	25

The top performers with combined scores to average successful legislation.

The next columns will describe those legislators who proposed "attaboys". The average number which becomes our benchmark is four. There were a total of 22 who scored above average. In the event of a tie, they were listed in alphabetical order. Some people may interpret these results on a positive note, while others may think the legislature is spending too much time patting people on the back when they should be passing significant legislation. That is just a matter of personal opinion and I can see how an argument could be made for either case.

NAME	NUMBER
Hewes	18
Horhn	15
Dearing	12
Jackson, R.	10
Powell	10
Stone	10
Michell	08
Tollison	07
Hyde-Smith	06
Kirby	06
McDaniel	06
Blount	05
Burton	05
Carmichael	05
Davis	05
Dawkins	05
Albritton	04
Browning	04
King	04
Lee, P.	04
Watson	04

Senators who proposed an above average number of "Attaboys".

The next columns will describe those legislators who co-sponsored "attaboys". The average number which becomes our benchmark is 44.

NAME	NUMBER
Butler, K.	177
Jackson, S.	175
Jackson, R.	103
Fraizer	089
Dearing	086
Burton	075
Lee, P.	061
Montgomery	061
Watson	059
Stone	056
Davis	050
Jones	046
Hyde-Smith	044

Senators who co-sponsored an above average number of "Attaboys".

The only Senator to score above average in all categories was Terry Burton.

Have you ever been in a group and tried to get each member of the group to agree on one thing? It could be something as simple as what toppings to put on a pizza you are ordering over the phone. If there are only two people ordering, it may be a fairly easy solution. However, if there are six people having pizza, one person may want pepperoni, another may want Italian sausage, and yet another may want ground beef. The more parties in the argument, the harder it is to reach a consensus. Obviously at some point you have to compromise or throw the idea out altogether and order hamburgers instead of pizza, or go without eating.

The same is true for the size of our legislature. I repeat a previous observation which is a good reason we need to downsize our legislature. It could, in turn make it easier to reach a consensus with less people arguing over the pizza. Again, we have 52 senators and 120 representatives for a total of 172. California has only 120 members altogether. It is the third largest state in the union, with

163,696 square miles, and represents almost 40 million people, compared to Mississippi, which represents less than three million people, and has only 48,430 square miles. Might you ask, "What's wrong with this picture?"

The bottom line (literally) on the chart is the fact that when an individual senator proposes a bill, not knowing how many, if any co-sponsors he/she will get, the likelihood of getting that bill passed is only 17% based on 2011 calculations. However, when senators join together, and work with each other to try to get a bill passed, that likelihood increases to 51%. Unfortunately, when you combine the two, and divide them by two for an average, the total effectiveness of our senators getting any bills passed is seen as only 25 percent.

If the number of debaters was lessened, and our senators would quit putting trash into the hands of their colleagues just to satisfy their constituents, there is no doubt, their effectiveness would increase sharply. I for one am not happy with 25 percent effectiveness from our leaders. My last five years in the military were spent trying to defend our military installations against attacks. Our success was measured to determine our effectiveness. For instance, we used certain types of pop up barriers that were designed and tested to stop a speeding truck loaded with a certain number of pounds of explosives. We demanded a pop up device that could guarantee us that if a truck of certain weight, going a certain speed, with a certain amount of explosives, came speeding through, the barrier would be one hundred percent successful at stopping a target of that description, if deployed in time.

We knew we couldn't possibly protect ourselves from all known attacks but we may be able to measure our effectiveness at preventing such an attack, or minimizing the damage likely to be done by mitigating the damage, using other devices or policies. We could determine that putting a regular sailor in Navy uniform on a gate to control traffic might be 60 percent effective. However, putting a sailor trained in traffic control, who is armed and wearing a black uniform with a badge and police hat, might be 100 percent effective.

As instructors training our personnel, we used the same descriptors in measuring the abilities of our students by putting in the lesson plan that we will (in this case):

- Measure the legislator's behavior (submission and co-sponsoring bills)
- Under specified conditions (during a regular session while working with colleagues)

- To a specific degree (numbers will be at, or above an established benchmark, i.e. propose at least 30 bills with 50 percent, or more success rate, and co-sponsor at least 50 bills with 80 percent or more success rate)

We deserve to know how well our legislators are performing their duty we empowered them to do. That is not being done currently, but this process would allow that measurement. We examined the senate, and now move to the house.

House of Representatives	Intro	Pass	Percent
Esther Harrison	1	1	100%
Bobby Shows	1	1	100%
Sarah R. Thomas	1	1	100%
Clara Burnett	5	4	80%
Jimmy Puckett	5	4	80%
Willie Bailey	8	6	75%
William J. McCoy	8	5	63%
Noal Akins	4	2	50%
Kelvin Buck	8	4	50%
Kimberly Buck	2	1	50%
Tyrone Ellis	6	3	50%
David Gibbs	4	2	50%
Wilbert L. Jones	4	2	50%
Warner F. McBride	8	4	50%
Preston E. Sullivan	2	1	50%
Mary H. Coleman	7	3	43%
Francis Fredericks	15	6	40%
Jerry R. Turner	8	3	38%
J. P. Compretta	11	4	37%
Johnny W. Stringer	19	7	37%
Linda F. Coleman	3	1	33%
Bobby B. Howell	3	1	33%
Joseph L. Warren	43	13	30%
Sherra Hillman Lane	7	2	29%
Edward Blackmon Jr.	12	3	25%
Scott DeLano	16	4	25%
Mary Ann Stevens	4	1	25%
Tom Weathersby	4	1	25%
Greg Ward	13	3	23%
Alyce G. Clarke	9	2	22%
Billy Broomfield	15	1	20%
Thomas U. Reynolds	21	4	19%
Greg Snowden	37	7	19%
Cecil Brown	49	9	18%
Percy W. Watson	66	12	18%

The chart above shows that there were 36 representatives who are above average in successfully proposing bills and 86 representatives (not shown) are at, or below average in successfully proposing bills.

Representative	Intro	Pass	Percent
Kimberly Buck	23	8	35%
Greg Ward	17	6	35%
Brian Aldridge	6	2	33%
Billy Broomfield	12	4	33%
Tad Campbell	3	1	33%
Becky Currie	6	2	33%
Blaine Eaton	3	1	33%
Bobby B. Howell	12	4	33%
Mac Huddleston	6	2	33%
Alex Monsour	26	8	33%
Ken Morgan	9	3	33%
Johnny W. Stringer	6	2	33%
J. Shaun Walley	9	3	33%
Frank Hamilton	23	4	32%
Credell Calhoun	13	4	31%
Greg Snowden	10	3	30%
Jerry R. Turner	10	3	30%
Noal Akins	7	2	29%
Mark Baker	17	5	29%
Andy Gipson	24	7	29%
Eugene F. Hamilton	24	7	29%
Sam C. Mimms, V	7	2	29%
Willie J. Perkins Sr.	7	2	29%
Ferr Smith	7	2	29%
Tyrone Ellis	11	3	27%
Mary Ann Stevens	11	3	27%
Wanda Jennings	19	5	26%
Adrienne Wooten	19	5	26%

Representative	Intro	Pass	Percent
David Norquist	1	1	100%
Casey Eure	4	3	75%
Mark DuVall	11	8	73%
Tracy Arinder	4	2	50%
Reecy L. Dickson	2	1	50%
Roger Ishee	6	3	50%
Sherra Hillman Lane	2	1	50%
Warner F. McBride	6	3	50%
Margaret Rogers	6	3	50%
Jessica Upshaw	21	10	48%
Scott DeLano	11	5	45%
Jimmy Puckett	9	4	44%
John Reed	9	4	44%
Toby Barker	12	5	42%
Cecil Brown	17	7	41%
C. Scott Bounds	10	4	40%
Deryk R. Parker	5	2	40%
RDiane C. Peranich	10	4	40%
Thomas U. Reynolds	10	4	40%
Omeria Scott	30	12	40%
Jeffrey C. Smith	5	2	40%
Henry Zuber III	10	4	40%
Joe Gardner	20	8	39%
Brandon Jones	16	6	38%
Harvey Fillingane	11	4	36%
Rita Martinson	11	4	36%
John Mayo	22	8	36%
Tom Weathersby	22	8	36%

The above chart shows that 56 representatives were above average in co-sponsoring successful bills and 66 representatives at or below average in co-sponsoring successful bills.

Jimmy Puckett	62%	Cecil Brown	30%
David Norquist	59%	Wilbert L. Jones	30%
Bobby Shows	59%	Thomas U. Reynolds	30%
Esther Harrison	53%	Reecy L. Dickson	29%
Sarah R. Thomas	52%	Greg Ward	29%
Greg Snowden	49%	Billy Broomfield	27%
Rita Martinson	44%	Linda F. Coleman	27%
Willie Bailey	43%	Jessica Upshaw	27%
Kimberly Buck	43%	Brandon Jones	26%
Clara Burnett	43%	Mary Ann Stevens	26%
Noal Akins	40%	Tracy Arinder	25%
Sherra Hillman Lane	40%	George Flaggs, Jr.	25%
Tyrone Ellis	39%	Francis Fredericks	25%
Casey Eure	38%	Roger Ishee	25%
Mark DuVall	36%	Warner F. McBride	25%
David Gibbs	36%	Diane C. Peranich	25%
Scott DeLano	35%	Margaret Rogers	25%
Johnny W. Stringer	35%	J. Shaun Walley	24%
Jerry R. Turner	34%	Mark Baker	22%
Bobby B. Howell	33%	Alyce G. Clarke	22%
Kelvin Buck	32%	John Mayo	22%
William J. McCoy	32%	Alex Monsour	22%
Preston E. Sullivan	32%	John Reed	22%
Mary H. Coleman	31%	Joseph L. Warren	22%
Tom Weathersby	31%		

The 49 representatives (above) were above average in a combined proposed and co-sponsored bill calculation.

Sixty-three representatives (not shown here) were at or below average in that category.

Omeria Scott	62	0	0%	Ray Rogers	3	0	0%
Bob Evans	55	0	0%	Tommy L. Woods	3	0	0%
John Moore	38	0	0%	Jack Gadd	2	0	0%
Bill Denny	27	0	0%	Jeffrey S. Guice	2	0	0%
Mark DuVall	25	0	0%	Frank Hamilton	2	0	0%
Credell Calhoun	23	0	0%	Eugene F. Hamilton	2	0	0%
Henry Zuber III	23	0	0%	Randall Patterson	2	0	0%
Becky Currie	19	0	0%	Bill Pigott	2	0	0%
Andy Gipson	17	0	0%	Rufus Straughter	2	0	0%
Phillip Gunn	13	0	0%	Brian Aldridge	1	0	0%
Steven A. Horne	12	0	0%	Harvey Fillingane	1	0	0%
Jim Ellington	11	0	0%	Robert E. Huddleston	1	0	0%
Joe Gardner	10	0	0%	Bennett Malone	1	0	0%
Deryk R. Parker	10	0	0%	America C. Middleton	1	0	0%
James Evans	9	0	0%	Dannie Reed	1	0	0%
W.T. Mayhall, Jr.	7	0	0%	Ferr Smith	1	0	0%
Kevin McGee	7	0	0%	Larry Baker	0	0	0%
Ken Morgan	7	0	0%	Toby Barker	0	0	0%
Larry Byrd	6	0	0%	Charles Jim Beckett	0	0	0%
Tracy Arinder	5	0	0%	Donnie Bell	0	0	0%
Blaine Eaton	5	0	0%	Richard Bennett	0	0	0%
Sidney Bondurant	4	0	0%	Tad Campbell	0	0	0%
Chuck Espy	4	0	0%	Casey Eure	0	0	0%
Herb Frierson	4	0	0%	Mac Huddleston	0	0	0%
Billy Nicholson	4	0	0%	Russ Nowell	0	0	0%
Jeffrey C. Smith	4	0	0%	John Reed	0	0	0%
Linda Whittington	4	0	0%	Margaret Rogers	0	0	0%
C. Scott Bounds	3	0	0%				
Roger Ishee	3	0	0%				
Robert L. Johnson III	3	0	0%				
David W. Myers	3	0	0%				

The first 47 representatives in the tables above were unable to obtain successful passage of any of bills they proposed.

The remaining 11 representatives made no attempt at proposing any bills of their own.

Robert E. Huddleston	38	0	0%
Gary Chism	32	0	0%
Gregory Holloway	10	0	0%
Linda Whittington	9	0	0%
Steven A. Horne	4	0	0%
William J. McCoy	3	0	0%
J. P. Compretta	2	0	0%
Charles Jim Beckett	0	0	0%
Donnie Bell	0	0	0%
Richard Bennett	0	0	0%

The first seven representatives in the table above were unable to obtain successful passage of the bills they co-sponsored.

The last three representatives made no attempt to co-sponsor any bills.

Chapter Thirteen

POLITICIANS IN GENERAL

"Politicians are like diapers; they both need changing regularly and for the same reason."

Author unknown

Let's make sure we understand the meaning of the word politician, so we don't attack anybody's Christian ways. Many are often members of the biggest churches with the largest congregations of registered voters and they show up for church most often just before elections. They have already told us how honest they are, and how much they want to serve us, but now let's look at other sources with more than one definition for the other side of the coin.

According to Wikipedia, a politician is "a person who acts in a manipulative and devious way, typically to gain advancement." Understandably Wikipedia can be questioned as a source, because anybody can edit that information. However, most would agree that Mr. Webster's credibility is unquestioned. The Merriam-Webster dictionary says, "a person primarily interested in political office for selfish, or other narrow, usually short-sighted, reasons." Thefreedictionary.com says a politician is, "one who seeks personal or partisan gain, often by scheming and maneuvering." But the most critical definition comes from: urbandictionary.com which says, "'politics' is derived from the word 'poly' meaning 'many' and 'tics' meaning 'blood-sucking parasites." They also say a politician is "one who has perfected the art of lying, and is a highly paid yes-man."

Please consider this quote:

"When buying and selling are controlled by legislation, the first things to be bought and sold are legislators."
PJ O'Rourke

Obviously, they aren't all bad, but the bad thing is they don't clean up their own messes. A recent ABC Nightline program aired a story about legislators across the country. One was seen reaching back and casting an electronic vote for a member who was not even present (but most likely drawing per diem).

Another legislator was on the golf course at a lobbyist-sponsored game when he was supposed to be at the capitol. Confronted by a journalist on camera, he pulled out a golf club from his bag, and threatened the journalist with it if he didn't leave.

Could this be at least one reason why they rank near the bottom of the approval list in national polls?

Albert Einstein once said, *"Try not to become a man of success but rather to become a man of value."* I wonder if some of our leaders took that the wrong way, thinking value meant their bank accounts.

What causes this problem? I believe it is a "power thing." In the late 1800's Lord Acton said, *"Power tends to corrupt, and absolute power corrupts absolutely. Great men are almost always bad men."*

Award winning novelist David Brin said, *"It is said that power corrupts, but actually it's more true that power attracts the corruptible."* But it is not only novelists who feel that way.

Justice Louis D. Brandeis of the US Supreme Court said, *"The government is the potent omnipresent teacher. For good or ill it teaches the whole people by its example. Crime is contagious. If the government becomes a lawbreaker, it breeds contempt for law; it invites every man to become a law unto himself; it invites anarchy. To declare that the end justifies the means—to declare that the government may commit crimes—would bring terrible retribution."*

Martin Luther King Jr., said, *"Injustice anywhere is a threat to justice everywhere."*

Lastly, Clarence Darrow wrote, *"Justice has nothing to do with what goes on in the courtroom; justice is what comes out of a courtroom."*

Politicians are often thought to have narcissistic tendencies. Did you ever look up the symptoms of a person with a narcissistic personality disorder? I did, and here they are:

- Reacts to criticism with rage, shame, or humiliation
- Takes advantage of other people to achieve his or her own goals
- Has excessive feelings of self-importance
- Exaggerates achievements and talents
- Preoccupied with fantasies of success, power, or intelligence
- Has unreasonable expectations of favorable treatment
- Needs constant attention and admiration
- Disregards the feelings of others, and has little ability to feel empathy
- Has obsessive self-interests
- Pursues mainly selfish goals

Leading psychiatrists say most are very intelligent, base grandiose fantasies on their natural advantage of intellect, and are pathological liars, who sometimes can't even distinguish themselves between the truth and a lie.

Have you noticed any of these traits in any of the politicians you might be voting for soon? If you know anybody like this that is running for office, you probably should reconsider electing a candidate with personality disorders. Examine your candidates closely, and use the narcissistic list as a checklist. If they meet most of the above criteria, think twice.

Every year since 1976, Gallup has conducted a poll to determine how their respondents rate the honesty and ethical standards of 22 professions. The latest results from November 2010 showed little change over the previous year. It is sad to see that our integrity, in all professions, has fallen in the eyes of the public to the point that no profession has enough integrity to receive a score of 100, any place in the 90's and only in the lowest of the 80's. That, in itself, should be considered criminal. Have we become that dishonest in dealing with our fellow man? If so, which professions are dragging us down the lowest?

Nurses, not surprisingly, ranked number one with a numerical score of 81. However, that profession dropped by two points in 2009 and three points in 2008.

I am glad to say that I recently retired as a military officer, and we hold the second highest position on the scale with a score of 73. Serving the Navy as a reservist, and often returning to active duty, gave me the time to pursue a dual career with 14 years of law enforcement in Mississippi. I am also glad to report that law enforcement earned sixth place in this survey with a score of 57. (*I am very proud that both my professions scored higher than judges/lawyers.*)

Wait until you hear the lower scores. Let's drop to the bottom of the list. They are the people I am most concerned about. Local officeholders scored 15th on the list of 22 professions. Lawyers were next lowest in 16th place, immediately followed by business executives at 17. State officeholders scored the next lowest in 18th place out of 22 professions. Members of congress got a score of 9 putting them in 20th place of 22 and my favorite, (lobbyists), scored lowest on the poll with a score of 7, ranked lower than car salesmen.

Honesty/Ethics in Professions

Please tell me how you would rate the honesty and ethical standards of people in these different fields -- very high, high, average, low or very low?

Nov. 19-21, 2010

% Very high/High

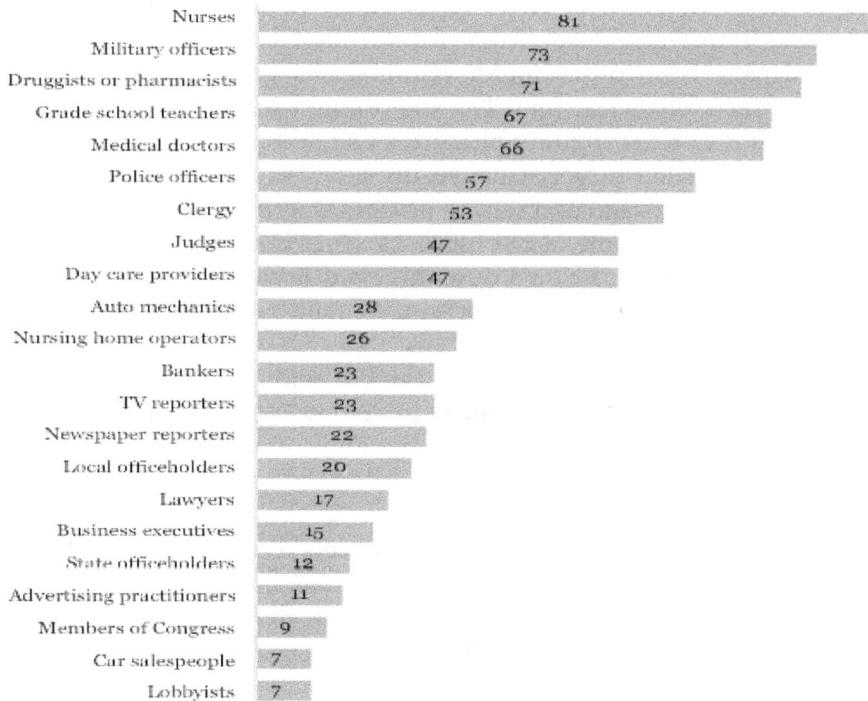

Profession	Score
Nurses	81
Military officers	73
Druggists or pharmacists	71
Grade school teachers	67
Medical doctors	66
Police officers	57
Clergy	53
Judges	47
Day care providers	47
Auto mechanics	28
Nursing home operators	26
Bankers	23
TV reporters	23
Newspaper reporters	22
Local officeholders	20
Lawyers	17
Business executives	15
State officeholders	12
Advertising practitioners	11
Members of Congress	9
Car salespeople	7
Lobbyists	7

GALLUP

What does this tell us? Well, these are the people I wanted to talk to you about, local office holders, lawyers (sometimes one and the same), business executives (often lawyers and local, or state officeholders), members of congress (also often lawyers and/or businessmen), and lobbyists (the lowest of the low). These are the very professions I have seen in my investigator roles over the years that are likely to conspire with each other to commit crimes.

During the mid-1990s, I worked as an investigator for Attorney General Mike Moore, back when we were still pursuing politicians, and public corruption. Jim Hood seems to have a different agenda and is doing a great job on child pornography. I just wish he could do both. Anyway, the unit I worked in was called, "Public Integrity". However, public integrity was not something I found very much of during those years, and I expect not much has changed. The phrase itself has almost become an oxymoron.

In approximately a two year period, I was personally responsible for charges on two sheriffs. One killed himself following his arrest, and the other served time in federal prison. I was also responsible for the first statewide elected public official ever resigning from office under criminal charges, State Auditor Steve Patterson. I didn't actually arrest him. He was brought to the courthouse by his lawyer Joey Langston to enter a guilty plea after I signed the affidavit. Everybody thought Patterson was such a nice, trustworthy guy. As a businessman, he was caught again just a few years ago and sent to prison for attempting to bribe a judge along with others who were some of our highest regarded lawyers. His lawyer Joey Langston couldn't take him to the big house this time, because Joey was caught up in the scam himself, and also went to prison. (Thank God for that judge who turned them in.)

That case surfaced about the same time the FBI sent another judge to federal prison for telling lies about his involvement in yet another reported bribe. Mike Moore's old tobacco lawyer friend Dickie Scruggs and son went to prison.

I charged two mayors for self-serving and illegally earning money from the entities they presided over. I assisted in the investigations that led to arrests of county supervisors, courthouse employees, a Chancery Clerk, and of all things, a funeral director. Remember, all these arrests were made in a period of only about two years while I was also jailing scores of drug dealers, and other common criminals. Did you notice that most of these came from our "bottom-feeders" list (local officeholders, state officeholders, businessmen, judges, and lawyers)? These are the people that we should be able to trust the most. Sadly, there are so few good ones that they are overshadowed by all the bad ones -- a noble profession suffers with a bad name.

Less than a year ago, the Department of Justice released this press release:

Department of Justice

Office of Public Affairs

FOR IMMEDIATE RELEASE
Monday, October 4, 2010

Alabama Legislators, Staff Members, Lobbyists and Businessmen Charged in 39-count Indictment for Roles in Wide-ranging Conspiracy to Influence and Corrupt Votes Related to Electronic Bingo Legislation

Former Lobbyist Pleads Guilty for Her Role in Scheme

WASHINGTON – Eleven individuals, including four current Alabama state legislators, three lobbyists, two business owners and one of their employees, and an employee of the Alabama legislature have been charged for their roles in a conspiracy to offer to and to bribe legislators for their votes and influence on proposed legislation, announced Assistant Attorney General Lanny A. Breuer of the Criminal Division and Assistant Director Kevin Perkins of the FBI's Criminal Investigative Division.

The defendants are charged in an indictment returned by a grand jury on Oct. 1, 2010, in Montgomery, Ala., which was unsealed today. Various defendants are charged with a variety of criminal offenses, including conspiracy, federal program bribery, extortion, money laundering, honest services mail and wire fraud, obstruction of justice and making a false statement. They will make initial appearances today in U.S. District Court for the Middle District of Alabama before U.S. Magistrate Judge Terry F. Moorer.

These incidents happened only 250 miles from our own capitol. The same has happened in our neighboring state of Tennessee. Do you really think similar activity isn't happening here?

I believe if the feds ever make a case on a Jackson lobbyist, or legislator who turns snitch, they will take down other lobbyists and members of the legislature like dominoes dropping on the bottom of an old wooden Coca-Cola case. However, it will never, ever, be done by any state law enforcement agency. Our state agencies are incapable of policing themselves, or their fellow agencies, not because of insufficient law enforcement experience or desire, but rather because of politics.

The feds have done it in other states but they have not made any arrests in Mississippi, from this category. I believe this has led Mississippians to believe it doesn't, and isn't, going to happen here. If you believe the crimes are not occurring here, I have some swamp land to sell you. I encourage every person that reads this to contact your US Attorneys, and ask them to make lobbying, and legislative crimes a number one priority. They call it "public corruption" and sometimes state it is a priority, but we have not seen a focus on that group here yet. The lack of arrests on the part of Mississippi legislators, and lobbyists is not an indicator of the lack of criminal activity. I have even been told by a lobbyist how members of the legislature might conspire with a lobbyist or businessman to receive favoritism on a law. I'll tell the FBI that, but nobody else.

If you have information that could be helpful to law enforcement agencies regarding corruption, don't contact local or state officials. They have many capable investigators, but the political machine will not allow them to charge officials. You might occasionally see the state auditor go after a few over financial crimes but that is only part of our problem. That job is a good springboard for climbing the ladder, but it doesn't help fix our legislature.

You can start with the FBI if you like, but they pretty much have their hands tied without concurrence from the US Attorney's Office in prosecuting these type crimes. Most of all, they need our help. They have done it before at the Congressional level, and need to do it even more at the state level because it would be very difficult, if not impossible, to prosecute a state politician in our courts. So burn up your phone lines to the US Attorneys, write those letters, send e-mails if you have any information, or suspect crime on the part of your bottom feeders.

I know many of you have been convinced in the past that nothing will be done, and I have even heard comments that "all public officials are crooks; nobody's going do anything about it." Although I don't necessarily agree that they are ALL crooks, I believe people get disgusted by the lack of prosecution, and just accept it.

Chapter Fourteen

CAN'T HEAR, CAN'T SMELL, CAN'T SEE, CAN'T COMPREHEND

"Develop a built-in bullshit detector."

Ernest Hemingway

Do we need a governor so devoid of senses? My first encounter with Phil Bryant was at Drug Enforcement School in New Orleans where we were both students in 1977. I recall to this day a bell bottom suit he wore in the class picture. I still have the picture.

I believe my next encounter with him was when he was an officer in the Jackson Chapter of the Jaycees, and I was trying to put together a Ridgeland Chapter in 1983. They sponsored us. We went to the state convention, and won every award a new chapter could win, but we had only been a chapter for a few months. However, the Jackson Chapter coveted the "Speaker's Awards", and they had the best of their best contender groomed for that contest. They were certain they would win it.

Every time they won an award they would play the Rocky theme song on their boom box. However, when our speaker got to the stand, and spoke on the subject of why he loved to be a Mississippian, I don't think there was a dry eye in the Biloxi Coliseum. We laughed and jested that most of the tears shed by Jackson Jaycees were due to sadness -- knowing they wouldn't win that award. And they knew it only halfway through our speaker's address. The rest of the tears came from proud souls and patriots. They didn't expect us to walk away with so many awards, but it made them look good for sponsoring us -- except for the Speaker's Award.

My next dealings that had anything to do with Phil Bryant were when I charged State Auditor Steve Patterson with a crime, and he resigned in lieu of further prosecution. Phil Bryant was appointed by Governor Fordice to replace him. At any rate, Phil got his opportunity to use that office as a stepping stone for lieutenant governor. It was ten years in the making.

The next time I met Phil Bryant was during his transitional period for the State Auditor position. I applied for a job with him. He gave me his typical politician response, and when I left, I never heard from him again. In hindsight, I am so glad it happened that way.

The next time I attempted to talk to Phil Bryant was just after he was elected as lieutenant governor. I intended to talk to him face-to-face about some of these issues. I sent him e-mails, left him phone messages, and so on. He refused to even respond to me. Instead, he had one of his people call me to tell me I would have to talk to him first about whatever I was concerned about, and he would see what happened from there. I was insulted and refused the offer.

I didn't hear from them again for several months, even though I gave them my e-mail address and cell phone number. Then one day I was invited to appear on the Paul Gallo Radio Show to discuss bingo corruption. I explained to Paul that one of the reasons it was difficult to prosecute bingo halls was the fact that they had legislative protection bringing the roof down on investigators who attempted to charge them. I told him that during my tenure at the MGC we even had a lieutenant governor who was on one of the boards.

I left the radio show a few minutes after those comments, and was driving down I-55. Ironically, I was just passing the Capitol Building off to my right when my cell phone rang. It was the same employee of Phil Bryant who tried to get me to go through him months before. He asked me if I still wanted an audience with the lieutenant governor. I told him I would talk to the lieutenant governor at any time. I told him I was available right then, and he told me to "come on down."

When I got there, Phil, his assistant, and his lawyer (Chief of Staff) were all there. I am not sure why that was necessary, but it didn't bother me. Neither of them ever noticed or questioned a small digital voice recorder in my pocket, but they must have suspected it because nobody said much. I did most of the talking after Phil fired me up. They probably had their own recorder running. Phil's first comment to me was that he "took offense" with me telling everybody on the radio show that he was involved with corrupt bingo. I was shocked. I had not said that at all. I had told them it was the lieutenant governor that was there during my tenure, (Amy Tuck). He told me that was not true, and that they all heard it (as he looked at the other two while they shook their heads up and down). I again denied it and offered to apologize if I turned out to be wrong. I suggested they get the tape from the radio show, and listen more closely. They indicated they would. We moved on from that subject. He asked me what I had wanted to talk to him about.

I asked him how he could audit the MGC only twice in ten years, and find nothing in the final audit. I explained that his background as a former police officer should have been enough for him to notice we were paying an entire division of law enforcement officers at the MGC to do nothing but "regulate." I explained they were required by law to enforce the laws as well as regulate the industry.

I confronted him about the laws not being enforced, and I told him he had to know what was going on there because of the annual report. His question to me was, "What annual report?" He had supposedly never seen one when the law clearly requires that the report be provided to him each year. I quoted him the statute number, and he had somebody bring him a copy. Below is an excerpt from that bingo laws our legislators passed requiring report distribution:

103- Commission **shall** prepare/provide COMPREHENSIVE
annual reports and rules/regulations to:
LT Governor
Speaker of the House
Chairman of the House and Senate Judiciary Committees
Chairman of the House Ways and Means Committee
Chairman of the Senate Finance Committee

Budgets were apparently being approved for the MGC without even reviewing their annual performance reports. That was ironic, because as State Auditor, Bryant had waved a red flag to then Lieutenant Governor Amy Tuck concerned that the "Performance Based Budget Plan" enacted by the legislature nine years before was not being implemented. See proof of that in the next two documents:

STATE OF MISSISSIPPI

OFFICE OF THE STATE AUDITOR

PHIL BRYANT
AUDITOR

December 15, 2003

Honorable Amy Tuck
Lieutenant Governor
New Capitol
Jackson, MS

Dear Lieutenant Governor Tuck:

Per your request, the Performance Audit Division of the Office of the State Auditor (OSA) performed a review of Mississippi's current practice regarding the 1994 legislation mandating performance-based budgeting. OSA has completed this project and now submits this report for your review.

We trust that the information included in this report will be beneficial to you and other parties interested in this subject.

Sincerely,

Phil Bryant
State Auditor

Office of the State Auditor
Phil Bryant

A Review of Performance-Based Budgeting in Mississippi

Report Summary

At the request of the Lieutenant Governor, the Performance Audit division of the Office of the State Auditor (OSA) conducted a review of the philosophy of performance-based budgeting, as well as its functions in the Mississippi appropriations process.

Over the last ten years, many states across the country have transformed their appropriations process to a performance-based budgeting system. Similarly, during the 1994 legislative session the Mississippi Legislature updated Mississippi's budgeting law to mandate performance-based budgeting. Even though nine years have passed since the performance-based budgeting law was enacted, the law has yet to achieve its full potential. In light of this, as well as the recent economic downturn in Mississippi, the Lieutenant Governor is proposing a fresh review of performance-based budgeting and its benefits.

This review encompasses the definition and philosophy of performance-based budgeting in general, the current appropriations process in Mississippi, as well as the degree to which the 1994 legislation is having an impact on Mississippi's budgeting process. Further, other states that maintain successful and efficient performance-based budgeting systems were studied to determine the best practices for success. States reviewed include Texas, Florida, Virginia, and Louisiana. These states have all implemented performance-based budgeting systems that are generally accepted as standards in performance-based budgeting.

As a result of this review, the following recommendations are suggested:

Fully Implement the Law

The law passed in 1994 has never been fully implemented. This law maintains potential to achieve results if implementation is effected.

Bryant should have noticed that the charitable gaming division was not making arrests (and had not in eight years), compared to my 46 arrests in two years. The problem was that it was the legislature that prevented them from doing their job--not wanting to infuriate the bingo operators--so they were only "regulated administratively." That was exactly the reason I quit even after the director asked me to stay, and Chairman Gresham all but begged me to stay. Mine and your tax dollars paid for law enforcement officers, not regulators who just request that the commission take administrative action.

At any rate, just before leaving Phil's office that day, I told him they were all wrong about what they supposedly heard me say, and that I had not said that he was involved. They insisted that they heard me say it by nodding their heads up and down when Bryant asked. So I suggested again they get the tape from the radio show, and if I said what they were accusing me of, I would gladly come back and apologize personally. I assumed he was an honorable man as well.

Then the tensions subsided as I got those things off my chest. He then suggested, as many politicians do, that the law needed to be changed and said he would get a senator to work with me on it. I told him the law worked as it was, but it wasn't being enforced. At any rate, I went down the hall, and saw Senator Joey Fillingane and a legal assistant from the legislature "ready" to draft new laws. I knew that was a joke and would never happen. I told them to use the law we had in place. He told me he couldn't force the gaming executive director to do his job. I told him it was the legislature not allowing him to do his job. He then said if I wanted something done, I needed to recruit more people in the fight. He and his assistant asked me to come back later and help them with verbiage. I left and never went back. I had been down that old political road before, wasting my time with a senator who was going to help with a bill. I will stop long enough to go back in time a few years, and tell you about that experience.

In 1999, after catching one charitable director misusing charity money, one of her board members (Senator Terry Burton) offered to help get the bingo laws changed with more teeth. We went easy on the charity's director, had her pay the money back, pay a small fine and put her on a compliance agreement. We sat down with Burton to change the law. We could have arrested her for felony embezzlement, but thought the tradeoff to get a stronger bingo law justified it.

I called him often during that session asking him about the status of the bill, and he kept on encouraging me, telling me it looked good. Then the day came for its consideration and it wasn't presented. "What happened?" I asked Terry Burton. He said, "I am sorry Rick, the document I am looking at says it's "LOST".

So I said, "We will send you another copy." To that, he said, "It is too late, we have passed the deadline and I don't think I can get the rule suspended." Bottom line, he reneged on his promise.

Here is a copy of an excerpt that came out later. All this happened back in 1999.

Lost
AMENDMENT No. 2 PROPOSED TO

House Bill NO. 997

By Senator(s) Burton

```
1        AMEND by inserting the following after line 11 and by

2    renumbering subsequent sections accordingly:

3        SECTION 1.  Section 97-33-75, Mississippi Code of 1972, is

4    amended as follows:
```

I believe it is a common ploy for legislators to tell you, "Oh yeah, I agree with you on that (Mr. Voter), and I am going to introduce a bill in the legislature to change that law." Then they walk away thinking, " *I am going to introduce one to get this guy off my back or make him believe we are going to get it passed, knowing all the time, there is no way in hell it stands a chance. Then I will just tell him I tried but that other side, those damn (democrat or republican, whichever the case may be) legislators just wouldn't go along with it.*"

Oh well, that was a ten year old history lesson. Back to leaving Phil Bryant's office after he accused me of making a statement about him that I didn't make. I drove home and got a call a couple of hours later from his chief of staff who had gotten a copy of the radio show disk. He told me the lieutenant governor asked him to call me, and tell me I was right -- that I had not said what they originally thought I said. I told him I already knew that, and asked him if his call amounted to an apology. He told me that the lieutenant governor had not authorized him to apologize. I then asked, what about the lieutenant governor, why didn't he call me? He couldn't answer me.

I felt like I had been totally disrespected by Phil Bryant, and that I deserved as much respect as he did. He had already disrespected me a year or so before by ignoring my e-mails. Then he passed them off to his crony for me to talk to but I refused. Then when he thought I had done something wrong, he was quick to have his same crony call me to come to the Capitol immediately. That amounted to more disrespect. But then to accuse me of something I hadn't done and have his two cronies agree with him that was more than I was willing to take.

At any rate, I was sitting on the couch at home accessing the internet with my laptop while searching for books on Amazon. Knowing that Amazon sold more than books and that Phil Bryant might have a hearing problem, I looked for a hearing aid. I quickly found one, purchased it, and had it delivered to him with a personal message. A screenshot of the web page is shown below. I felt like I had avenged myself from some of his disrespect.

The Mississippi PEER Commission had already concluded and printed their concern about the MGC not doing its job, breaking the law themselves, letting unqualified people be licensed, and stating that there was a known propensity for mob activity reported by the FBI.

Considering how big the gaming industry is in Mississippi, and the issues pointed out by PEER, you would think our state "watchdog" would look at them very carefully. The truth is Phil Bryant audited them only two times in his ten years as State Auditor. His first audit showed some minor problems, but his second one was a glowing accolade. Even as a former law enforcement officer, he couldn't see that none of the officers in the Charitable gaming Division were not enforcing any laws, but our tax dollars paid their salaries as police officers. Our tax dollars also paid for annual trips for agents from all over the state to go to Clinton for firearms proficiency qualifications. As far as I know, they are still not enforcing the law, and only imposing administrative sanctions. Stevie Wonder could have seen trouble there, but I guess Phil couldn't see it.

Imagine a police officer in the town you live in, not making an arrest in a year. What would you think about him? Imagine the whole police force not making an arrest in a year. Now imagine a whole police force not making any arrests in 8, even 10 years. Would you as a citizen tolerate that? Wouldn't you be in the mayor's office jumping up and down? I would, and that is basically what I am doing now because the Mayor's equivalent has not listened.

I never attempted any more contact with Bryant. However, I did keep up with him a little bit following the oil spill on the Gulf. It appeared the coast had seen him as trying to cover up the fact that the spill was serious. In one of many Sun Herald reports, this statement was found:

"To people saying they can smell the oil, he says, "No, you can't." The gas smell may be coming from their lawn mowers, he said. "That is not gasoline coming out of the Gulf."

Anyway these are my Phil Bryant stories. I have no doubt he will win the republican nomination, but it won't be because I helped. I feel that way because it has been my experience that if things don't directly affect us, we don't care enough to take action. If the things I mentioned to you about him made any difference to you, just like me, you wouldn't vote for him. You had better prepare yourself though for what you may be getting, and expect similar treatment to what I got. Some of the narcissistic tendencies I shared with you before were glowing in our "meeting".

I am not just bringing up personal issues between Phil Bryant and me, or any other politician, just for the sake of it. I am trying to help you see, especially for the benefit of those who don't know him personally, what he is really like. Can you imagine the arrogance of a lieutenant governor calling a citizen to his office to browbeat him over something bad he heard that the person said about him (true or not)? When I wanted to talk to him, there was no way. I had to go through subordinates. But when he wanted to talk to me, it was like he thought I was one of his state employees that he was calling in on the carpet.

In addition to not being able to see, hear or smell, there are certain things he can't seem to comprehend either. One is that he is a public official, in the public eye, subject to public scrutiny and opinions, and that we have an addition to the US Constitution called the First Amendment. Unless somebody told a lie about him, knew at the time it was a lie, damaged his reputation to the point that he suffered loss, and did so with malice, he is in the public eye, and subject to public criticism. That will often include remarks about him that he doesn't like. But as I told him in his personal note attached to his hearing aid, if he spends all his time calling in citizens every time they say something he doesn't like, he will be a very busy man, but he sure won't get much done.

He apparently wasn't worried about the fact that the laws were not being enforced, and a taxpayer/voter was complaining about his taxes being misused to pay for law enforcement officers that should have been paid for administrative clerk regulators. He must have only been concerned about himself and angered by what he thought was a lie against him. That is truly a narcissistic trait. Although he is the most senior person by statute to receive the MGC report, and it was all but smeared in his face that they were not complying with the law, he still has taken no action that has fixed that problem. He wanted me to do it with his "buddy rub" senator.

I told a member of the legislature in my district about this story, and he accused me of being disrespectful. That is just another example of the arrogance from our elected officials that think we should take a licking from our politicians, and still respect them. (Again, refer to the narcissistic symptoms.) While that may be his opinion, you have to earn my respect to get it. You don't get respect by title alone. I think Phil Bryant understands that well by now – at least from me anyway. Had he handled my first contact with him differently, all this could have been avoided. Do you remember in the 2011 legislative session when the need arose to establish new voting districts? Phil Bryant as lieutenant governor was president of the senate and as such was expected to lead the senate to resolution. The senate worked very hard to pass its version of a redistricting plan, hopefully with support of him as president of the senate. However, he decided to introduce his own bill in opposition of the senate bill presented by Terry Burton. That was unheard of. As it turned out neither of them worked, but they might have, had he been a team player. It was all about Phil getting his version passed and getting the credit for doing so. He had a real feeling of self-importance. Although I have not been the president of Terry Burton's fan club, I have to give him credit for his willingness to ignore his leader's self-centered actions. I hope that was not some sort of staged act for some unknown political reason. I just don't trust them anymore.

Chapter Fifteen

WHAT YOU SEE AIN'T WHAT YOU GET

"You can fool all of the people all of the time if the advertising is right and the budget is big enough"

Joseph Levine

Mississippians are good people, proud people and mostly country people. Most of us would rather have a home grown tomato at times than a T-bone steak. We know how to tell a home grown tomato from a market tomato. When I say "market" I mean something that has been marketed to us as a "down home" treat but bears all the marks of a rotten politician. The stores can polish a tomato, leave the stems on, wax it, display it under droplets of water, add signs that say, "vine-ripe," from Smith County and every other thing they want to, but we Mississippians can tell when we are being duped.

Somewhere out there in the tomato selling world is a marketer. He researches the best variety of tomato, the one with the best appearance, the one that has the most appeal, the one he can market to the most people and then....he dresses it up. That is when marketing and strategy comes together. They want us to believe this tomato is something it's not. They want it to look good. They want it to be the number one tomato on the market and are willing to spend countless dollars on its promotion that will come back to them, if not in sales, at least in business expense write-offs.

There is nothing better than a Mississippi home-grown tomato from Mt. Olive or Pelahatchie, Tunica or Sebastopol or anywhere else in Mississippi where a hard working farmer gave it his own touch, a man of his own, not owned by business ventures. They never try to fool us. They don't have to dress up their products. God already did it for them. Some country tomatoes may have a seam down the side that looks like grandma's big fat rear-end. Some may have cracks around the stem or occasional brown spots.

They don't always look perfect, but you know what? Just wipe away that dirt, spots of bug spray, bird poop and occasional spray from old Bubba, the big black Lab on your shirt or pants leg and bite into it. You will know right then, you have the real thing. Unfortunately, when it comes to politics in Mississippi, it's just not that easy.

The politicians team up on good hearted Mississippians who would like to see the good in everything and everybody. They bring in the high-faulting, big wigs from Washington, DC that call themselves political strategists. They may live here but that's where the tricks of their trade come from. They come from people already in office who have learned the tricks of the trade like Haley Barbour, millionaire DC lobbyist and his business friends and associates. They pull out all the stops and look for that one tomato that they can polish, shine, add color to, show off a country vine here in there and they do everything they can to advertise it using money that will come back to them in the end. They spend it like crazy gambling on getting it all back and then some, if they can interest you in just the right pick of the bunch.

Mississippians fought most of the Civil War with inferior weapons. The north had long since had its Spencer rifles far superior to our muskets. Those northern tacticians from New York and Washington, DC are among us now, trying to defeat us from within. Their weapons of today are forked tongues, signs, newspapers, scholarly perfected speeches, image polishing, magazines, internet, painted-up buses, radio, television, and the nuke of all nukes....business interest.

We have gone from a society of politicians voting for our best interests, to voting for the special interest groups that poured in the money during pre-campaign undertakings. Why should your representative vote for something a lobbyist wants? This is somebody who is going to make his job easier by drafting the legislation for him. He is going to take your representative for a big steak dinner and on to the bar where bourbon flows free like nature's own water at Dunn's Falls. Our representatives and their colleagues have failed to pass legislation that would limit the amount of money a lobbyist can spend on them to influence them on legislation. What happened to the influence they used on us to get our vote? Do we not count?

That's the problem in a great big nutshell "influence". If you don't believe me, think about this for a moment. Everybody thinks Phil Bryant is the greatest thing since toilet paper. You may too. Now, stop for a moment and meditate, especially if you don't know him personally and ask yourself, why. He likes to tell everybody he has experience, he will hold the state accountable, he wants what is right for Mississippi. He wants you to know he is a family man and Christian conservative. He wants to appear as a down to earth guy just like you and me and that he is honest and trustworthy. How many times have we heard that from politicians only to know if your grandmother was still around, she would wash their devious mouths out with lie soap?

So let's get started on that little Phil Bryant exercise and ask ourselves these 12 questions.

1. Do I know him personally and know his claims to be genuine?
2. Will a Methodist represent the needs of a predominantly Baptist state?
3. What did he really do as State Auditor.... better yet what did he not do?
4. What experience does he have as governor (not lieutenant governor)?
5. Why has he overlooked gaming corruption and failed to do anything about it?
6. Why did he support raising our taxes six times after taking an oath he wouldn't?
7. Why was he trying to help his business buddies in land deals that got uncovered?
8. Why should he be promoted....does his record justify it?
9. Why should we promote a senate leader whose house is only 25 percent effective?
10. Why should we promote a candidate who opposed his own senate's districting plan?
11. Why should we elect a man that has been groomed by big marketing dollars?
12. Why should we elect a man that has used northern strategies to fool us?

Take out a dozen eggs and use them for this exercise. Throw one away for every question you can't answer to the best of your ability. If you have enough eggs left over to feed your family breakfast tomorrow, then vote for Phil Bryant. If you can't, then vote for anybody else. I am not pushing a candidate. I am just trying to show you the strategically marketed product we have been sold is not that home grown tomato, he and his business buddies would like us to think he is. I am not going to just make that claim. In the following pages, I am going to provide you proof of those techniques, millions of dollars spent on strategy, marketing and promotions. I judge Phil as that store-bought tomato and I can't stand them.

After reading the rest of this, tell yourself what you think, and if you voted republican in the primary, encourage people who didn't vote to vote democrat. The parties don't mean anything. Most of your state representatives and senators are of that party simply because the majority of the voting citizens in their districts are of that party. To run as any other party would be fruitless. They are not devoted to those party lines. Unfortunately, with our closed primaries, we are stuck with them once we commit in the primary. You might have wanted Republican Ron Williams in the primary, but since he doesn't show up in the runoff, you may favor Democrat Bill Luckett over Dupree but can't vote for him in the runoff, but all bets are off in the general election, we can vote either party.

Call voting what you like. It may be considered a duty, a right, a privilege or anything else you may want to call it. I like to call it a by-product of freedom more closely related to a right. We have a right to vote and a right not to vote because of the freedoms our fighting men and women have preserved for us over centuries. Why should we be compelled if only by political pressure to vote for someone on a ballot that we don't like? We shouldn't and I won't. I should stay home runoff day because I voted republican. But let's get beyond the rhetoric and look at the candidates closely and try to find that home grown tomato in this mess.

Who is really pushing Phil Bryant? Is it you and me, the voters, or is it business? He likes to brag about the money he has raised and the cash he has (or once had) in his campaign funds. Let's try to determine from this data who really wants him in office. Is it the "worker bee" or the businessman? When preparing this first spreadsheet, I used information directly from Phil Bryant's campaign finance reports on file at the Mississippi SOS office. I pulled data that will show you the real story when arranged under certain headings. This one shows real people like you and me, retirees, homemakers, county workers, insurance agents and so on. It does not depict owners, CEO's, presidents, executive officers or the like. These are the common people that financially supported Phil Bryant in the first three month reporting period of his campaign with $500 or less.

Phil Bryant Gov Campaign — Donations May 1-May 31, 2011
Contributions of $500 or less from individual "workerbees or retirees", not shown as owning or solely operating a business.

Last Name	First Name	City	State	Occupation	Employer	Date	Amount	Aggregate
Russell	Bill	Walls	MS	BOS	DeSoto County	1/14/2011	$250	$250
Morgan	Bob	Brandon	MS	Analyst	Department of Public Safety	4/30/2011	$250	$250
Sherill	Bobby	Meridian	MS	Insurance Agent	Insurance Advisory Group	3/14/2011	$250	$250
Zachow	Christine	Jackson	MS	Physician	Zachow	3/14/2011	$250	$250
Harbarger	Claude	Brandon	MS	Administrator	St. Dominic Hospital	2/28/2011	$250	$250
Koger	David	Diamondhead	MS	Retired	N/A	3/21/2011	$250	$250
Wimbish	Dianne & Jon	Brandon	MS	Sales	Insurance	1/28/2011	$300	$300
Roberts	Donna Ruth	Oxford	MS	Retired	N/A	1/20/2011	$350	$350
Rouse	Douglas	Hattiesburg	MS	Orthopedist	Southern Bone and Joint	1/20/2011	$500	$500
South	Dwalia	Hernando	MS	Physician	North MS Primary Care	2/9/2011	$250	$250
Edens	Fred	Brandon	MS	Attorney	US Legal, Inc.	4/30/2011	$250	$250
Price	Fred	Floowood	MS	Retired	N/A	4/29/2011	$250	$250
Barrett	Gelinda	Jackson	MS	Homemaker	Homemaker	2/9/2011	$500	$500
Rosen	John Charles	Carriere	MS	Retired	N/A	4/19/2011	$500	$500
Gillespie	Lamar	Hattiesburg	MS	Physician	Retired	1/18/2011	$250	$250
Heinmiller	Lowell	Hattiesburg	MS	Retired	N/A	1/14/2011	$250	$250
Stockstill	Marie	Carriere	MS	Homemaker	Homemaker	4/19/2011	$500	$500
Barnett	Mitch	Columbia	MS	General Manager	Crain Tractor & Equipment	2/9/2011	$300	$300
Wallace	Susan	Columbia	MS	Homemaker	Homemaker	2/9/2011	$500	$500
Bailey	Thomas	Lucedale	MS	Pilot	Retired	1/26/2011	$250	$250
Windham	W.A.	Laurel	MS	Director	US Dept. of Agriculture	2/9/2011	$300	$300
Tucker	Walter	Brandon	MS	Deputy Sheriff	Retired, Rankin County S.O.	2/11/2011	$500	$500
Rhodes	William	Vancleave	MS	Retired	Retired	4/29/2011	$250	$250
								$7,700

There weren't a lot of common people with small donations that supported Bryant, were there? You can go to the SOS web site and see the succeeding reports of one month long each. I don't want to bore you with more of the same. I want to move on and show you other spreadsheets I have put together to tell the rest of the story. http://www.sos.ms.gov/elections.aspx

The next spreadsheet shows what I like to call "legitimate corporate donations". Corporations are limited to a $1 thousand dollar contribution for political candidates. These corporations have made those type donations.

Corporations	City	State	Date	Amount	Aggregate
Adams Mobile Home Supply	Yazoo City	MS	1/26/2011	$1,000	$1,000
Bayer Health Care	Madison	MS	4/30/2011	$1,000	$1,000
Citizen's Bank and Trust	Marks	MS	2/9/2011	$1,000	$1,000
Columbia Auto Parts and Machine	Columbia	MS	2/9/2011	$1,000	$1,000
Construction Equipment, Inc	Philadelphia	MS	2/4/2011	$1,000	$1,000
Denbury	Plano	TX	4/30/2011	$1,000	$1,000
Digital Engineering and Imaging	Kenner	LA	4/29/2011	$2,500	$2,500
Dungan Engineering	Columbia	MS	2/9/2011	$1,000	$1,000
First Tower Corp.	Jackson	MS	4/30/2011	$1,000	$1,000
First Tower Loan	Jackson	MS	4/30/2011	$1,000	$1,000
Gary Hanning Equipment & Construction	Escatawpa	MS	4/19/2011	$1,000	$1,000
Gulfco of Louisiana	Flowood	MS	4/30/2011	$1,000	$1,000
Gulfco of Mississippi	Gulfport	MS	4/30/2011	$1,000	$1,000
H & H Towing and Recovery	Laurel	MS	4/29/2011	$1,000	$1,000
Hankins Lumber Company	Grenada	MS	1/26/2011	$1,000	$1,000
Hazmat Services Inc.	Pascagoula	MS	1/14/2011	$1,000	$1,000
Maggie Clark Media Services	Brandon	MS	2/28/2011	$1,000	$1,000
Matthews Brothers, Inc.	Pass Christian	MS	4/29/2011	$1,000	$1,000
Morris & McDaniel, Inc.	Jackson	MS	4/19/2011	$1,000	$1,000
Provine Flying Service, Inc.	Greenwood	MS	1/26/2011	$1,000	$1,000
R & J Construction	Laurel	MS	4/29/2011	$1,000	$1,000
Superior Asphalt Inc.	Jackson	MS	1/2/2011	$1,000	$1,000
The Yates Companies	Philadelphia	MS	1/1/2011	$1,000	$1,000
Timbs Enterprises	Indianola	MS	1/14/2011	$1,000	$1,000
Tower Loan of Missouri	Flowood	MS	4/30/2011	$1,000	$1,000
Watkins Partners	Jackson	MS	4/19/2011	$1,000	$1,000
					$27,500

As you can see, each corporation followed the law with maximum donations of $1 thousand dollars with the exception of the one highlighted that donated $25 hundred (a Louisiana firm). I am not sure why a Louisiana business owner would be interested in swaying Mississippi's elections anyway but his money in excess was sent back. Notice though that like the "worker bees" in the previous spreadsheet, there aren't a whole lot of corporations donating their limit. The Maggie Clark Media Services will come up again and you will see why they have no problem donating to the Phil Bryant campaign.

Remember me telling you in an earlier chapter how John Grisham, in his novel *The Appeal* revealed to us through one of his characters how to circumvent campaign donation limitations? Also remember the official SOS records I showed you from his buddy Bobby Moak (current candidate for Speaker of the House) and how he received thousands of dollars from different associates within casinos and how they had the appearance of circumventing campaign finance laws? Okay, I will let you be the judge on the corporate donations to Phil Bryant in this spreadsheet. Notice that the employers are all corporations and notice that the occupations of the donors are in controlling positions within these purported corporations. But...pay particular attention to the aggregate amounts of money donated by those corporate leaders that far exceed a $1 thousand dollar limit. So how did that do that? They claim the donation was from them individually, not the corporation. There is no limit on an individual contribution. Sheriff candidate and bingo entrepreneur Rudy Johnson donated $150 thousand dollars to his brother Tim "Elvis" Johnson for a statewide position that went nowhere. Elvis left the building and although he flexed his microphone as a senator, county supervisor and high paid bingo employee himself, he no longer represents our citizens. This big money may have the same effect on Phil Bryant. I only listed those on this spreadsheet that donated $2 thousand dollars or more with the exception of Gary Harkins who donated $15 hundred dollars each month for an aggregate of $6 thousand dollars, up to the primary.

Phil Bryant   Gov   Campaign   Donations Jan 1-Apr 30, 2011

Contributions claimed to have been given by individuals who exercise control within businesses/corporations

Last Name	First Name	City	State	Occupation	Employer	Date	Amount	Aggregate
Prewett	Bruce	Southaven	MS	Pres/CEO	Prewett Enterprises	2/9/2011	$7,000	$15,000
Patel	Chandresh	Oxford	MS	Manager	The Hampton Inn	2/9/2011	$5,000	$5,000
Lee	Deanna	Carriere	MS	Owner	HRL Contracting	2/9/2011	$20,000	$20,000
Vice	Diane	Moss Point	MS	Owner	Vice Construction	2/9/2011	$7,500	$7,500
Wright Jr.	Douglas	Saltillo	MS	Executive	Community Eldercare Srvcs	2/9/2011	$2,500	$2,500
Mallette	Frank	Vancleave	MS	Sec/Director	Mallette Brothers	2/9/2011	$2,500	$2,500
Dyess	G.	Hattiesburg	MS	President	M.G. Dyess	2/9/2011	$2,000	$2,000
Harkins	Gary	Flowood	MS	President	Harkins Realty	2/9/2011	$1,500	$6,000
Kleinpeter	George	New Orleans	LA	President	Burk-Kleinpeter, Inc.	2/9/2011	$5,000	$5,000
Mallette	Glen	Gautier	MS	Pres/CEO	Mallette Brothers	3/14/2011	$5,000	$5,000
Dyess	Glen	Carson	MS	CEO	M.G. Dyess	4/1/2011	$2,000	$2,000
Goings	H. Wesley	Jackson	MS	Sec/Treasurer	Telepex (Telepak?)	4/19/2011	$5,000	$5,000
Meena	Hugh	Jackson	MS	President	Cellular South	4/19/2011	$4,000	$4,000
Creekmoore	James	Jackson	MS	Chairman	Cellular South	4/19/2011	$7,500	$7,500
Barksdale	James	Ridgeland	MS	Pres/CEO	Barksdale (Management?)	4/19/2011	$7,500	$7,500
Hoskins	James	Pass Christian	MS	CFO	S.H. Anthony	4/19/2011	$5,000	$5,000
Borries	James	Vancleave	MS	Owner	J. B. Borries, Inc.	4/19/2011	$5,000	$5,000
McRaney	Jena	Bassfield	MS	Officer	M.G. Dyess	4/19/2011	$2,000	$2,000
Hill	Jody	Falkner	MS	Officer	Hill Brothers Construction	4/19/2011	$2,333	$2,333
Sanderson Jr.	Joe	Laurel	MS	Chairman/CEO	Sanderson Farms, Inc.	4/19/2011	$10,000	$10,000
McNulty	Joe	Magee	MS	Pres/CEO	Pioneer Health Services	4/19/2011	$25,000	$25,000
McCaskill	Joseph	Jackson	MS	Producer	Wellington Associates	4/29/2011	$5,000	$5,000
Hill	Kenneth	Falkner	MS	Officer	Hill Brothers Construction	4/29/2011	$2,334	$2,334
Hill	Kenny	Falkner	MS	Officer	Hill Brothers Construction	4/29/2011	$2,333	$2,333
Pratt Jr.	Larry	Pope	MS	CEO	First Pharmacy	4/29/2011	$5,000	$5,000
Johnson	Larry	Jackson	MS	President	Landmark	4/29/2011	$10,000	$10,000
Dyess	Michael G.	Sumrall	MS	Vice President	M.G. Dyess	4/29/2011	$2,000	$2,000
Dunlap	R.H.	Batesville	MS	CEO	Dunlap and Kyle	4/29/2011	$10,000	$10,000
McRae Jr.	Richard	Jackson	MS	VP/Tres/Director	Macco Investments?	4/29/2011	$10,000	$10,000
Dyess	Ricky	Columbia	MS	Vice President	M.G. Dyess	4/29/2011	$2,000	$2,000
Jacobs	Robert	Jackson	MS	CEO	Weight Watchers	4/29/2011	$2,500	$2,500
Applewhite	Roger	Gautier	MS	Owner	Applewhite Rubbish Landfill	4/29/2011	$5,000	$5,000
Anthony	Sean	Gulfport	MS	Owner	S.H. Anthony, Inc	4/29/2011	$10,000	$15,000
Irby	Stewart	Jackson	MS	Vice President	Stuart C. Irby Co.	4/29/2011	$5,000	$5,000
Lovelace	Terry	Jackson	MS	President	Utility Constructors	4/29/2011	$2,500	$2,500
Elmore	Thomas	Aberdeen	MS	CEO	Eutaw Construction	4/29/2011	$10,000	$10,000
Denny Jr.	Walter	Ridgeland	MS	CPA	Barksdale Management	4/30/2011	$2,500	$2,500
								$237,000

I encourage you to ask yourself two questions based on the information in this spreadsheet. Do you really believe the money in the last spreadsheet (almost a quarter of a million dollars) in less than three months was taken from pockets of individuals? Do you believe if elected, Phil Bryant will be controlled by business interests instead of "worker bee" voters? Remember, there were several more spreadsheets to follow bringing these donations into the millions. All of them are available on the SOS website.

A former prosecutor friend of mine told me that corporate executives often manipulate campaign finance laws by claiming the large donations and personal donations. They also continue donations through the general election in November. They get their money back if it did come out of their pockets by a simple scheme of paying themselves a Christmas bonus at, or above the amount they donated. Nobody will ever know the difference and the lawyers/legislators that made our shoddy campaign finance laws, just duped us again with a great big loophole they created themselves. When are we going to get tired of being manipulated and put our foot down? The best way is, don't re-elect anybody and don't elect any politicians.

Now, let's move past individuals and look at Political Action Committees (PAC). These are groups of special interest that pool money that may or may not go to a particular candidate but rather go to a cause or a person supporting that cause. If a group of fat-friendly doctors trained in liposuction want legislation and/or support from the governor on promoting their businesses, they may donate to the PAC in hopes of their pooled money going to a candidate most likely to support their business interests. Here is an example of that for the Phil Bryant campaign. I only listed those who gave a thousand dollars or more in the first three months of the reporting period, so the total is actually higher than it appears in this spreadsheet and all of the spreadsheets for that matter.

PAC Name	Business Sector	City	State	Date	Amount	Aggregate
ATMOS Energy PAC	Energy	Dallas	TX	4/30/2011	$2,500	$2,500
Bankplus PAC	Banking	Ridgeland	MS	3/14/2011	$6,000	$6,000
Contractor's PAC	Contracting/Building	Jackson	MS	4/29/2011	$2,500	$2,500
Denbury Resources PAC	Oil and Gas	Plano	TX	4/30/2011	$1,500	$1,500
Homebuilders Association of MS PAC	Homebuilding	Jackson	MS	4/29/2011	$20,000	$20,000
LEN Pac	Consumer Finance	Jackson	MS	4/30/2011	$5,000	$5,000
Mississippi Chiropractors PAC	Chiropractic	Flowood	MS	4/29/2011	$1,000	$1,000
MS Coalition for Progress PAC	Mississippi State University	Jackson	MS	4/30/2011	$10,000	$10,000
NUCOR Steel Recycler's of MS PAC	Steel Recyclers	Flowood	MS	1/18/2011	$1,000	$1,000
Renasant Bank PAC	Banking	Tupelo	MS	2/9/2011	$1,000	$1,000
Spectra Energy Group PAC	Natural Gas	Houston	TX	4/30/2011	$5,000	$5,000
						$55,500

Okay, so now we see all this money that is coming in and where it comes from, so now I want to show you connoisseurs of tomatoes how it is spent. After you read all this, I hope you go through your bushel baskets, remove all the rotten tomatoes and pass them out to your friends so they can throw them at the candidates in need at the next stump party.

From the beginning of the New Year until the last month before the primary, this is what Phil Bryant spent to strategize in order to get your vote. These strategists look at everything from the color of ties that depict just the right message, down to the amount of grease to put on the yellow Caterpillar ball cap. They tell their candidates what to say, how to say it, when to say it and who they should say it to. If 10 thousand people are expected at the annual coast crawfish festival and the candidate hates crawfish, he WILL learn to like it before he speaks to that crowd. Give them what they want, is the mentality whether it is genuine or not. They mess with your mind. Frontier Strategy Group (friends of Bryant and Barbour who offer advice and an airplane) make sure you know that on their website by showing you what the right brain contributes as opposed to what the left brain contributes. Click the link below and see what I mean. Did you know strategists and marketers were messing with our minds? Cigarette companies have done that to us and our children for decades.

http://www.frontier.ms/

Vendor	Services Purchased	City	State	Date	Amount	Aggreate
Jena T. Abrams	Campaign Strategies	Meridian	MS	6/30/2011	$1,000.00	$1,000.00
John Ayers	Campaign Strategies	Ridgeland	MS	6/30/2011	$1,000.00	$1,000.00
Elizabeth Bosarge	Campaign Strategies	Ocean Springs	MS	6/30/2011	$1,000.00	$1,000.00
Classic Connections LLC	Campaign Strategies	Brandon	MS	1/3/2011	$1,825.00	
Classic Connections LLC	Campaign Strategies	Brandon	MS	2/15/2011	$1,800.00	
Classic Connections LLC	Campaign Strategies	Brandon	MS	2/28/2011	$2,000.00	
Classic Connections LLC	Campaign Strategies	Brandon	MS	3/31/2011	$2,000.00	$14,029.72
John Downs	Campaign Strategies	Pearl	MS	6/30/2011	$1,774.89	$1,774.89
Jessica Freeman	Campaign Strategies	Brandon	MS	6/30/2011	$1,350.00	$1,350.00
Johusha Gates	Campaign Strategies	Madison	MS	6/30/2011	$750.00	$750.00
Brandon Hannah	Campaign Strategies	Morton	MS	6/30/2011	$1,712.04	$1,712.04
Elizabeth Henry	Campaign Strategies	Brandon	MS	1/5/2011	$200.00	
Elizabeth Henry	Campaign Strategies	Brandon	MS	1/5/2011	$200.00	$400.00
Frontier Strategies LLC	Campaign Strategies	Jackson	MS	1/3/2011	$20,940.62	
Frontier Strategies LLC	Campaign Strategies	Jackson	MS	1/3/2011	$19,056.52	
Frontier Strategies LLC	Campaign Strategies	Jackson	MS	1/3/2011	$8,990.27	
Frontier Strategies LLC	Campaign Strategies	Jackson	MS	2/28/2011	$40,811.20	
Frontier Strategies LLC	Campaign Strategies	Jackson	MS	3/15/2011	$19,821.68	$350,928.56
Scott Hotchkiss McClintock	Campaign Strategies	Tunica	MS	6/30/2011	$1,295.48	$1,295.48
Stephn Heard Moore	Campaign Strategies	Brooksville	MS	6/3/2011	$1,500.00	$1,500.00
Alan Moran	Campaign Strategies	Kiln	MS	6/30/2011	$1,000.00	$1,000.00
John Myers	Campaign Strategies	Pellahatchie	MS	7/7/2011	$2,901.73	$2,901.73
Politicap	Campaign Strategies	Raymond	MS	1/6/2011	$10,000.00	
Politicap	Campaign Strategies	Raymond	MS	1/11/2011	$100,192.00	
Politicap	Campaign Strategies	Raymond	MS	1/25/2011	$524.34	
Politicap	Campaign Strategies	Raymond	MS	1/31/2011	$10,000.00	
Politicap	Campaign Strategies	Raymond	MS	2/3/2011	$176.17	
Politicap	Campaign Strategies	Raymond	MS	2/28/2011	$10,000.00	
Politicap	Campaign Strategies	Raymond	MS	3/31/2011	$10,000.00	$175,509.33
Matthew Wayne Rigel	Campaign Strategies	Hattiesburg	MS	6/30/2011	$1,797.84	$1,797.84
Lindsey Robinson	Campaign Strategies	Laurel	MS	7/6/2011	$1,000.00	$1,000.00
Rose Strategies	Campaign Strategies	Washington	DC	7/14/2011	$14,674.00	$14,674.00
Stanley Shows	Campaign Strategies and Expenses	Brandon	MS	1/3/2011	$3,000.00	
Stanley Shows	Campaign Strategies and Expenses	Brandon	MS	1/13/2011	$93.50	
Stanley Shows	Campaign Strategies and Expenses	Brandon	MS	2/15/2011	$568.14	
Stanley Shows	Campaign Strategies and Expenses	Brandon	MS	3/10/2011	$144.33	
Stanley Shows	Campaign Strategies and Expenses	Brandon	MS	3/15/2011	$735.00	
Stanley Shows	Campaign Strategies and Expenses	Brandon	MS	3/21/2011	$403.41	
Stanley Shows	Campaign Strategies and Expenses	Brandon	MS	3/31/2011	$3,000.00	
Stanley Shows	Campaign Strategies and Expenses	Brandon	MS	4/8/2011	$521.73	
Stanley Shows	Campaign Strategies and Expenses	Brandon	MS	4/25/2011	$417.69	
Stanley Shows	Campaign Strategies and Expenses	Brandon	MS	1/31/2011	$2,632.50	
Stanley Shows	Campaign Strategies and Expenses	Brandon	MS	1/31/2011	$473.00	
Stanley Shows	Campaign Strategies and Expenses	Brandon	MS	1/31/2011	$2,632.50	$25,845.04
Katie Ryan VanCamp	Campaign Strategies	Brandon	MS	6/30/2011	$1,500.00	$1,500.00
						$582,794.93

This is what big money from corporations gives you, big money like almost $6 hundred thousand dollars to manipulate your conscience. Did you realize the job of governor only pays $122 thousand dollars a year? But that's not all. Wait until you see what is behind door number three. He has now spent all that money learning how to manipulate you so he now has to make it work for him, getting the message out to you. If you have ever placed ads on radio or TV you know how effective they are, but also know how expensive they are. But who cares....it's not their money they are spending. It's mine, yours and all big business owners.

I won't mention all the small tomatoes, like local printing/advertising, etc., but rather the big tomato farm that gets his name and picture out while you eat breakfast, drive down the road, access the internet, watch late night news and so on. Here's how Phil Bryant really spent his campaign money convincing you he is the right choice for governor:

Media Outlet	City	State	Date	Aggregate
Maggie Clark Media Services	Brandon	MS	7/22/2011	$1,615,062.82

Keep in mind, this is prior to the primary and does not include additional payments that may have been made for the runoff or the November general election. Remember when you saw the $1 thousand donation from Maggie Clark Media Services? I told you it would come up again. Don't get me wrong. This lady is a professional and the go-to person to go to if you want to be elected. She and her staff are very good at what they do. They even got Steve Patterson elected!

At any rate, I would like to sum it up and finalize my comments to you about Phil Bryant before moving on to the next candidate. Phil has spent almost $600 thousand dollars on strategists to learn how to manipulate his image to one you like best because you really don't know anything about him for sure. He has also spent more than $1.6 million dollars in media coverage to get that marketed image and made-up slogans out to you. That alone is almost $2 million dollars, not including any other expenses again for a job that pays $122 thousand dollars a year.

Candidates who have not been politicians, or in a place to do good things for existing businesses, or make promises to them, are at a handicap in this game. The money businesses gave allowed him to be plastered into your mind with nothing but the promised-land down the road. We are influenced by all those strategic techniques and media coverage whether we want to admit it or not.

I will give you an example of what I mean. Recently a concerned Christian lady was visiting one of my relatives' small business and heard about the first edition of this book. While visiting my relative as I spoke with him on the phone, she asked to speak to me about Phil Bryant. I spoke to her and I asked her this question. "Why Phil Bryant other than what you have seen on advertisements, why Phil Bryant....what do you know for sure about him that either he or his followers are telling you?" All she could think of was that she heard through her church that he was a good conservative Christian man. I didn't argue that point with her, but rather asked her to read edition two of my book before proceeding to the polls.

Here's my take:

- Experience – He has never been governor any more than Haley Barbour had been before he was elected. None of our presidents or governors in recent times have been in that position before, so the experience of the office he seeks just isn't there.

- Accountability – He wants you to think he will hold the state agencies accountable. He certainly hasn't done it with regards to gaming commission even after it was smeared in his face. I don't know what audit protocol would be in terms of the frequency needed for auditing agencies bringing in big bucks but I can tell you as state auditor he only audited the gaming commission two times in ten years and both were laughing stocks. He raised the issue of noncompliance to then Lt. Governor Amy Tuck nine years after the legislature mandated Performance Based Budgets and now seventeen years later after heading the senate, what has he done about that?

- Popularity – Absolutely, bought and paid for. He has escalated himself to the status of a Hollywood and/or Nashville celebrity showing off to the state in custom designed tour buses and a Provost Coach like this one that costs well over a million dollars:

Nothing but corporate class for this old boy. Remember that as you drive your old Studebaker truck to the market and come back to park it next to your old

Farmall tractor. Last but not least, think about this….how popular could the other candidates have been if they had started out the primary with over $2 million corporate dollars (compared to the $7 thousand from "worker bees")? Does that mean that either one of them would not have been the best candidate for us? "Bought and Sold" should be the campaign slogan instead of "for the right reason".

~

There are two democrats in the runoffs. They are Bill Luckett, a non-politician lawyer from Clarksdale and Mayor Dupree from Hattiesburg. Mayor Dupree has so many errors on his campaign finance reports, in my opinion, he shouldn't even be in the race and the Secretary of State should be ashamed for allowing documents with so many omissions. I wanted to compare the difference in corporate owners' donations in excess of $1,000 to each other by examining their donor's occupation and employer. I could not do so on his reports because he left so many blank. He also has donations listed as receipts in odd amounts like $433.17 (example). I would be willing to bet that number is an expenditure, not a donation. At any rate, his reports were such a mess, I gave up. If his administrative and/or oversight skills are no better than that, I don't want him in a state office anyway. However, as an overall observation, there were many donations by corporate owners in excess of $2 thousand dollars that are said to be from individuals. He also had many payouts to media and political strategies.

Mr. Luckett has raised a considerable amount of money. However, his campaign finance reports show that the majority of his donations were from the average citizen in amounts of $250 to $500 dollars. Later in his reports they begin to rise with quite a few over $2,500 dollars, but you won't find the questionable donations in the thousands that say they came from an individual but really looks like it came from a corporation. That tells me Luckett is not owned by business interests. Also, I didn't find any major expenditure on his part for campaign strategy to manipulate the voters, or major media deals that might make him look like somebody he is not. His only major supporter is his business partner in a blues restaurant in Clarksdale, Hollywood Actor Morgan Freeman. Mr. Freeman gave him $175 thousand dollars to date. He's not a politician, not owned by big business and what you see is what you get. He doesn't try to be somebody he is not.

Chapter Sixteen

"BUDDY RUBS" WANT CONTROL OF OUR MONEY

"The only thing worse than a liar is a liar that's also a hypocrite"

Tennessee Williams

Stacy Pickering previously came under fire about personal use of a state car just last year. That was about the time Bill Maxey resigned for the same thing. Other long time members of the Mississippi Department of Public Safety (DPS) were also accused. Blogs after the story pointed fingers at newspaper reporters, political opponents and everything else. A closer look inside Pickering's top staff might reveal old ties to some of those people inside the DPS that may have had axes to grind. From the articles I read about the issue, it sounds like Maxey paid his debt owed and went away quietly. Pickering, on the other hand, still maintains his office and still continues to pursue other people for what he was accused of doing himself and may still be doing. That is sort of ironic when you go onto the Office of the State Auditor's website and read the "holier than thou" quotes from Stacey Pickering. Read the one below he is so proud to display:

"No one is above the law. We hold all stewards of taxpayer dollars accountable, to the highest degree of the law."
State Auditor Stacey Pickering

One thing Mr. Pickering needs to realize is that the law is a set of codified statutory decisions by the legislature to make a violation of their expected behavior, a violation of the law. The law carries with it certain punishments as a crime upon conviction of the offense. However, if Mr. Pickering uses the color of law to collect a civil debt, he has not enforced the law or caused any other person or agency to do so. He has used the "pay up or go to jail mentality" to make his job easy and put another tally mark on his bulletin board to be stored away for the next election. A demand notice (with payment) itself does not qualify as enforcing the law. It usually means you don't have enough evidence or enough go-nads to go after the man, but you still want that trophy on the wall.

Convicting a person of a crime, using the jury system requires that the crime be proven beyond a shadow of a doubt. The defense only has to convince one juror that a reasonable doubt exists and the suspect goes free. Proving that a debt is owed in a civil matter requires that preponderance of the evidence points toward the accused.

The test of these cases is often described as "more likely than not," meaning more likely than not that the accused committed the offense so he will have to pay up.

That is a much easier burden to prove but still brings the headlines to the auditor that lays another stone on the path to his next higher position. He will need to show his worth by making more cases than his predecessor to show his worthiness of a promotion to the voters of Mississippi. More cases mean more media exposure. What we really have in the auditor's office, is mostly good people, humble attorneys, great auditors and investigators as well as other loyal employees. Unfortunately, these offices are often led by self-serving, ladder climbing, narcissistic, headline seeking, back stabbing politicians and the names that should be honored for good, hard work are tarnished by being a part of an organization led by crooks. The no-named investigators and auditors just fade away in time, only to possibly appear on the horizon again as a low-paid, contract humble servant. Their worth or value to the auditor becomes evident when their rates of pay are compared to others closer to, or considered more loyal to the auditor without regard for number of years' experience, education or dedication.

In a Clarion Ledger report by Jerry Mitchell on July 6, 2010, the issues of criminal versus civil are discussed. Excerpts from his report follow:

> *In addition, each state employee who drives a state-owned vehicle must read and sign a book put out by the state Department of Finance and Administration that says a state-owned car cannot be used for personal business. Employees are required to keep a daily log with beginning and ending odometer readings, miles traveled and locations noted.*

> *Since Maxey and his supervisors would not comment, it's unclear if he has complied with these requirements.*

> *Usually allegations involving personal use of state vehicles are "dealt with by the auditor's office," said Tom Hood, executive director of the state Ethics Commission. "They can bring a civil claim, or it could be criminal."*
> *Mike Keys, manager for technical assistance at the state auditor's office, said civil actions are most common.*

Has our state auditor become a bill collector?   Pickering is a republican and Attorney General Jim Hood is a democrat. Although they have somewhat of a working relationship, it does not mean that they are "social buddy rubs" by any stretch of the imagination. Pickering has no prosecutorial authority. All he can do is forward a case to the Attorney General. If Hood wants to prosecute it, he will. Otherwise, unless Pickering takes the case to a local district attorney, it goes nowhere. The problem with that is most of the accused are public officials or long time public employees with about as many connections (including registered voters) in the district as the district attorney. Prosecution is not likely there either unless the DA wants to commit political suicide. I know that's not right, but it is just the way it is. So you may see 20 cases pursued and only one or two where the law was used in anything but arm twisting. To see for yourself, go to Pickering's website and read the press releases of cases pursued and compare them with cases prosecuted in criminal court. You may even find someone who was prosecuted to the max, while others committing far more serious crimes were not prosecuted at all.

http://www2.osa.ms.gov/forum/forumdisplay.php?f=22

Here is one of Mr. Pickering's quotes that I like the most. It will make sense when you read about my latest contact with his office.

"Accountability and transparency are critical to government. It is important that taxpayers know their money is spent correctly and responsibly."

State Auditor Stacey Pickering

I recently learned that one of Pickering's former full-time state employees (now independent contractor), is currently working for my state senator (and candidate for State Treasurer) Lee Yancey part of the week. I say "my" state senator, but I mean only that he is the senator in my district. I don't own any state senators, although I am sure there are those that do. He is another one of the losers I contacted when I was seeking action against the gaming commission two years ago and even after providing him positive proof of the state violating its own laws, he did nothing that I ever saw. As far as I am concerned, Lee Yancey was just as responsible as the governor and his worthless chain of command below him. He strikes me as just an outsider who moved to a specific district that would become open, with the biggest church for backing.

At any rate, I suspected that whether Pickering's actions were right or wrong, neither he, nor his representatives would want the details of his activity known. However, Mr. Pickering is big on "transparency" so I didn't think there would be a problem if we, the public, asked about this cozy arrangement with his buddy rub republican Lee Yancey.

I had heard last year that Pickering's public relations employee Lisa Shoemaker had worked as a media consultant or in some other similar capacity for a U.S. Congressional candidate on the Gulf Coast. Ms. Shoemaker's Linked-In page showed both jobs but she appeared back at the auditor's office as "Communication's Director" for the Office of the State Auditor (and still does). However, I learned through the state transparency website that she was not an employee, but rather a contractor and two contracts were listed on the transparency site. Her rate of pay was listed as $60 per hour.

Having worked as a division director for the state in the past and knowing few, if any raises had been granted to anybody, I suspected that with the title "director", she made around $53 thousand dollars, or probably around $25 to $27 per hour based on a 2,087 hour work year. Unable to find any transparency information on her prior salary, I decided to go to the source (Auditor's Office) and request public records, not naming her individually but any former employees in the previous year who were allowed to leave and come right back under contract. I wanted to know if Pickering was paying her for her worth compared to other former, or retired employees also under contract. I wanted to prove or disprove his statement that he said **"It is important that taxpayers know their money is spent correctly and responsibly."** I wanted to know if her pay was responsible compared to other employees.

On August 9, 2011, I specifically asked for public "records", not mere information or details of the past, but rather, records that showed preserved evidence of the transactions in question. The young lady attorney took one look and told me it would probably only take one day to respond. I contacted her several times over the next few days to determine if the records were available and she stalled me with problems like updating computers, etc. I don't blame her though. I know what was going on inside (damage control) by the Auditor's office. The law changed last year giving agencies seven work days to respond. She eventually took six. Here is my first response:

STATE OF MISSISSIPPI
OFFICE OF THE STATE AUDITOR
STACEY E. PICKERING
STATE AUDITOR

August 16, 2011

VIA EMAIL at Rick Ward <rickward47@hotmail.com>
And US Mail

LCDR Ricky W. Ward, USN (Retired)
126 Dogwood Trail
Brandon, Mississippi

Re: Public Records Request

Dear Mr. Ward:

The Office of the State Auditor received your Public Records Request on Tuesday, August 9, 2011, where you requested the following information:

> Names and titles of any and all persons who are currently, or have been on contract in the State Auditor's office within the past year, but were previously working therein as a state employee. Please list the employee's date of departure and rate of pay (hourly or annually) as of their last day of service, along with their new rate of pay as a contractor. Also please provide the start date of the contract.

Per the Office of the State Auditor's public records policy, costs of the production of the requested documents include a charge of ten cents ($0.10) per page and actual cost per hour of reproduction. In addition, search/collation of the records by staff personnel shall be at actual cost per hour. There are no documents to be reproduced, but there is a one-half hour charge for research by staff personnel. The total cost of the information to be provided to you is $17.50.

POST OFFICE BOX 956 • JACKSON, MISSISSIPPI 39205 • (601) 576-2800 • FAX (601) 576-2650
www.osa.ms.gov

Mr. Rick Ward
August 16, 2011
Page 2

Upon receipt of your payment of $17.50, the information will be provided to you. You may pick up the information upon delivery of the payment or it can be emailed to you. If you have any questions, you may contact me at 601.576.2728.

Sincerely,

Melissa C. Patterson
Special Assistant Attorney General

MCP:ld

cc: Mr. Stacey E. Pickering, State Auditor

The next to the last statement on the previous page said, "***There are no documents to be reproduced***, but there is a one-half hour charge for research by staff personnel. The total cost of the information to be provided to you is $17.50." (See the next page.) I was bum-fuzzled. I wanted records that provided me answers to the questions I was posing. Not knowing how they operated internally, what software they used, or in what forms the records were maintained, I didn't know the specific document to ask for, but I think you will agree that I spelled out what I wanted.

Now, let me offer a suggestion. Since the Supreme Court has ruled that public information stored on computers is still considered public records and in order to use this type software the agency cannot use software that would prohibit access by the public. Therefore employee data was in storage. All it would have required is a screen print of a computer screen page depicting her employment dates and rate of pay. Any other personal information like social security number, etc., could have been redacted with a black marker after printing out the document, if that had been an issue. Secondly a copy of the contract could have been reproduced from within their office or the state's transparency site with little effort. It would have shown the date her contract started, rate per hour, dates of service and any caps on entitlement. Both of these steps would have taken probably less than 15 minutes and would have answered every question I posed. They could have handed me two documents, a screen print of her employment dates with rate of pay and a copy of the contract. Why then, did they not provide those documents and claim there "are no documents to be reproduced." The e-mail below says "There are no tangible documents to reproduce"….Really?

Upon my arrival at the Office of the State Auditor, on August 17, 2011 they also handed me a letter dated August 17, 2011 by the same AG representative. Just like the previous letter, they refer to the fact that I requested "information" in their line, just before quoting my request verbatim. However, they didn't address the line above my descriptive quote which said:

"Please accept this letter as a request for public _records_ as described below:"
But their response was, **"There are no documents to be reproduced."** *(Really?)*

STATE OF MISSISSIPPI
OFFICE OF THE STATE AUDITOR
STACEY E. PICKERING
STATE AUDITOR

August 17, 2011

VIA HAND DELIVERY

LCDR Ricky W. Ward, USN (Retired)
126 Dogwood Trail
Brandon, Mississippi

Re: Public Records Request

Dear Mr. Ward:

The Office of the State Auditor received your Public Records Request on Tuesday, August 9, 2011, where you requested the following information:

Names and titles of any and all persons who are currently, or have been on contract in the State Auditor's office within the past year, but were previously working therein as a state employee. Please list the employee's date of departure and rate of pay (hourly or annually) as of their last day of service, along with their new rate of pay as a contractor. Also please provide the start date of the contract.

The Office of the State Auditor does not have any contract employees that fit the description of your request. The Office does have one Independent Contractor which it will include in this request out of an abundance of caution.

Lisa Shoemaker, Director of Communications, had an annual salary of $52,535.15 plus fringe benefits of approximately 30% (for a total compensation of approximately $68,295.70) when she resigned from the Office of the State Auditor on September 30, 2010 to pursue additional opportunities. Ms. Shoemaker signed a contract with the Office of the State Auditor as an Independent Contractor to provide media services for the State Auditor. Ms. Shoemaker's

Mr. Rick Ward
August 17, 2011
Page 2

contract start date was October 1, 2010, for a limit of $51,395.00 for the 2011 fiscal year. Ms. Shoemaker was paid a total of $39,960.00 for the 2011 fiscal year.

If you have any questions, you may contact me at 601.576.2728.

Sincerely,

Melissa C. Patterson
Special Assistant Attorney General

MCP:ld

cc: Mr. Stacey E. Pickering, State Auditor

So, they decided to offer information in their own words which read to me like an explanation or justification. Please read it and see what you think (last paragraph, continued on next page).

Here is the first page of the contract they spoke of (but didn't have it to reproduce). It was taken from the state transparency site, the word Stacey Pickering likes to use – TRANSPARENCY.

CONTRACT FOR PROFESSIONAL SERVICES

This Personal Services Contract ("Contract") is made by and between entered into as of this the _____ day of September 2010, by and between the Office of the State Auditor, State of Mississippi, 801 North West Street, Suite 801, Jackson, Mississippi, 39201, hereinafter referred to as the "Agency", and on the day of , 20 and Lisa Shoemaker, hereinafter referred to as "Consultant", whose address is 106 Heights Drive, Clinton, Mississippi 39056, under the following terms and conditions:

TERMS AND CONDITIONS:

1. **Scope of Services:** At the request of the State Auditor, Consultant will provide advice and consulting assistance as may be necessary to the State Auditor and to the Agency; assist with special projects; and provide strategic communication, public relations and media relations services. At the request of the State Auditor, Consultant may be authorized to speak to the media about certain aspects of projects or assistance she may be providing to the Agency. Consultant shall report directly to the State Auditor.

2. **Contract Period:** The period of performance of services under this Contract shall begin on October 1, 2010 and end no later than June 30, 2010. This Contract may be renewed at the option of the Agency for a period of one year.

3. **Consideration:** As consideration for the performance of this Contract, Consultant shall be paid a fee not to exceed in accordance with the terms of this Contract: Consultant shall receive compensation in an amount not to exceed $51,395.00. This compensation is based on an hourly rate of rate of $60.00. The hourly rate includes all expenses with the exception of any travel expenses outside of the Jackson Metropolitan Area. Travel expenses will be billed as provided per State of Mississippi travel regulations at the state rates as set out in the State Travel Policy, www.dfa.state.ms.us/Purchasing/Travel/TravelManual.pdf, with a limit of $10,000.00, for a contract total of $61,395.00. In no instance will payment be made above and beyond the contracted amount.

   Ms. Shoemaker shall submit monthly invoices to the State Auditor. A copy of the invoice to be used is attached to this Contract as Exhibit "A". The invoice shall outline the work performed and detail the hours worked. The State Auditor shall approve each invoice prior to the invoice being submitted for payment

   The State Auditor may from time to time request changes in the scope of services of Ms. Shoemaker to be performed hereunder. Such changes, including any increase or decrease in the amount of compensation, must be mutually agreed upon by and between the State Auditor or his duly authorized representative and Consultant, and shall be included in written amendments to this contract.

4. **Payment:** The Agency agrees to make payment in accordance with Mississippi law on "Timely Payments for Purchases by Public Bodies", Section 31-7-301, et seq. of the Mississippi Code of 1972, as amended, which generally provides for payment of undisputed amounts within

1

Now, on the surface, you may read what they want you to read. Her pay and benefits as an employee exceeded what she would make as a contractor without benefits (therefore she was worse off, not better off). On September 27, 2010, Lisa Shoemaker was still an employee at the Office of the State Auditor. On that date, she signed the contract basically described in the letter. Her contractual period would begin on October 1, 2010 so she was never gone a single day from one status to the next. The benefit she gained that she didn't have as a state employee was the ability to work for a politician's campaign and be paid for those services. She did so while working on Congressman Steven Palazzo's campaign. Her last official state "tweet" on her Twitter account was in September 2010 when she reported that Pickering's bumper stickers were in. By the way, the reason her total pay was $39,960 instead of the full amount of the contract, is that it was executed beginning the fourth month of the fiscal year (the fiscal year ended June 30).

The phone number she uses for the State Auditor site is the same that is posted on the Lee Yancey's flyers. I will check to see if that is a state cell.

The plot thickens. What the Auditor's Office omitted in their "information" was the fact that there was another, more recent contract that made her arrangement look a lot more attractive. By now she had a new contract that still paid her $60 dollars per hour, but this time it had a cap of $78 thousand dollars, plus up to $10 thousand in expenses. This $88 thousand is sounding better, plus she has formed a corporation with the Secretary of State called "Southern Strategies" and has earned over $15 thousand in the last couple of months (reported) on Lee Yancey's campaign finance report. With one successful candidate behind her (Palazzo) and another wannabe out front (Lee Yancey), along with her company, she is well on her way. Maybe next year, her new contract will be $98 thousand and still under the legal requirement of $100 thousand that would have to be approved by a board of reviewers. He kept her under the approval wire.

PERSONAL SERVICES CONTRACT

THIS PERSONAL SERVICES CONTRACT ("Contract") made and entered into this the 1st day of July, 2011, by and between the OFFICE OF THE STATE AUDITOR of the State of Mississippi, whose address is 501 North West Street, Suite 801, Jackson, Mississippi 39201, hereinafter "OSA", and Southern Strategies, LLC, whose address is 106 Heights Drive, Clinton, Mississippi 39056, hereinafter "Consultant", under the following terms and conditions.

WITNESSETH:

In consideration of the mutual covenants contained herein, and subject to the terms and conditions hereinafter stated, it is hereby understood and agreed by the parties hereto as follows:

1. **SCOPE OF SERVICES:** At the request of the State Auditor, Consultant will provide advice and consulting assistance as may be necessary to the State Auditor and to OSA; assist with special projects; and, provide strategic communication, public relations and media relations services. At the request of the State Auditor, Consultant may be authorized to speak to the media about certain aspects of projects or assistance she may be providing to OSA. Consultant shall report directly to the State Auditor. Consultant shall coordinate the performance of the services to be provided hereunder through the State Auditor and consult with the State Auditor on specific courses of action which should be pursued.

2. **CONTRACT TERM:** The period of performance of services under this Contract shall begin on July 1, 2011 and end no later than June 30, 2012. This Contract may be renewed at the option of the State Auditor for a period of one (1) year.

3. **CONSIDERATION:** As consideration for the performance of this Contract, Consultant shall receive compensation in an amount not to exceed $78,000.00 (Seventy-eight thousand dollars). This compensation is based on an hourly rate of $60.00 (sixty dollars). The hourly rate includes all expenses with the exception of any travel expenses outside of the Jackson Metropolitan Area. Travel expenses will be billed as provided per State of Mississippi travel regulations at the state rates as set out in the State Travel Policy, www.dfa.state.ms.us/Purchasing/Travel/TravelManual.pdf, with a limit of $10,000.00 (ten thousand dollars), for a total of $88,000.00 (Eighty-eight thousand dollars). In no instance will payment be made above and beyond the contracted amount.

   Consultant shall submit monthly invoices to OSA. The invoice shall outline the work performed and detail the hours worked. The State Auditor shall approve each invoice prior to invoice being submitted for payment.

4. **PAYMENT:** OSA agrees to make payment in accordance with Mississippi law on "Timely Payments for Purchases by Public Bodies", Section 31-7-301, et seq. of the Mississippi Code of 1972, as amended, which generally provides for payment of undisputed amounts within forty-five (45) days of receipt of the invoice.

1

However, the fact that she is well on her way is commendable for her, but the question of whether or not Pickering is seeing that our money is being spent correctly and responsibly still remains. Let's compare her to other employees/former employees. Their contracts are on the transparency sight. I won't bore you with reading the rest of them but this is what you find if you look yourself:

Lisa Shoemaker $60.00 per hour, cap of $88,000, ($10 thousand expenses)

Norman R. McLeod $36.94 per hr. cap of $14,776 (no pre-approved expenses)

Rodney Zeagler $36.94 per hr. cap of $38,400 (no pre-approved expenses)

Scott Rankin $27.50 per hr. cap of $27,700 (no pre-approved expenses)

http://www.transparency.mississippi.gov/contracts.php

I would just like to make a few observations and leave the suspicions and assertions up to you. Lisa Shoemaker is in her 20's with about 4 years documented job performance as well as some membership in professional organizations and holds a Bachelor's degree. Note her rate of pay. Go to her Linked-In web page and view her qualifications, then compare them to the others.

http://www.linkedin.com/pub/lisa-shoemaker-apr/8/400/a45

Norman McCloud and Rodney Zeagler are very experienced college graduates and hold CPA certifications. They have been certified state auditors for collectively over a half century. Norman has served as Division Director for State Audit during previous administrations and both have served as Deputy Auditors.

Scott Rankin has a law degree and has served in various high level state positions over the past 20-30 years. He has previously served as the Executive Director of the Mississippi Ethics Commission (the job now held by Jim Hood's brother Tom Hood). Note their rates of pay, caps and expenses and ask yourself if our auditor could have found us a better deal that could be available full-time as the title suggested. How many times has he whined about more auditors? Maybe this is why he can get what he needs.

Let's go back for a moment though and address the issue about the records available being records denied. Who was responsible for that? Is the Office of the

State Auditor or the Office of the Attorney General? That is a very important issue that needs to be addressed. I would like to hear from all the people who have ever sought public records and got these responses or responses very similar:

- You will have to hire a part-time temp employee to do this much research.
- You will have to pay for the research that will cost in the hundreds of dollars.
- You may come and inspect our records yourself (not knowing what to look for).
- Here is a big box of documents for you, go find what you want in it.
- The records are not available.
- The records are not public.

Most all of the state-agency lawyers work for Attorney General Jim Hood. They are embedded in the agencies and in my opinion, often forget their loyalty and when need be, assist in the cover-up of mistakes made by their client agencies. It is as if those of us who seek documents are the bad guys and the lawyers (that we pay for too) put themselves in a defense attorney mode and block us from what another law (Public Records Act) says we are entitled. So what we are stuck with is no citizen's advocate. So if we don't know exactly what to ask for, or how to ask it, we get into a war of words with the attorneys, sparring with them armed only with layman terminology. That justifies them not giving you what you asked for. It seems to me if they sometimes play like they are brain dead or speak some other language. Please, if you have had this experience, let me know and if this appears on a blog site, spell it out.

~

I have to bring up one more issue about our auditor and his buddy rub Lee Yancey, both of which want to look out after our money. I tried to get the auditor to listen about crimes committed by state officials two years ago. He would not respond to me or my complaints filled out on his website. I then notified David Huggins, his Chief Investigator whom I have known for over 40 years. My e-mail and his response can be seen here, but I never heard from him again and nothing was ever done. They knew my allegations from the form I filled out on the website.

New   Reply Reply all Forward   Delete Junk Sweep ▾ Mark as ▾ Move to ▾   📧 ⟳   Options ▾ ⊙ ▾

RE: BINGO   Back to messages ⬇ ⬆
To see messages related to this one, group messages by conversation.

▫ David Huggins   11/02/09
   To rickward47@hotmail.com   Reply ▾

Rick:

Thanks, This may surprise you but, I have already thought about your knowledge on this topic. Lunch sounds good for me

David R Huggins
Director
Investigative Division
Office of The State Auditor
601-576-2724
800-321-1275

From: rickward47@hotmail.com [mailto:rickward47@hotmail.com]
Sent: Monday, November 02, 2009 6:57 PM
To: David R. Huggins
Subject: BINGO

David:

I've got a feeling if you haven't already, in the near future you might be tasked with some bingo or charity money audits/recovery. If you do and you want the inside scoop on these things, I can save you a lot of time. Will be glad to sit down over lunch and do a data dump if you want. Just let me know.

Rick

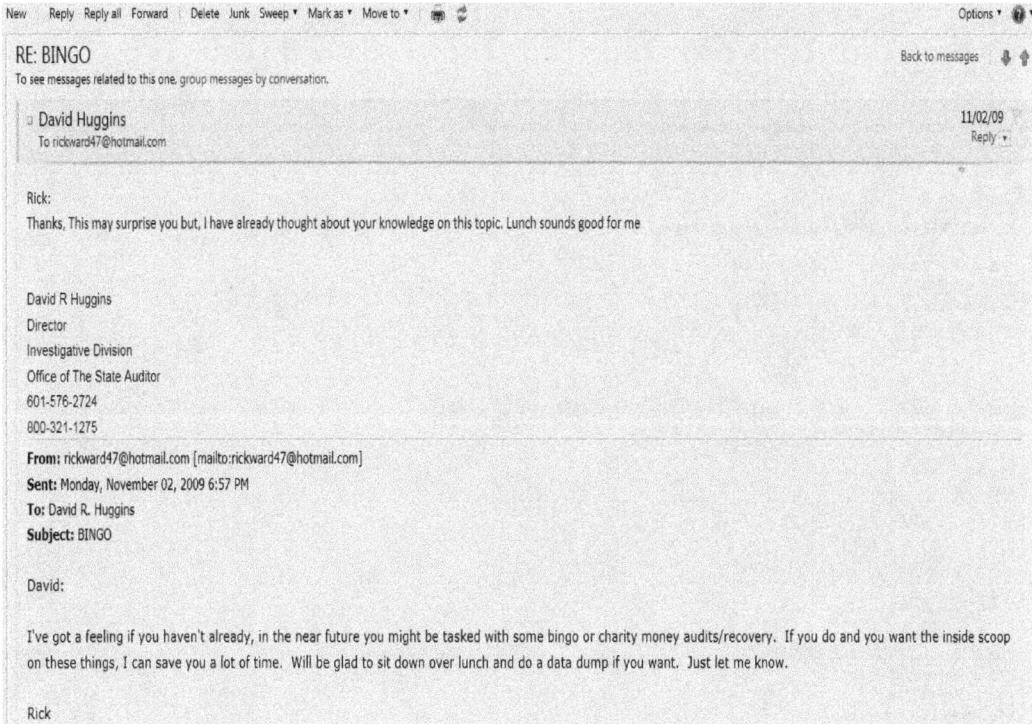

I took the battle to Lee Yancey too. He was going to do something. Please read the e-mail string between us. You will see he "entertained" me and never lifted one finger that I am aware of. I know nothing ever changed but even if he had tried, he should have contacted me and told me what he had done but what he ran up against. So he gaffed me off as a senator and now he wants my vote for State Treasurer? Ain't gonna happen pal.

Responding to someone with news (good or bad), is common courtesy. I have seen so many politicians like those mentioned in this chapter that think they are above the law or above their voters and they don't realize what goes around comes around. If I needed a good dog catcher, I would look elsewhere.

Lee Yancey   12/10/08
To rickward47@hotmail.com   Reply :

Hi Rick. I have not submitted the letter. I have had several conversations with people who share your point of view who are former employees of the Gaming Commission. I am continuing to gather information. Thank you for all the data you have provided. I am planning to do something.

Lee

--- On Tue, 12/9/08, rickward47@hotmail.com <*rickward47@hotmail.com*> wrote:

> From: rickward47@hotmail.com <rickward47@hotmail.com>
> Subject: RE: E MAIL
> To: "Lee Yancey" <jlyancey@yahoo.com>
> Date: Tuesday, December 9, 2008, 4:14 PM
>
> Lee:
>
> I never head back from you after my response so I don't know if you revised the letter, trashed it as I indicated if that was what you wanted to do or what. I would like to know one way or the other.
>
> Thanks,
> Rick
>
>
>
>
>
>
> > Date: Tue, 21 Oct 2008 06:52:02 -0700
> > From: jlyancey@yahoo.com
> > Subject: RE: E MAIL
> > To: rickward47@hotmail.com
> >
> > Dear Rick,
> >
> > I am studying the request for the attorney general's opinion on this matter. You have written this (I think) as if I were the one writing it and I want to make sure it is what I would say. You have had at least a decade to get frustrated over this issue and it is very new to me. I understand your frustration but ask for your patience in letting me get a grasp of this important issue. I do plan to submit the request when I am more than a letter carrier for you. I will be the one receiving all the questions and I want to be fully prepared to answer them. I have a Finance Committee meeting Thursday to discuss tax issues for the coming session so I will not be at the Gaming Commission's meeting. I will be in touch.
> >

~

I have one more contractor to talk to you about. I do this because again, our State Auditor has an obligation to spend our money frugally with our best interests in mind. That doesn't include his best interest for future political positions or requiring us (taxpayers) to pay for his own personal politicos.

Talk about a loser, here is a guy who has more political connections on his "resume" than a country dog has got fleas. He was named eight months ago as the Republican National Committee's Senior Advisor. He apparently looks good in big circles and rubs elbows with all those other buddy rubs I talked about, but he lost an election in his own home town for City Council Ward Three in Laurel last election. Check him out though on the next link though. Maybe Pickering coming from Laurel owes him, or maybe he wants to benefit from his political resume. Either way, it looks to me like we are paying for his politico and possibly an occasional driver with an expense account to and from Laurel. At any rate, the leadercall.com says this about James (Jim) Johnson:

Johnson has spent many years on Republican campaigns and fundraising, originally going to Washington to serve as Deputy Undersecretary of Agriculture under President Reagan.

Johnson also served on the staff of former U.S. Sen. Trent Lott (R-Miss.), and was the founder and first executive director of the New Republican Majority Fund (Lott's political action committee).

He also worked in a fundraising capacity for lobbyist group Barbour, Griffith and Rogers, and worked on Mississippi Governor Haley Barbour's campaign.
Click here for the full story:

http://leadercall.com/local/x1894467075/Johnson-named-RNC-senior-advisor

Oh yeah, I want to make sure you know, our frugal auditor looking out after our dollars contracted this man at the same hourly rate as his "Communications Director". Oh, by the way, did I mention that our auditor himself only makes about $45 an hour or so himself? That is no slouchy paycheck, but why would a state official pay two employees, contractors or whatever you want to call them, at an hourly rate some $15 an hour more than his?

PERSONAL SERVICES CONTRACT

THIS PERSONAL SERVICES CONTRACT ("Contract") made and entered into this the 20th day of July, 2011, by and between the OFFICE OF THE STATE AUDITOR of the State of Mississippi, whose address is 501 North West Street, Suite 801, Jackson, Mississippi 39201, hereinafter "OSA", and James H. Johnson dba Capitol Associates, whose address is 1525 Parker Drive Laurel, MS 39440, hereinafter "Consultant", under the following terms and conditions.

WITNESSETH:

In consideration of the mutual covenants contained herein, and subject to the terms and conditions hereinafter stated, it is hereby understood and agreed by the parties hereto as follows:

1. **SCOPE OF SERVICES:** At the request of the State Auditor, Consultant will provide advice and consulting assistance as may be necessary to the State Auditor and to OSA; assist with special projects; and, provide strategic planning and local government services. At the request of the State Auditor, Consultant may be authorized to speak to civic clubs and other organizations on behalf of the Auditor and OSA. Consultant shall report directly to the State Auditor. Consultant shall coordinate the performance of the services to be provided hereunder through the State Auditor and consult with the State Auditor on specific courses of action which should be pursued.

2. **CONTRACT TERM:** The period of performance of services under this Contract shall begin on July 20, 2011 and end no later than December 31, 2011. This Contract may be renewed at the option of the State Auditor for a period of one (1) year.

3. **CONSIDERATION:** As consideration for the performance of this Contract, Consultant shall receive compensation in an amount not to exceed $31,200.00 (thirty-one thousand and two hundred dollars). This compensation is based on an hourly rate of $60.00 (sixty dollars). The hourly rate includes all expenses with the exception of any travel expenses. Travel expenses will be billed as provided per State of Mississippi travel regulations at the state rates as set out in the State Travel Policy, www.dfa.state.ms.us/Purchasing/Travel/TravelManual.pdf, with a limit of $10,000.00 (ten thousand dollars), for a total of $41,200.00 (forty-one thousand two hundred dollars). In no instance will payment be made above and beyond the contracted amount.

   Consultant shall submit monthly invoices to OSA. The invoice shall outline the work performed and detail the hours worked. The State Auditor shall approve each invoice prior to invoice being submitted for payment.

4. **PAYMENT:** OSA agrees to make payment in accordance with Mississippi law on "Timely Payments for Purchases by Public Bodies", Section 31-7-301, et seq. of the Mississippi Code of 1972, as amended, which generally provides for payment of undisputed amounts within forty-five (45) days of receipt of the invoice.

Lastly I would like to make a point that our auditor likes to show on his website just like his other buddy rub (Phil Bryant) likes to repeat. They like to quote Ronald Regan:

"Each generation goes further than the generation preceding it because it stands on the shoulders of that generation. You will have opportunities beyond anything we've ever known."

Ronald Reagan

I gotta give them this much, they certainly have opportunities they might not have ever known. However, for three men who claim to be guardians of our funds, I would like to propose a different role model for them. That is former President Harry Truman. Let me give you some points about him that directly relates to our former auditor, our present auditor and our wannabe state treasurer who cares not enough about his voters to even respond with a simple e-mail:

- *Truman refused per diem because he knew he would have to eat, one way or the other.*
- *He refused to write family back home using government stamps or envelopes. He bought and licked his own.*
- *Rode home only with his wife when leaving office and refused Secret Service because of the cost and the fact that he didn't want anybody "making a fuss" over him.*
- *After leaving office, was offered numerous high-paying executive jobs with major corporations. He responded, "You don't want me. You want the Office of the President, and that does not belong to me. It belongs to the American people and it's not for sale."*
- *Congress chose to change the rules for the Congressional Medal of Honor and award it to him for what he did to end WWII. He refused to accept it writing, "I don't consider that I have done anything which should be the reason for any award, Congressional or otherwise."*
- Lastly, he said, *"My choice early in life was either to be a piano player in a whorehouse or a politician and to tell the truth, there is hardly any difference."*

Truman was a man who could make a decision that could impact the world and move on without thinking about it again. Our politicians today can't even pledge not to raise taxes without re-considering. Unlike most our politicians, I have not found a single narcissistic characteristic in Truman's background. We need a hero that has truly fought the battles, not one that movies and commercials have painted as one. We need to fill all our leadership positions in the state with Harry Truman wannabees. We don't need liars. We don't need hypocrites and we don't need narcissistic power mongers who couldn't care less about their common man.

Could it be that Stacey Pickering had something to hide by not finding documents that could be reproduced to respond to my request? Could it be that the Attorney General's embedded lawyer had a reason not to provide the information? Has that ever happened before?

Summary

It's pretty obvious that the governor had a reason for leaving out any reference to gaming, casinos or bingo in his state of the state addresses. His constant accolades to other businesses, some of which were already here when he took office, his speeches about added revenue that new business brings in, jobs they create and so on, are a clue that he didn't want to say one word about gaming. When he was talking about the recession, the hurricanes, the floods, lost revenue, and lost income, he couldn't have helped but talk about gaming, unless he consciously chose not to. His state of the state speeches were incomplete without talking about gaming.

He is the man at the top of the ladder responsible for laws, and obedience to those laws, and he insists he must obey them himself. Therefore, there is no legitimate or lawful reason he would want to give instructions himself, or have his MGC commissioners or the executive director give instructions to stop enforcing the law if it weren't for protecting the gaming industry.

With Phil Bryant at the top of the chain required by law to receive the annual gaming reports, there is no excuse for him not taking action to require the MGC to abide by the law. The fact that I sat face-to-face with him the first week of November 2009, and told him about the laws being broken, and he did not take action is proof positive, that he too, had no desire to see the MGC, or gaming industry suffer any unfavorable publicity, whether it was due or not. I laugh (while throwing up) every time I see his commercial where the guy says he is not scared to do the job. I haven't seen that in him. He sure hasn't done anything about the MGC worth bragging about. Two audits in ten years on the MGC is sad. His wife says in a commercial that he goes after everything he does one hundred percent, well, he must not believe in law enforcement.

The legislature is too large, and can't agree on hardly anything. When it gets that large, it becomes counterproductive, as the figures show. The ones that are there have a poor record of performance when you compare the number of bills introduced, with the number of co-sponsored bills, with the number of bills that are passed. Their size, as I pointed out compared to California's Legislature, considering the square miles, and number of people they represent, is a no-brainer to the question of whether or not our legislature is far too big.

Since laws don't apply to the gaming industry, governor or members of the legislature, we are in a lawless society, except for those of us they desire to prosecute.

216

With district attorneys taking bribes, judges in federal prison, lawyers who partnered with the attorney general in prison, his (Scruggs) son in prison, the former State Auditor serving time, his lawyer serving time, what state is our state in? It certainly is not the state that Governor Barbour has described in his state of the state addresses. That is why the title of this book is *Mississippi: The Real State of Our State* ….the real/whole truth.

Attempting to take action on one state agency for a violation when the attorney general lawyers are embedded in each agency, and the agency with oversight is run by the attorney general's brother, is like peeing into the wind. It all comes back on you. Even if you present prima facie evidence to the Mississippi Ethics Commission that a governing body has violated the law, the maximum fine is only a $100. (The legislature made sure of that.) And that fine will not be charged anyway as long as they can play Monty Hall and work out a deal.

The MGC lawyers in my case must have spent more time on damage control than they should have taken on properly advising the commission of their legal responsibilities. Instead of me feeling that they were providing a service to me as a citizen when asking for public records, I have no doubt they were running interference for the bumbling actions the MGC had taken which also cast them into a suspicious light. They should be non-biased in their response to the public, and should offer legal advice up front to keep the MGC from making errors that cause them to run interference and set up damage control procedures.

Attempting to get anything done through PEER -- when they have no authority to do anything but investigate, and their commission is made up of members of the legislature who determine their scope of work and edit their final report -- is useless. That to me is one of the saddest issues, considering what high quality investigations, and reports they have provided in the past. But again, it was just a waste of our tax dollars knowing they had no enforcement authority, and the legislature was not about to do anything about it. If you don't believe it, go back and look at the findings in all of the reports on the MGC, starting with the first. Follow them forward, and note how often you see the same finding years later. The legislature just laughs it off.

Laws that would hold public officials accountable for violations of ethics, public record laws and public meeting laws that carry up to a $100 fine maximum are absolutely useless. I wonder how many cases the Mississippi Ethics Commission has taken up for action and filed suit as they did in the previous administration before the Hood brothers came to town.

Laws that are supposed to regulate lobbyists, but do nothing, may as well have not been printed. They are a waste of paper they are printed on. They are just killing more and more trees. The same goes for campaign violations.

The legislature and governor have clearly made anything they do wrong, at best, a slap on the wrist. However, they are first to offer lip service to hang drug dealers or murderers. When we elect a governor from the least credible occupation (lobbyist) based on Gallup polls, we deserve what we get. The favored candidate for governor now is from near the bottom of the list on the poll as a current state office holder. Maybe these are the reasons we stay at the bottom of any list compared to other states.

When the governor complains about having to release minimum security prisoners because of budget cuts he initiates instead of further taxing the gaming industry, and then he releases murderers and rapists on our society, you can see what kind of state our state is in.

When our legislative committees tasked with overseeing an industry and passing laws to protect our people, do nothing but write laws to protect the industry, and then take money from the industry in campaign funds, we are already in trouble.

When these people in power are allowed to stay in power, and gain more power, they are – if they are not already -- prime candidates for corruption.

For the governor to cut crucial services needed for our well-being because he doesn't want to increase anybody's taxes, that is sad, and incompetent. I can almost understand politicians seeking re-election not wanting to raise voter's taxes, knowing they probably won't get re-elected if they do. However, I can't see protecting one industry -- especially one industry known for hundreds of years by the corruption that comes with it.

When our legislators as a whole can't have a better rate of success than 23 percent passage rate across the board, we need to change their pay to performance based salaries. We need to establish a benchmark for the number of bills submitted versus the number passed, and the same goes with co-sponsored legislation, while determining a reasonable number of "attaboys". If they don't reach our expectation, cut their pay five percent for every five percent they fall below the benchmark. When the redistricting takes place, they need to consider larger districts for representatives, resulting in fewer representatives. Per diem should not be paid to those within 50 miles of Jackson and they should have to fill out detailed vouchers just like state employees, who, by the way, have a much better reputation for honesty anyway.

If somebody doesn't convince the state officials that we deserve to hear about gaming (good and bad), gaming/legislative/lobbying corruption is going to take over this state -- if it hasn't already. It is sort of funny, from all this research I have done over the last five years, the e-mails, letters, complaints, phone calls, visits to governmental offices that I have made, all I want is for the MGC to make arrests, and our governors to include them in the state of the state addresses. Is that too much for a citizen, registered voter, retired, disabled military person whose entire adult life has been in many facets of nothing but public service to ask for? Whether you join me in this senseless fight, or not, you at least know the "real" state of our state now.

Appendix I
MGC Commissioners

Chairman Jerry St. Pe' from Pascagoula, term expires September 30, 2012

Commissioner Nolen Canon from Tunica, term expires September 30, 2011

Commissioner John M. Hairston from Gulfport, term expires September 30, 2013

Appendix II
Legislative Gaming Committee Members

Bobby Moak, Chairman

http://billstatus.ls.state.ms.us/members/house/moak.xml

Clara Burnett, Vice-Chairman
http://billstatus.ls.state.ms.us/members/house/burnett.xml

Members:

Willie Bailey http://billstatus.ls.state.ms.us/members/house/bailey.xml

Earle S. Banks http://billstatus.ls.state.ms.us/members/house/banks.xml

J. P. Compretta http://billstatus.ls.state.ms.us/members/house/Compretta.xml

George Flaggs, Jr. http://billstatus.ls.state.ms.us/members/house/flaggs.xml

John W. Hines, Sr. http://billstatus.ls.state.ms.us/members/house/hines.xml

D. Stephen Holland http://billstatus.ls.state.ms.us/members/house/holland.xml

Bennett Malone http://billstatus.ls.state.ms.us/members/house/malone.xml

John Mayo http://billstatus.ls.state.ms.us/members/house/mayo.xml

David Norquist http://billstatus.ls.state.ms.us/members/house/norquist.xml

Randall Patterson http://billstatus.ls.state.ms.us/members/house/patterson.xml

Diane C. Peranich http://billstatus.ls.state.ms.us/members/house/peranich.xml

Sara R. Thomas http://billstatus.ls.state.ms.us/members/house/thomas.xml

Henry Zuber III http://billstatus.ls.state.ms.us/members/house/zuber.xml

Appendix III

FBI Offices in Mississippi

FBI Jackson Field Office
1220 Echelon Parkway
Jackson, MS 39213
Phone: (601) 948-5000
Fax: (601) 713-7550
E-mail: fbijn@leo.gov

Columbus
2500 Military Road, Suite 4
Columbus, MS 39705
Phone: (662) 328-5299
Fax: (662) 328-5307

Greenville
342 Washington Avenue, Suite 205
Greenville, MS 38702
Phone: (662) 332-6331
Fax: (662) 332-6332

Gulfport
1317 26th Avenue, Suite 2
Gulfport, MS 39501
Phone: (228) 864-6131
Fax: (228) 214-2335

Hattiesburg
6635 Highway 98 West, Suite 400
Hattiesburg, MS 39402
Phone: (601) 579-8436
Fax: (601) 579-8447

Meridian
2100 9th Street, Room 207
U.S. Post Office Building
Meridian, MS 39302
Phone: (601) 693-6000
Fax: (601) 693-6001

Oxford
2109 University Avenue, Suite 201
Oxford, MS 38655
Phone: (662) 234-1713
Fax: (662) 232-3340

Pascagoula
421 Delmas Avenue, Suite 200
Pascagoula, MS 39567
Phone: (228) 769-7920
Fax: (228) 938-2612

Southaven
8710 Northwest Drive, Suite 301
Southaven City Government Building
Southaven, MS 38671
Phone: (662) 280-0717
Fax: (662) 280-0722

Tupelo
500 West Main Street, Suite 214
Federal Building
Tupelo, MS 38804
Phone: (662) 842-9411
Fax: (662) 841-2404

Appendix IV

US Attorney Offices in Mississippi

John Marshall Alexander, (interim)
U.S. Attorney
Northern District of Mississippi
900 Jefferson Avenue
Oxford, MS 38655-3608
(662) 234-3351

John Dowdy
U.S. Attorney
Southern District of Mississippi
 501 East Court Street
Suite 4.430
Jackson, Mississippi 39201

and

1575 20th Avenue
2nd Floor
Gulfport, Mississippi 39501

Appendix V

How to check up on State Government

You may like to know who contributed to a specific elected official's campaign. This site shows little about Political Action Committees (PACs), and shows nothing pertaining to fish fry, or barbeque cash that is often hauled away in garbage bags. Don't forget all that bingo cash that is available to those who help them stay out of jail. However, the SOS site will give you considerable information from those bold enough to report payments. It may give you an indication in the future about how these politicians will vote or act on certain issues under their cognizance. Type in your internet address bar:

http://www.sos.ms.gov/elections3.aspx

Scroll down to Reports and select the time frame you are interested in. It will take you to a screen that will allow you to search by candidate or committee. If you choose to search by name, the next screen will allow you to enter the candidate's information, last name first. The next screen will show you all the reports in date order submitted by the candidate. Choose the one you are interested in, and click the "pdf" red block to the far right. An actual copy of the report will appear. You may view it on your screen, save it to a file or print it out. That's all there is to it.

Let's say you want to know how much a lobbyist makes for trying to influence the legislators that you have voted to put in office. Keep in mind all the dinners and parties they invite your candidate to so they can influence him --often with spirits. Now ask yourself how much time that legislator spent with you, the person who helped put him in office, and allowed you to offer your influence on proposed bills.

At any rate, you can go to this site:

http://www.sos.ms.gov/elections_candidates_lobbyists_center3.aspx

Scroll down and select the lobbying compensation report. The next screen will allow you to choose the year, the name, or even a total compensation report. That's all there is to it.

What if you want to check on your legislator to see things like, what bills he/she introduced, how many they introduced, how many of those passed or failed, how many they co-sponsored and how many "attaboys" they vote on. I will get to that in a moment but first I want to explain the "attaboys." Those are recognition type resolutions. You may see your lawmaker recognize a girls' basketball team in their home district. It may be recognition for a long time state employee or a musician who has achieved celebrity status. It also may be for a fallen soldier, and they certainly should be recognized. However, think about this for a moment, this serves as a means for the legislator from that district to campaign for more votes, so they win in the long run, regardless of their intention. I often look at legislators, and use my own technique to determine their performance and effectiveness. It is not scientific or official, but I think you will agree that it is a fairly reasonable method.

I give no credit for the "attaboys" because that is something everybody votes for. It is just understood that anybody that recommends one will sooner or later vote on a colleague's that wants a positive vote too. There is no need to vote no. So those are a given, and I don't even pay attention to them, for the purpose of their ability to work as a team player.

When a legislator proposes a bill and it passes, under my system, he gets one point. If it doesn't pass, he gets no points. Remember, these people are expected to help draft and propose legislation and work with their colleagues to get it passed. Failure to do so at some point could make them ineffective.

So, when a member of the legislature co-sponsors a bill, it is an indication of how much they want that bill to pass, and how much they want to take ownership on it, rather than riding the fence, casting a vote only when they have to. If they co-sponsor a bill that passes, I give them another point because they are partially responsible for the bill passing. In my final calculation, I divide the total number of bills proposed into the number that passed and get my first number. I then do the same thing with total number of bills co-sponsored and divide them into the number that passes for the second number. I then add those two numbers and divide by two to get an average score for the lawmaker. Don't forget the legislature passed a bill in the early 90's mandating performance based budgets for state agencies. Why shouldn't a performance measure apply to them as well?

Here's how you do that. Type this address in your internet address field:

http://billstatus.ls.state.ms.us/

Choose Bill Status on the left side of the screen. The pop up screen will give you several options for searching bills. But let's just say for the sake of this guide, we want to look at a previous session. Scroll down to the next to the last option which is Previous Sessions and click on it. Choose the year, and session you are interested in. There are several options on the next page for both the house, and the senate. For our practice, choose, List of Measures by Author either under the House or Senate heading, whichever you are interested in.

Find your legislator's name on the next page in alphabetical order and click on it. The next page will have a listing of the bills proposed or co-sponsored by your legislator. If his/her name is on the far right of a page on a particular line, that means he sponsored it. If another name is shown on that line, that person is the sponsor, and your legislator is only a co-sponsor.

If you choose my methodology, scroll down until you get to the "attaboys" and ignore them. The will always be at the bottom. Count going back up the page, the number of times your legislator introduced a bill. Look to the far left to see the status of the bill. In most cases for past sessions, it can either be "Approved by the Governor" (passed), or "Died in Committee" (failed).

If the legislation passed, but was "Vetoed by the Governor", I give credit for passing to the legislator. If you find your legislator introduced (sponsored) 20 bills but only two passed, divide .20 into 2. That will tell you that his successful performance for introducing and getting his/her bills passed is ten percent. If he/she co-sponsored 15 bills and 11 of them passed, you would divide .15 into 11, and his successful performance for getting co-sponsored bills passed is 73 percent.

Now to get his average performance, add 15 and 73 together, and divide it by two. The average performance grade I have awarded to this individual is 44. You may find by using the same methodology in a larger group instead of just one, that your legislator's score is pretty good. If you have a better methodology, I suggest you use it. However, it is of utmost importance that you know what they are doing, whether they are being a leader, or a follower, and whether or not they have the ability to work with other members in getting bills passed.

I will show you an example by using my own State Representative Mark Baker, who is running for reelection, and my Senator Lee Yancey, who is running for State Treasurer. I will use the 2011 regular session.

Mark Baker introduced 19 bills and only four passed which gives him a 22 percent success rate using my calculations. Mark co-sponsored 16 bills, and only four passed, which gives him a 25 percent success rate. He has an average of 23.5 percent success rate which is only half a percent higher than the legislature as a whole.

I am not trying to show a 100 percent success rate as being the best, rather comparing each with their peers. All of the members of each house are graded against their colleagues by giving the one with the highest score a place at the top of the list, and the one with the lowest score at the bottom of the list. If the highest score is 50, that number now represents a hundred by grading on a curve.

I suggest you recommend your legislators post proposed bills on their sites before the session also depicting their stance, so you will know their interests, and whether or not they represent you or lobbyists. It would also give you time to call them before action is taken on a bill.

I must say, I was pleasantly surprised when I checked on the current State Auditor's performance. You may go to this site and look at it yourself:

http://www.osa.state.ms.us/

When you get there, click on Press Room on the top bar. It will take you to press releases of each action he has taken. I only caution you to notice in the cases of politicians stealing money, as to whether or not they are held accountable criminally, or just made to pay back the money. You may have to re-visit the site later to see an update. I also encourage you to keep following it for the last two years before the next election (not the one about to start). If the incumbent wants to stay, or reach for higher stars, he may get lenient on politicians knowing he will need their support.

I would encourage you to go to the MGC site but I don't think it is worth looking at. The Watkins, Ludlam, Winter and Stennis site is much better, more truthful, with less omissions, and very informative:

http://www.msgaming.com

They do a great job at keeping up with what's going on in the casino industry, although, it has been my experience that what you see on the minutes is not wholly representative of what was said in the public meeting. For that reason, if you want to know, go to the commission meetings. Also, the information they provide on charitable gaming is miniscule. Their "Mission Statements" are downright comical if you look at what they say they do, and what they really do. I won't waste my time looking up that link but you can Google it if you like.

If you want to find out what the attorney general is doing, you can go to his website at:

http://www.ago.state.ms.us/

He has done a great job on computer crime, sex offenders, consumer protection and identity theft. However the division I once worked in, "Public Integrity", under Mike Moore's administration appears to either be slacking off or not getting their due credit. They are responsible for investigating and prosecuting public officials and white collar crime. I don't see much of that when I click on his Press Release tab. You may want to follow it yourself.

Going from Attorney General Jim Hood's office to his brother Tom Hood's office, the Mississippi Ethics Commission, I can't find anything that they have done. I know they have good, qualified investigators, and receive complaints that the commission should act on. Should we not be made aware of their work and findings? Look at this site if you are interested:

http://www.ethics.state.ms.us/ethics/ethics.nsf/webpage/A_main?OpenDocument

They are supposed to investigate violations of the law committed by public servants. At least their commission has more than just legislators on it, but we deserve to know what they do. I sure couldn't find it on their web site.

The Mississippi PEER Commission has a lot of good information on their site. However in the cases where they have found the state agencies in wrong-doing themselves, you will have to go further to see what happened. That is especially true with regards to findings at the MGC. PEER is only an investigative/reporting arm of certain members of the legislature that form the PEER Committee, and has been called, as I said before, a "Tiger with no Teeth". Their site is:

http://www.peer.state.ms.us/

The last state agency I will refer you to is the Mississippi Insurance Commission/State Fire Marshal. Their web site is:

http://www.mid.state.ms.us/

From the looks of their Press Release section, there aren't any "balls of fire" in either of their offices. Most of the releases are warnings to be careful of certain dangers. You be the judge.

I might add though that many of the media clips I have seen in the past for the DPS or DOT have depicted worker-bees, (Troopers, etc.). However as a new election approached, we saw the commissioner's smiling face talking about seatbelts and DUI. (At least one highway commissioner followed the same practice.)

This site will tell you just about anything you want to know about your state officials including legislative voting records, campaign finance, positions, election results, and much more. If they weren't scared to respond, it shows the results of their political courage tests.

http://www.votesmart.org/official_state.php?state_id=MS&dist=&go2.x=18&go2.y=17

Heads up though, your governor, and wannabe governor, have chosen not to respond to the courage test.

About the Author

Rick Ward is a retired Naval Reserve Lieutenant Commander who spent 20 years as a Physical Security Officer in the United States Navy. He retired from his last assignment at the Naval Criminal Investigative Service (NCIS) in Washington, DC in early 2006. He enjoyed a dual career of 14 years in law enforcement in Mississippi as a result of his reserve status. He has served in all facets of law enforcement including uniformed municipal police officer, county investigator, state narcotics agent, attorney general investigator, and division director over charitable gaming enforcement. He has a total of 34 years of experience in all areas of the law enforcement and police discipline.

He has served as a United States Army Contract Investigator for Federal Employment Compensation Act Fraud, and as a Navy Contract Advisor in the Antiterrorism, and Force Protection field. He has been a National Guard Military Police Officer, and served both as an enlisted, as well as an officer in the police field in the US Navy. He served as the Regional Security Officer for Navy Region Northeast, and was onsite in New York during the attacks of September 11, 2001.

He has a Master's Degree in Education from the University of Hawaii, a Bachelor of Science in Criminal Justice from the University of the State of New York, and an Associate Degree in Law Enforcement, from Mississippi Gulf Coast Community College. He is a Certified Protection Professional (CPP) in the American Society of Industrial Security and is also certified at Level V as a Homeland Security Expert in the American Society of Homeland Security.

Rick Ward is a graduate of the Mississippi Law Enforcement Officer's Training Academy at Pearl, Mississippi, the United States Army Military Police School at Fort McClellan, Alabama and the Federal Bureau of Investigations (FBI) National Academy at the United States Marine Corps Base in Quantico, Virginia.

Rick is currently in the Creative Writing Program at Belhaven University, and is a member of Sigma Tau Delta. He has published two legal suspense novels, *The Lawmaker* (2008), *Blood Stained Justice* (2009) and an historical research novel, *Blood for Molasses: A Mississippi Massacre* (2010).

Rick has conducted genealogical and other historical research as a hobby for more than 25 years. He has been featured in countless newspapers and has appeared on numerous television and radio shows. He has traveled extensively throughout the United States, as well as Europe, Africa, and the Middle East on military assignments. He voluntarily served in the Pentagon Command Center during his last two months of service providing support for Katrina oversight.

www.ingramcontent.com/pod-product-compliance
Lightning Source LLC
Chambersburg PA
CBHW081147270326
41930CB00014B/3072